CHILDREN'S CONCEPTS AND THE PRIMARY CURRICULUM

C. J. Willig taught in East London primary schools for twelve years until taking up a post as Lecturer (later Senior Lecturer) in Education at Coventry College of Education. In 1966–7 he served as a Senior Research Fellow at Bradford University.

He was then appointed Principal Lecturer in Education at the Froebel Institute (now Roehampton Institute of Higher Education) where he taught students working for advanced diplomas and higher degrees in primary education until his retirement. He has also contributed to many initial and in-service teacher-education courses at the Roehampton Institute and elsewhere. His current interest is in the contribution developmental psychology can make to understanding children's thinking in the various curriculum subjects.

Previous research work includes investigating the social implications of streaming in the junior school and the influence of children's self-concepts on academic performance.

His academic qualifications include an MEd (with mark of distinction) and a PhD in psychology.

CHILDREN'S CONCEPTS AND THE PRIMARY CURRICULUM

C. J. Willig

P·CP
Paul Chapman
Publishing Ltd

First published 1990
Paul Chapman Publishing Ltd
144 Liverpool Road
London N1 1LA

British Library Cataloguing in Publication Data

Willig, C. J. (C. James)
    Children's concepts and the primary curriculum.
    1. schools. Teaching. Applications of research on
    cognitive development of children
    I. Title
    371.1'02

ISBN 1-85396-101-9

Typeset by Burns & Smith Ltd., Derby.
Printed by St Edmundsbury Press, Suffolk
Bound by W.H. Ware, Avon

A B C D E F G 5 4 3 2 1 0

CONTENTS

Preface   ix

Acknowledgements   xiii

1   CONCEPTUAL DEVELOPMENT AND EDUCATION   1
    Introduction   1
    Children's views on the nature of academic disciplines   1
    Discovering children's concepts   3
    The development of children's concepts   5
    Research into conceptual development and extending children's
        learning   12
    Summary and conclusions   22
    Further reading   23

2   THE LANGUAGE CURRICULUM: WRITTEN EXPRESSION   24
    Introduction   24
    The nature of writing and writing in school   25
    Psychology and the teaching of written expression   28
    Summary and conclusions   43
    Further reading   45

3   MATHEMATICAL EDUCATION   46
    Introduction   46
    The nature of mathematics and mathematical education   47
    Psychology and mathematical education   51
    Summary and conclusions   67
    Further reading   67

4 SCIENCE EDUCATION   69
   Introduction   69
   The nature of science and science education   70
   Psychology and science education   73
   Summary and conclusions   94
   Further reading   95

5 EDUCATION IN HISTORY   96
   Introduction   96
   The nature of history and the nature of education in history   97
   Psychology and the teaching of history   100
   Summary and conclusions   114
   Further reading   115

6 GEOGRAPHICAL EDUCATION   116
   Introduction   116
   The nature of geography and geographical education   117
   Psychology and geographical education   120
   Summary and conclusions   136
   Further reading   137

7 ART EDUCATION   139
   Introduction   139
   The nature of art and art education   140
   Psychology and art education   143
   Summary and conclusions   158
   Further reading   160

8 MORAL EDUCATION   161
   Introduction   161
   The nature of morality and moral education   162
   Psychology and moral education   165
   Summary and conclusions   181
   Further reading   182

Postscript   183

References and Bibliography   186

Author Index   200

Subject Index   203

DEDICATION

To the memory of my parents and to my one-time colleagues, Marjorie Branch, Harry Davis, Alfred Rogers and Harry Wepfer, who guided and supported me in my first teaching post.

PREFACE

This book is intended to help teachers make sense of what children say and do, and to use that knowledge to improve the quality of pupils' learning. Essentially, it aims to link the study of conceptual development with the practicalities of teaching in seven representative curriculum areas – language, mathematics, science, history, geography, art and moral education. It covers pupils' developing concepts of phenomena as varied as flotation, historical time, mapping and justice, as well as describing strategies children use in counting, spelling and drawing.

Patchy though the literature is, there is a steadily growing body of knowledge about children's concepts related to many aspects of the primary-school curriculum, but much of it lies buried in specialist professional journals and does not receive the exposure it deserves. My aim is to draw extensively on that literature and to make its methodology and findings more accessible to teachers.

The field might be a little more closely defined if, by way of introducion, we touch briefly on the concept of shopping – a basic economic transaction examined in Chapter 6. According to Jahoda (1984), 6-year-olds see buying and selling as a sort of game played with people who sell things. A little later on it is realized that shop assistants are actually paid employees but children at this point have no idea where the money comes from to pay their wages. In fact, the wholesale/retail principle is not fully grasped until well into the primary-school years and, of course, until that stage is reached, children's understanding of trade in general (a concept central to geography) remains hazy.

In the related field of learning strategies, Heege (1985) has identified methods for solving mathematical problems children have worked out for themselves. In multiplying 5 by 6, a common practice is to go straight to 10 × 6, which is easily remembered, and to halve the answer. Then there is the doubling principle, which pupils use in arriving at 4 × 7. This time they go to 2 × 7, which they already know, and simply double the answer. Among the many other strategies Heege found was one based on the commutative principle where children had already grasped the fact that 6 × 7 and 7 × 6 give the same product.

The full educational implications of all this research activity still need to be worked out in practice, and that is a task mainly for educators and not psychologists. In the meantime, however, teaching must go on and we must make the most of the data we have. At the very least, research into conceptual development warns us that we cannot assume that children and adults always see things in the same way; and because it demonstrates how slowly understanding develops, it also brings home to us the need to return to the same concepts again and again throughout a child's school life. There are other reasons why a knowledge of this research could have a powerful influence on the practice of teaching.

First of all, if we accept that education involves an exchange of ideas between pupil and teacher, we must first of all try to understand and take account of the concept or learning task from the pupil's point of view. Second, a knowledge of the developmental sequence can make the planning of work much easier and ensure a better match between the learner's ability and the standard of work aimed at.

Third, the research shows how a knowledge of stages of development can be used in extending learning. Fourth, the research articles themselves often contain useful material that can easily be adapted for teaching purposes as well as providing models for questioning techniques and for structuring children's learning. This is a particularly neglected use of research and for this reason some studies are reported in greater detail than is usual in an introductory text.

In brief, this book aims to introduce basic information about the development of thinking that is of practical concern to teachers, and to act as a source for ideas about teaching material and method.

In Chapter 1, the framework used in the seven curriculum chapters is set out and elaborated on. It describes methods for identifying and analysing children's concepts in addition to outlining some approaches to extending children's thinking. We shall concentrate on the educational implications of research into conceptual development. It would be inappropriate in a short introductory text to attempt to cover all the aspects of learning, or to comment on the many complex and controversial theoretical issues that abound in developmental psychology. However, for readers who wish to explore these matters, a list of sources for further reading is included at the end of Chapter 1.

Each of the seven curriculum chapters conforms more or less to the same pattern. There is an opening section on the nature of the discipline and its particular contribution to children's learning. Where it exists, we then examine empirical work on teachers' and children's conceptions of the area of learning concerned, addressed to children's response to such questions as 'What is history?' and 'Why do we write stories in schools?' The main part of each chapter is given over to illustrating the development of particular concepts or skills; for example, in science, concepts of living; in language, spelling; and in art, understanding paintings. The research described in this section is intended to be representative only, but references to more general surveys are made where they exist. Finally, controlled experiments designed to advance learning are reported, in which educators or psychologists have designed teaching programmes or demonstrated the application of particular teaching methods in that subject area.

The emphasis throughout is on the contribution empirical studies can make to the teacher's work, but references dealing with general aspects of teaching in the seven curriculum areas we shall be considering are included in the further-reading lists.

My hope is that this standard format – discovering children's concepts, matching the new material to the learner's needs and stimulating learning – will contribute to giving a structure, unity and coherence to professional curriculum courses in initial teacher education in addition to providing serving teachers with a consistent approach to curriculum-based in-service education. Despite its diversity, there are common threads running through the curriculum, not least the general pattern of cognitive development that can be observed in every academic discipline – whatever its content.

Lastly, I must explain why this review of conceptual development is linked to specific areas of the curriculum. In the first place, the introduction of a National Curriculum has stimulated interest in defining stages of learning in the academic disciplines. This book addresses the same problems and complements the DES National Curriculum documents by filling in the necessary psychological background. A further reason is that professional courses in teacher education and in-service training (INSET) initiatives are frequently curriculum-subject based and it is therefore convenient to present the material under these headings. But there is another, deeper, justification. The academic disciplines emerged and continue to develop because they serve us well in making sense of the world, and it is for this reason they feature so prominently in the school curriculum. Few of us would dissent from the proposition that primary-school children should be introduced to the areas of knowledge that have made such an impact on the human mind and that touch on so many of the things children are struggling to understand. The current debate, and it is a very fierce one, is really about how we should do so, and whether or not the processes of learning should take precedence over content.

I have no space to follow these controversies but it follows that whatever policy is adopted, whether it is subject-based, a topic approach, some form of integration or child-initiated learning, the subject-matter of the academic disciplines must directly or indirectly be integral to much of what is learnt in schools. I would also suggest that the form of organization schools adopt may well be secondary to observing such principles as fostering children's curiosity, taking heed of and following up children's interests wherever we can, learning by discovery and the emphasis on first-hand experience that are central to child-centred education and that inform the chapters that follow.

C. J. Willig
London

ACKNOWLEDGEMENTS

I am deeply grateful to my wife, Ann, who has contributed to the writing of this book in many ways, not least in making valuable comments on the manuscript from the point of view of a practising primary school teacher.

I should also like to thank the many friends and colleagues who read and made helpful comments on all or part of the manuscript.

The following permissions for use of copyright material are gratefully acknowledged:

J.M. Dent Ltd. for copyright material from Buxton (1984) summarized in Table 3.1.

Geographical Association for copyright material from Matthews (1984) reproduced in Figure 6.2.

International Reading Association for copyright material from Gentry (1982) adapted in Table 2.3.

International Thomson Publishing Services Ltd. for copyright material from Piaget and Inhelder (1970) reproduced in Figure 1.1.

Macmillan Publishing Company for copyright material from Lowenfeld and Brittain (1987) adapted in Table 7.1.

Oxford University Press for copyright material from Wilkinson et al. (1980) summarized and adapted in Tables 2.1 and 2.2.

Scottish Academic Press (Journals) Ltd. for copyright material from Ives (1984) adapted in Figure 7.3.

Society for Research in Child Development at University of Chicago Press for copyright material from Peterson, Peterson and Seeto (1983) used in Table 8.1, Dolgin and Behrend (1984) used in Table 4.2 and Anooshian and Young (1981) used in Figure 6.3.

Taylor and Francis Ltd. and the authors for permission to use copyright material from Dentici et al. (1984) reproduced in Table 4.3.

John Wiley and Son Inc. for copyright material in Selman et al. (1982) and Sneider and Pulos (1983).

1
CONCEPTUAL DEVELOPMENT AND EDUCATION

INTRODUCTION

This chapter sets the scene for the rest of this book. It suggests a framework for understanding research into conceptual development and it attempts to show its practical applications in helping teachers to discover, analyse and extend children's concepts.

We shall be addressing four central and interrelated questions:

1. What are children's views on the nature of academic disciplines?
2. How can research help teachers to discover children's concepts?
3. What are the common characteristics of concepts at various stages of development?
4. How can research assist teachers to develop children's thinking in the major curriculum areas?

Some discussion of the difficult theoretical and controversial issues these questions raise is inevitable, but it is kept to the minimum necessary to make sense of the research findings reviewed.

CHILDREN'S VIEWS ON THE NATURE OF ACADEMIC DISCIPLINES

Scattered throughout the psychological literature are indications that having clear intentions helps people to learn more efficiently. This has prompted several investigators to ask children what they believe such basic everyday school activities as reading and writing are about. The results are instructive but not always reassuring. For example, Southgate, Arnold and Johnson (1981) discovered that the 7–9-year-old children they interviewed adopted severely practical, no-nonsense attitudes to reading. As they saw it, this activity was essentially a means of furthering learning, to help with spelling and to obtain information. Only a very small minority mentioned reading for its own sake; perhaps worse still, 13 children of the 50 questioned either could not say what reading was about, or could not see the purpose of it.

Much the same applies to children's writing. Some colleagues and I (Tamburrini, Willig and Butler, 1984) once tried to discover the purposes of different forms of writing as seen through the eyes of 40 academically able and articulate 10- and 11-year-olds.

To give just one indication of our findings, most of the children had only hazy ideas about poetry, and over half could give no reason at all why people should want to write poems. We were often told that the principal subject-matter of poetry was nature and all its works, such as the girl who thought 'poems are all about spring; we write about blossoms and the breeding of animals, etc.'. But when pushed there was ready agreement that poetry covers a much wider range of topics than that. There were rare exceptions, however. One boy I spoke to had groped his way to the conclusion that poems could be 'about ugly as well as beautiful things, like living in slums', and as we talked, he came up with the thought that 'you can put exactly what you like and how you feel in a poem ... you can put your heart in it and get involved'. This boy realized that feelings are central to poetry, but our findings as a whole suggested that nearly all the children we spoke to would benefit from explicit guidance about the function of poetry and writing for other purposes as well.

Reading and writing are not isolated cases. We shall be meeting other evidence to confirm that children do not always understand the reasons for studying various curriculum subjects or, come to that, the object of particular school activities. There is also some evidence suggesting that teachers, too, differ about the nature of curriculum subjects. Mathematics is a case in point, and so is moral education that, as we shall see later, is open to several interpretations.

Summary   We are often too busy teaching to ask ourselves what children make of the various curriculum subjects they are learning – yet psychology and common sense unite in the belief that it is better to know what one is about than not. This is why each of the curriculum chapters in this book begins with a brief outline of the nature of the discipline and its contribution to the curriculum followed by reports of research into children's and teachers' conceptions of the various curriculum areas. Despite some gloomy findings, there seems to be no reason why primary-school children should not be introduced to the purposes of academic disciplines at a simple level, or begin to learn, for instance, how scientists and historians go about their work.

DISCOVERING CHILDREN'S CONCEPTS

The psychological research you will meet in the following chapters suggests a number of methods for identifying children's concepts, which can be used as described or easily adapted for classroom use.

One common practice is to present children with written or pictorial material and then to ask specific questions about it. Looft (1974) used this tactic in a study of concepts of life reported in Chapter 4. He got children to look at pictures of living and non-living things and to sort them into two groups according to whether they thought the subject of the picture was alive or not. Next, to find out what they knew about the characteristics of living creatures, children had to decide whether each of the living things picked out needed to breathe, needed food and was able to reproduce.

In Looft's study, all children had to do was to make one basic judgement (living or non-living) and then respond to three 'yes or no' closed-type questions. This is a good technique to find out what children know, but if we want to avoid putting ideas into children's heads – and we very often do – an alternative method is to ask more open questions that allow children to express themselves freely. Even without supporting material, Stevens (1982) found this to be a simple and effective way of entering into children's minds. She got primary-school pupils to write or tell her about what the queen did and, as you will see in Chapter 5, this was sufficient to produce a rich store of information about children's concepts of the monarchy and its role in politics.

In yet another variation of method, Jahoda (1984) shows the value of persistent probing in his study of the wholesale/retail principle in trade, described in Chapter 6. Here is part of an interview with a 10-year-old boy:

I (interviewer): What happens to the [shopkeeper's] money at the end of the day?
S (subject): I think it gets counted out. I don't think they give it out until the end of the week.
I: Who do they give it out to?
S: They pay the people who've been serving.
I: Do they give it all out?

S: They keep some to buy more stuff for the shop.
I: Does the shop pay the same for the things?
S: I think they get them cheaper. If they got them at the same price they wouldn't be making anything.

Jahoda had specific objectives in mind and you will notice how the boy's responses are cleverly used and the discussion steered towards the wholesale/retail principle around which the interview was structured.

Piaget's methodology is widely copied or varied. Children are set a problem, sometimes involving manipulation of objects, sometimes not, and as they go about solving it the experimenter presses hard to get at the thought processes underlying what children say and do. Take as an example one of Piaget and Inhelder's (1970, p. 57 ff.) experiments concerned with the relationship between time and movement. They wanted to know whether young children's thinking would be dominated by the actual length of a path traversed, or simply by its beginning and end points. To find out, the investigators asked children to compare the progress of two model trams along the two tracks depicted in Figure 1.1. The first one (A1) is in a perfectly straight line. The second (A2) takes an indirect path, but all the segments are equal and at right angles to each other. The points of departure and arrival are common to both.

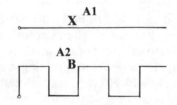

Figure 1.1   The paths traversed
(*Source*: Piaget and Inhelder, 1970)

In part of the experiment, the investigator moved a model tram along the path of the lower line stopping at point B. He then asked a boy, referred to as MIC, to move his tram along the top line stopping at a point where it had travelled as far as the investigator's. MIC did what young children often do and placed his tram directly above point X. The investigator then asked, 'Are you sure you have gone as far as mine?' and the child was then invited to trace both routes with his finger along the tracks.

Further question-and-answer sessions followed until finally the researcher was satisfied that MIC was well aware that A1 was the shorter of the routes. He even said quite definitely at one stage that A2 must be longer 'because of the squares'. But MIC still had not grasped the distinction between distance and movement. He worked on the principle that the two movements equal the same length when they arrive at the same finishing point. Any detours made *en route* were therefore dismissed as irrelevant.

This combination of an interesting game-like situation and intense and subtle questioning enabled Piaget and Inhelder to discover children's grasp of the complex relationships existing between distance and speed. However, although they do not apply in this case, there are legitimate criticisms of Piaget's methods we shall be touching on shortly. Even so, Piaget's basic approach still repays careful study.

The ideas of children, and in particular young children, are often most clearly and vividly expressed in drawing or painting, activities Copple, Sigel and Saunders (1979, p. 50) call 'visible thinking'. You will see what they mean in Chapter 7, where examples are given of children's drawings that reveal their thoughts and feelings about the world and what is important to them and what is not.

Summary Discovering children's concepts is not as simple a matter as it looks. Experimenters and children can confuse each other by the language they use and there is also the constant problem of devising situations that make sense to children but that also clearly reveal the concepts psychologists and teachers are interested in.

Nevertheless, the research literature reported in this book provides a rich source of material for teachers interested in understanding children's concepts and their development. Their attempts to solve the problems set by experimenters give us a glimpse of the world as children see it through the words they use, the actions they perform and through the drawing and painting they produce.

The importance of questioning is apparent throughout. Its effectiveness depends on knowing beforehand the appropriate questions to ask (and here a knowledge of intellectual development is very useful) and on persuading children to elaborate their answers so that we can know what they are really thinking. Questioning is once again coming to the fore in teacher education and, for teachers interested in the current state of the art, two excellent sources are given in the further-reading list.

THE DEVELOPMENT OF CHILDREN'S CONCEPTS

During the primary-school years, children acquire literally scores of concepts that cover the entire curriculum; to make matters even more complicated, these concepts change in character as new ways of thinking emerge. The problem for psychology, therefore, is to find a way of imposing system and order on this apparent diversity by identifying common characteristics in children's intellectual development.

Our first step must be to explore the nature of concepts. This discussion will lead us towards theories of cognitive development that aim to describe and to explain the acquisition and growth of concepts. We shall consider just two of these, Piaget's theory and Peel's interpretation of intellectual development.

The Nature of Concepts

Basically, concepts refer to the process of categorizing things and events in order to deal with them more efficiently. Take this simple example. Until recently my notion of word-processors was minimal but I can now operate my own machine with reasonable confidence and, to gain further experience, I have tried out other models whenever I can. I now have a concept of word-processors that can help me to understand the potential of machines far more sophisticated than my own. I bring to bear my knowledge of word-processors in general to that particular word-processor that, although different from mine, shares common properties with all other word-processors. That is the purpose of a concept: it enables us to classify phenomena and to draw on previous experiences to help us to cope with whatever faces us.

Attitudes serve much the same purpose, as do constructs, a term Kelly (1955) uses to explain how people control and order their lives. All of us, Kelly says, act in the manner of scientists. We note the repetition of events, we reflect on them and we use that information to anticipate future happenings. A construct denotes the meaning we attach to people and events or, come to that, any other phenomena that attracts attention. As Kelly (*ibid.* p. 105) says, constructs are like templates, through which we make sense of and structure the world.

The nearest equivalent terms to concept Piaget uses are 'schema' and 'scheme'. Roughly speaking, a schema is an elementary form of scheme. However, it will be easier here if we use the term scheme to cover all stages of development. A scheme is a mental representation built up from past experiences that is used to process incoming information. We have literally hundreds of schemes covering every aspect of our mental life, which range in complexity from the most abstruse mathematical principle down to the simple addition of number.

Now a critical point about schemes is that they have potential for change. Take lying, for instance. Children's earliest scheme of lying is very straightforward – a lie is a naughty word. Later on it is defined as something that is not true, even where false information is given unintentionally. Finally, the stage is reached where a lie is seen as something intentionally false only.

According to Piaget, schemes change when new knowledge no longer fits in comfortably with existing ideas. If, for example, a boy is accused of lying when he unwittingly misled his mother by saying his sister was in when she was out, he is given a mental jolt. In protesting his innocence it becomes clear to him that intention to deceive is a necessary condition of lying. That new insight has to be incorporated into the scheme but to make it compatible, the scheme of lying itself must change. In fact, mental development consists of a succession of such accommodations as this, which pushes thinking to a higher and higher plane.

Mental constructs change according to a definite pattern and it is the function of theories of cognitive development, which we move on to now, to throw light on these processes.

The Piagetian Approach

Inevitably, we turn first to Piaget's theory of conceptual development. Piaget himself was a prolific writer and energetic investigator whose work spanned over half a century, and the arguments and counter-arguments his ideas provoked have resulted in a substantial, not to say daunting, research literature. A brief outline of the stages of cognitive development relevant to primary schools is sufficient for our immediate purposes but, for readers wanting to know more about Piaget's ideas, several sources are given in the further-reading list.

Our concern is mainly with the pre-operational stage of thinking, which lasts from about 2 to 7 years of age, and the concrete operational stage, which very roughly covers the age-group from 7 to around 12. In the context of Piagetian theory, the great change in the primary years is from pre-operational thinking (which is rigid and somewhat unstable) to concrete operational thinking (which is associated with more flexible forms of thought).

Let us take one of Piaget's most familiar tests to illustrate this development (Piaget, 1967, p. 45). Children are shown two balls of clay of the same size and identical in appearance and then, as they watch, one of the balls is distorted into a sausage shape. Figure 1.2. shows how the two balls look now.

At the pre-operational stage, the child will say there is now more clay in the sausage because it is longer, or that it contains less because it is thinner. Only when the concrete operational stage is reached does it dawn on

Figure 1.2   The conservation task

children that the quantity of material remains the same whatever happens to its shape. Children are no longer deceived by outward appearances; they can now, to use Piaget's term, 'decentre'.

This little experiment illustrates the principle of conservation: the ability to recognize that nothing has been added and nothing has been taken away. Only the shape of the object has been altered. According to Piaget and Inhelder (1969, p. 136), the key to conserving is the ability to reverse; in other words, to go back to the starting-point of an operation. In the ball of clay illustration we have just considered, the concrete operational thinker knows full well that the process can be reversed restoring the distorted ball to its original shape – the pre-operational child does not.

Egocentricity is another key characteristic of young children's thinking, which we shall be meeting again and again throughout this book. To Piaget, the term 'egocentricity' takes on a particular meaning that has nothing at all to do with selfishness or self-interest. In this context, egocentricity means quite literally that thought is centred on the self and that viewpoints differing from one's own cannot be appreciated. As egocentricity is such an important landmark in thinking, we ought to see what it means in practice. The first example concerns the child's physical world.

In one of Piaget and Inhelder's (1956) well-known problems, models of three mountains of varying size and height are set out on a table around the sides of which four chairs are placed facing inwards. The child sits on one chair where he or she stays throughout. A doll is placed on one of the other chairs and the child is then asked to convey to the investigator by drawing, cutting out a model or selecting one picture or photograph from a number of others, what the doll could see from where it was sitting. The doll is moved on to the other vantage points and the procedure is repeated. This task makes heavy demands on children and you will not be surprised to learn that most do not get it right until around the age of 7.

For an example of social egocentricity, we turn to moral thinking where a recognition of the thoughts and feelings of others is essential in deciding between right and wrong (see Chapter 8). In one of Urberg and Docherty's (1976) tests, a picture was shown of two children fighting over the same toy; a second picture was then presented showing a woman giving the toy to one of the two children. The pupils taking part in the experiment had to say how they would feel if they were given the truck and then how the other child with no toy to play with might feel. Generally speaking, the older the children the better able they are to put themselves in someone else's shoes.

Considered as a whole, thinking at the concrete operational stage becomes much more coherent and systematic. Seriation – the arrangement of things in order of size – is no longer a problem; and classification becomes much easier now the relationships between groups and sub-groups can be worked out. Piaget sets out in full the logical and mathematical operations on which these new abilities are based. We need not go into this formal analysis but it would be helpful to keep in mind that children can now conserve, they can reverse mental operations, they can decentre and appreciate perspectives other than their own.

Now a few words of qualification and warning. After a slow start, Piaget's theory was enthusiastically taken up by educationists, but as is often the way with a new idea, greater claims were made for it than were sometimes warranted. What happened next is a matter of history. A reaction set in and we have now reached the position where some teachers who have raised the matter with me believe that Piagetian theory has been 'disproved'. Of course, it is nothing like as simple as that and, because of the possible effects of all these confusions on classroom practice, I ought to say a little about the current status of the theory.

Let us first take the problem of Piaget's methodology. Earlier I mentioned the 'mountains' experiment, which was designed to test children's ability to take perspectives other than their own. Most children under the age of about 7 found it difficult to manage but Hughes (1975) thought it was worth trying to test the same concept but in a much more familiar, everyday setting. Briefly, he devised a 'hide-and-seek' game-like situation using dolls. What the children had to decide was who could see whom from where. Significantly, most of the 30 children aged between 3 and 5 years were successful in doing so, with even the 3-year-olds showing few signs of egocentric thinking. This is just one of the instances where Piaget has appeared to under-estimate the abilities of young children. Donaldson (1978) believes that pre-school children find conventional Piagetian tests difficult because they are not really sure what to do. The 'hide-and-seek' task, however, is quite different, and is immediately understood because (as Donaldson points out) this scenario makes 'human sense' and gives children the confidence to tackle it.

A second source of difficulty is that Piagetian testing, in common with much experimental work with children, depends on language. Obviously, the investigator has to frame questions in a form that children can understand, but as anyone who has worked with young children knows, this is not as easy as it might seem. For example, we have long known that children have trouble in distinguishing the meaning of the expressions, 'more', 'bigger than' and 'less', which makes testing very difficult in some areas.

A third problem is associated with stage theory. Piagetian theory undoubtedly helps us to understand the course of children's thinking but there are, nevertheless, problems about stage theory. Each stage, so the argument goes, is marked by a unique set of mental structures that set boundaries on children's performance over a range of intellectual tasks. Thus, other things being equal, we might confidently expect children at the concrete operational on one logical reasoning test to be round about the same level on similar tests. But extensive research has shown the real picture to be much more confused than that. Of course, Piaget recognized that there is no sharp cut-off point between stages, and he reminds us that there are bound to be periods of transition when children hover uncertainly between one stage and the next. Even so, the discrepancies go deeper than that. Although the findings are not entirely conclusive, there is evidence to show that children's thinking is much more erratic than is commonly supposed (Brown and Desforges, 1979). For instance, an empirical study by Rest (1979) demonstrated that children's levels of judgement can differ widely from item to item in assessments of moral thinking, presumably because more sense is made of some moral problems than others. I mention this because we cannot assume that individual children operate at the same level in all aspects of learning. They do not.

All that said, it would be unwise to allow these criticisms and differences of emphasis to obscure Piaget's positive achievements. His original observations and the theory built up around them gave psychology a new and exciting point of departure and, because of his efforts, we now have much deeper insights into the course of cognitive development.

The newer developmental theories (see Sternberg, 1987) look to such fields as information processing for inspiration and play down the role of logic and mathematics, which are central to Piagetian theory. And again, contrary to Piaget's position, a much higher profile is given to environmental influences on development.

Nevertheless, in respect to understanding children's changing concepts, Piaget's work is as relevant as ever it was, subject to the qualifications just mentioned. Such characteristics as the ability to conserve, to decentre and to take on the perspectives of others can be commonly observed and, although we may not be able to label children as 'pre-operational' or 'concrete operational', we can nevertheless assess which stage a particular child is at in respect to a particular aspect of knowledge.

Peel's Theory of Conceptual Development

Peel's (1971) analysis of children's thinking is best explained through an experimental situation. We begin with a passage describing the closure of a railway station:

> Lynn is a large town with a busy railway junction which attracts boys who are interested in train-spotting. Burton is a small place not far away and so many people who live there do their shopping in Lynn because there are more shops. British Railways have recently decided to close Burton station and run no more trains from there to Lynn.
>
> (*Ibid.* p. 34)

Only one question is asked: 'Should Burton station be closed, and why do you say that?' The answers were graded using a three-stage system: level A, restricted responses; level B, circumstantial responses; and level C, imaginative responses:

1. A restricted answer is defined as one that is irrelevant and where tautology and inconsistency may dominate. Examples are: 'Yes. One day a train-spotter may get killed'. 'Yes. The trains have stopped running.' 'Yes. There are lots of other railway stations.'
2. A circumstantial answer is defined as one that is bound solely by the content of the passage, often taking account at first of only one element. Examples are: 'No. The people of Burton may depend on Lynn for their shopping'. 'Yes. People should do their shopping in their own town and this is good for trade.'
3. An imaginative answer is defined as a response involving the generation of independent ideas and an appreciation of cause-and-effect relationships. Examples are: 'It all depends whether the people can get to Lynn any other way'. 'It depends whether many people use the train and if they have other ways of travelling to Lynn.'

Peel (*ibid.*) tells us that among 11–12-year-old children, 2 gave restricted answers, 37 circumstantial and 25 imaginative answers in response to the railway-closure passage. This suggests that his developmental sequence could well be used in upper-primary and middle-school classes, especially as some of the low scores reported might well be due to children's unfamiliarity with this kind of experience. It is quite possible that, with practice, younger primary-school children could do quite well in exercises of this kind.

Summary   Concepts allow us to classify and to process incoming information by drawing on our past experiences.

New information inconsistent with an existing concept or scheme is rejected outright if it does not make sense, in which case the concept remains unaltered. If the new insight is credible and therefore inconsistent with the existing scheme, then the scheme must be modified to accommodate it.

Piagetian theory attempts to describe and to explain conceptual development. Although there are theoretical and methodological problems associated with his analysis, it has been widely and successfully applied in analysing concepts because it draws attention to a number of easily recognizable characteristics that broadly differentiate pre-operational from concrete operational schemes.

In Peel's model, thinking is labelled as restricted, circumstantial or imaginative. It is relatively easy to use and has been applied with particular success in the field of social studies.

By combining criteria from research into cognitive development, a rough-and-ready guide for assessing the quality of pupils' thinking for use in the classroom can be constructed. The checklist reads as follows:

1. Do the responses contain irrelevancies or inconsistencies?
2. Are there indications of pre-operational or concrete operational thought? More specifically, is the child able to conserve, to reverse a mental operation, to decentre or to take on a perspective other than his or her own?
3. Do pupils look for and establish relationships between one factor and another?
4 To what extent can children generalize?
5. Can all the relevant factors be identified and the relationships among them sorted out?
6. Is attention confined just to the facts provided or do pupils go beyond the information given and generate independent ideas that govern their solutions to problems?

RESEARCH INTO CONCEPTUAL DEVELOPMENT AND EXTENDING CHILDREN'S LEARNING

Let us assume that we have managed to obtain a fair idea of children's understanding of an aspect of, say, mathematics or history. What do these findings tell us?

The information gathered from testing children will tell us the stage most children in the class are at and where the extremes fall, but nothing at all about the circumstances that led up to these results – there is a good deal of evidence to indicate that competence in some areas is at a low level, not because children are incapable, but simply because they have never before thought seriously about the issues involved. Thus, for quite a long time, it was thought that the Piagetian stage of concrete operational thinking in history was not reached until around the age of 12, but later research showed that – if given the chance to think about cause-and-effect relationships in history – children's level of achievement could be raised dramatically. Therefore, and particularly when using research findings, we should look upon developmental data not as a norm or target to be aimed at but as a starting-point for extending children's thinking.

Essentially, knowing the level of children's present abilities helps to determine the shape of future learning experiences. More specifically, a knowledge of conceptual development underpins the techniques of matching teaching material to the ability of the learner, disturbing the learner's existing ideas, learning by telling, learning from observation and thinking about thinking. We shall now examine these five strategies.

Matching Teaching Material to the Ability of the Learner

Some time ago now, the DES (1978b) 'Primary Survey' expressed considerable concern about the generally poor match reported between the standard of work achieved and the level children were thought capable of reaching. Incidentally, the 'best' match was found in the areas of reading, mathematics, writing and PE; the 'worst' in science, geography, history and art and craft.

But what do we mean when we talk about match? The concept is defined by Harlen (1982, p. 184) as

> finding out what children can already do and what ideas they have, as a basis for providing experiences which will develop these skills and concepts. The keynote of matching is thus finding the right challenge for a child, the size of step that he can take by using but also extending existing ideas.

Harlen is insistent that matching means more than giving children more of what they can already do; its object is to challenge them to raise their thinking to a higher plane.

All teachers know how difficult it is to pitch work at a level that is neither too easy nor too hard. In fact in Bennett *et al.*'s (1984) empirical study, a satisfactory match was achieved on only 40 per cent of the tasks set: about a third of the assignments were too difficult and about a quarter too easy. The researchers traced the root of the problem back to inadequate teacher diagnosis where teaching mathematical procedures took precedence over discovering where children were going wrong in attempting to solve the problem. What this means in practice is well illustrated by Bennett *et al.* (*ibid.* p. 175) in one of their many fascinating snapshots of teachers at work in the classroom. In this instance, Fiona is having trouble dividing 54 by 2. We take up the story where she appeals for help:

> Teacher: Well you ought to be able to oughtn't you. And your pencil's thick and black for start. That's squashed together. You've forgotten how to do this? You'd better practise at home this weekend. How many two's in five?
> Fiona: Two.
> Teacher: Where does the two go?
> Fiona: In there.
> Teacher: Write it down at the top. How many left over?
> Fiona: One.
> Teacher: Now what do we say? How many two's in..?
> Fiona: Four.
> Teacher: In what? How many two's in..?
> Fiona: One.
> Teacher: No.
> Fiona: Five.
> Teacher: How many two's in..?
> Fiona: Four.
> Teacher: But that isn't four. What number is that?
> Fiona: One.
> Teacher: But you can't say how many two's in one can you? Because there aren't any, and that's your number. How many two's in..?
> Fiona: Fourteen.
> Teacher: Yes now come on. You were busy talking and you're stopping other people from working as well. You're getting a bad habit of talking Fiona. You're doing far too much. Right come on. Do this one 51 ÷ 3.

You can easily see that it is the mechanics of the exercise that pre-occupies the teacher. Over and over again she asks, 'How many two's in..?' However, there was no attempt to discover Fiona's understanding of the problem or how, if left to herself, she would go about solving it. Apparently it was the rules of 'carrying' that confused her and it was this aspect that needed to be worked on.

The authors analyse many classroom encounters in the same way and go on to offer practical advice on improving diagnostic skills. This book is one of the most important studies of primary schools in action published in recent years, and it is well worth reading for its down-to-earth advice on the everyday problems confronting teachers.

The extract I selected relates to the diagnostic element in the teaching/learning strategy. This was also a feature of Lancaster-Smith's (1985, p. 81 ff.) study, but he went on to show how the diagnosis could be used in structuring the learning experience from there on. He tells of a 9-year-old boy named Brian who continually had problems with written subtraction problems. His first effort at subtracting 87 from 261 was this:

$$\begin{array}{r} 261 \\ - 87 \\ \hline 226 \end{array}$$

He explained his thinking in this way:

Brian: 7 take away 1 is 6, 8 take away 6 is 2, and 2 take away 0 is still 2.
(The teacher then decided to give a problem using smaller numbers, i.e. 24 − 9).
Brian's answer was:

$$\begin{array}{r} 24 \\ - 9 \\ \hline 25 \end{array}$$

Teacher: If you had £22 and gave me £6 how much would you have left?
Brian: (Visibly he counted back 6 from 22 on his fingers). £16.
Teacher: Now write that down like the last question and tell me how you get the answer. [He wrote]:

$$\begin{array}{r} 22 \\ - 6 \\ \hline 24 \end{array}$$

Brian: 6 take away 2 is 4. And 2 take away nothing is 2.
Teacher: Is that the same answer as the one you worked out in your head?
Brian: No ... it can't be right. 22 take away 6 is 16. I must have added instead of taking away.

Brian knew how to subtract informally by counting backwards and he had also learnt that subtraction means you are left with a smaller sum of money than the amount started with. It was the formal, written procedure he could not manage, especially when the numbers became too large to deal with in his head. Lancaster-Smith decided that work with concrete materials such as the Dienes apparatus was needed initially, and that problems should be restricted to smaller numbers involving tens and units until the process was securely grasped. As we shall see in Chapter 3, there are scales showing the progression in understanding number that can be used for diagnostic purposes.

In Lancaster-Smith's example, the diagnosis dictated a return to earlier processes that had not been properly mastered. In some instances, where there is only a minor hiccup, further practice is all that is necessary, and in other cases pupils judged to be in danger of marking time are moved on to a more advanced level.

The key to satisfactory 'matching' lies in finding challenging, but still manageable, learning experiences for children. This sounds simple enough, but the problems encountered in putting this principle into practice are formidable. Bennett *et al.* (1984) and Southgate, Arnold and Johnson (1981) give sound advice on organizational matters, such as how to cut down on children queueing at the teacher's desk and how to diagnose the problems of individual children. What comes through strongly is the need to make the most of every encounter with pupils as individuals, in groups and as a class, and it is here that an understanding of the pattern of children's thinking is invaluable.

Disturbing the Learner's Existing Ideas

Good teachers have always asked penetrating questions or posed practical problems that surprise learners and force them to reflect on what they think they know – this is the basis of Piaget's cognitive conflict principle, which he sees as basic to learning. It operates as follows. When we come across something we do not understand we are thrown off balance. As this situation is difficult to tolerate we try to restore the balance by solving the problem, and in the process thinking is raised to a higher plane.

Although there are reservations about applying this strategy to all forms of learning (see Ginsburg, 1983; Meadows, 1983), the research evidence suggests it is a useful technique to bear in mind. For instance, the cognitive conflict principle is highly thought of in the moral-education literature. As Hersh, Paolitto and Reimer (1979) see it, it is quite possible for children to come up against the views of people at higher levels of moral development than themselves as they go about their everyday lives. This experience could well make them uneasy about their own moral position and bring about a change of attitudes without any formal teaching. However, if cognitive conflict does not occur 'naturally' then, so the argument goes, situations should be contrived to challenge or disturb deliberately the ideas children already hold. Few of us can tolerate a state of uncertainty for long and, to escape from it, children are forced to think about the ideas that have satisfied them so far, to justify them if they can and, if they cannot, absorb the new insights and move on to the next stage of moral thinking. One procedure (known in shorthand form as the +1 theory) is to expose children to the stage just above the one they are currently at, which most probably gives the best chance of making progress.

In the study by Selman and Lieberman (1975), summarized in Chapter 8, children were shown sound filmstrips illustrating levels of moral reasoning below, at and slightly above the stage of most children in the class. This was followed by class discussions led by teachers and, if you look ahead to Chapter 8, you will see that the results in terms of advancing children's moral thinking were most encouraging. The idea, of course, is not to give children the 'right' answer straight, but by force of skilful questioning to get children to inspect their own moral views and, if found wanting, to modify them to a position that will stand more rigorous scrutiny.

You will have noticed that Selman and Lieberman used class discussions, not individual methods, to promote moral understanding. Now while individual teaching is sometimes essential – Lancaster-Smith's (1985) example of teaching subtraction described earlier is one such example – class and group discussions have just as important a contribution to make, particularly where concepts are open to wide interpretation and 'right' answers are not expected. Apart from anything else, children can stimulate each others' thinking.

The cognitive conflict principle is also widely applied in science education. In Chapter 4 there is a reference to the work of Osborne, Bell and Gilbert (1983), who describe its use in their account of an attempt to change children's understanding of current flow in a conventional bulb battery circuit. In science there is a right answer that can be put to the test. In their class discussions, Osborne, Bell and Gilbert listen carefully to all the alternative explanations pupils put forward, but it is the accepted solution that they focus on and emphasize.

The questions teachers ask of their classes must have varying effects on the pupils. When faced with a new situation, the most able are likely to grasp the issues quickly and resolve the dilemma at a level well in advance of their original position. The middle group would still progress but not at so fast a rate, while the views of some less able pupils might well remain undisturbed by the questioning. In such class and group discussions children seem to take what they are ready for, no more and no less.

A good start has been made but we need more classroom-based research to show the relative advantages and disadvantages of individual-, group- and class-teaching methods in respect to match over a wide range of content.

Carefully thought-out questions lie at the heart of the cognitive conflict strategy. Peel (1971, p. 121), using an historical example this time, presented children with a passage comparing the abilities and knowledge of people living in the middle ages with those of children living in the present day. His key question was: 'Were the people of the middle ages clever or stupid? How do you know?' This was followed up with many supplementaries, such as: 'Are you always clever because you can read?' 'Why is it that many ordinary modern children of twelve know more about some things than very clever people of the past?'

You will note the insistence on evidence, on going beyond the information given and sorting out the relationships or causal links between one piece of information and another. In effect, this is an exercise in logic that enters into all academic disciplines, and there is every reason to believe that primary-school children would profit from learning its basic rules.

In other curriculum areas cognitive conflict is rarely mentioned, but we hear a good deal about problem-setting and solving that have a great deal in common with it.

Teaching by Telling

Teaching by telling or meaningful reception learning, as it is called in the literature, involves giving information directly to children. Perhaps because telling as opposed to discovering seems to go against progressive methods of education, deliberate imparting of knowledge may have suffered an undeserved eclipse. Ausubel (1968) is prominent among those anxious to reinstate meaningful reception learning in schools and, in arguing his case, he makes a careful distinction between rote and meaningful learning. The former, he says, is entirely dead knowledge. It stands by itself because it has no connection with information or insights acquired in the past. In contrast, meaningful learning fits in comfortably with existing concepts and is made the learner's own in a way that knowledge acquired by rote can never be.

Reception learning has sometimes been equated with passive learning because no physical activity is involved. However, as Piaget (1977, p. 712) himself says (in an unexpected outbreak of humour), 'it has been finally understood that an active school is not necessarily a school of manual labour' – and perhaps it is now more widely recognized that meaningful reception learning involves considerable mental activity on the part of children.

McClelland (1982a) specifies three conditions that must be satisfied if meaningful learning is to take place:

1. The material itself must be meaningful.
2. The meaning of the material must be within the learner's grasp. (This underlines once more the importance of the developmental sequence in ensuring a good match between the learner's present knowledge and new teaching material.)
3. The learner must intend to learn meaningfully.

Ausubel attaches much importance to what he calls 'advance organizers', which are essentially a means of alerting the learner to the link between existing knowledge and the new material. McClelland (1982b) gives several helpful examples of advance organizers he found useful in teaching science to 7- and 8-year-olds. For instance, the key statement he gives for energy, which sets the scene for subsequent learning, is 'Energy is the ability to make changes'.

Ausubel also wisely insists that new learning should be expressed in the children's own words. Education involves a re-formulation or re-coding of knowledge that takes account both of old and new learning. This combination of the pupils' informal language and the more formal language of academic disciplines allows learners to put their own personal stamp on the new knowledge and to make it their own.

Advance organizers help the learner to make sense of the exercise in hand, although whether tightly worded, key statements should always be given before children have had a chance to sort out their own ideas is open to question. Nevertheless, at some stage the principles embodied in advance organizers can usefully guide children's explorations and give their conclusions a generality they would not otherwise have.

The critical problem – and it is not an easy one to resolve – is when to tell and when not to. Giving the right answer to a moral dilemma would be self-defeating but there are some concepts, such as the scientific explanation of thunder, which children would never acquire if left to themselves. We have to wait for what appears to be the 'teachable' moment, and only a dialogue between teacher and taught can determine when that point is reached.

Learning from Observing

Teachers are constantly being urged to give children opportunities to observe at first hand. For example, paragraph 5.10 of the influential Department of Education and Science (1978b) *Primary Education in England* survey reads 'There is hardly any aspect of the curriculum in which children can make progress without taking careful note of what they see, hear or otherwise experience, and without thinking about their observations'. Later on, in paragraph 5.12, we are told that 'opportunities for discriminating, classifying and observing inter-relations arise in connection with work in all areas of the curriculum. They could be used more fully than they are'.

I do not imagine anyone would question the value of observation in education, but Dearden (1980, p. 24) makes a critical point when he says 'What we observe is relevant to our knowledge and interests'. If observation is going to be anything other than superficial, it must be backed up with knowledge: effective observation in history demands a knowledge of history; there is a complex group of skills necessary to interpreting maps properly; the work of the old masters cannot be fully appreciated without knowing what to look for; and so we could go on.

Let us take an example. The children taking part in West's (1981) experiment looked at the same pictures but 'saw' different things. A small group not only seemed unable to see clearly but also 'saw' things that were not there. For instance, some of them mistakenly picked out men walking in the flames in a picture of the Great Fire of London and, even more remarkably, the Victory's gun-deck was variously identified as a factory, a bakery, a gasworks and a supermarket.

There is another angle to children's perceptions of pictures. There is an obvious link between their judgements of paintings and their stage of cognitive development. The younger age-groups prefer a subject-matter they can understand and identify with, a simple and realistic composition and bright and contrasting colours. In contrast, adolescents look for relationships between such abstract criteria as form, style and emotional impact, which young children could not begin to understand.

If we do not think about it too deeply, it is easy to fall into the trap of supposing that the eye acts like a camera producing instant and 'accurate' copies of reality. However, it is the memory store that dictates the stimuli we attend to and those we ignore. It governs what we perceive and it determines our interpretation of the objects and events observed.

The strong message that comes through from the research literature is that children not only need help in learning to observe effectively but also that the help they are given should take note of the learner's stage of development. Children's attention needs to be directed towards the significant and diverted away from the insignificant. Methods for guiding observations are more conveniently discussed in Chapter 4 in the context of science education, but the principles described there can also be applied to other curriculum areas.

Learning by Thinking about Thinking

Piaget tended to minimize the role of adults in children's learning, and this is why the writings of Vygotsky (1962) and Bruner (1983) – who have done much to draw attention to the social context of learning – are now in the ascendant. Bruner, for example, talks about 'scaffolding' – a process in which, initially, adults provide a range of props for young learners that are gradually withdrawn as their competence increases. As is shown later, much teaching in schools follows this pattern with teachers acting not so much as givers of knowledge but as facilitators of learning.

One illustration of the partnership between the teacher and the taught comes from mathematics. We are just beginning to learn something about the informal and often ingenious methods young children use to solve mathematical problems that teachers can capitalize on and extend. For example, children who know the doubles principle $(5 + 5 = 10)$ might be encouraged to use it in solving such a problem as $5 + 9$, which can be broken down as $5 + 5 + 4$.

One contribution teachers can make is by encouraging children to acquire metacognitive skills. This is a shorthand, technical term used to describe the ability to monitor and control one's own thinking processes. The psychological literature, as always, is difficult to interpret, but Flavell (1979) – a distinguished developmental psychologist – is convinced that children who do more cognitive monitoring are better learners in and out of school than those who do not. He is supported by Short and Ryan (1984), who report that the use of metacognitive skills is one of the major distinguishing characteristics of good readers. They cite evidence to show that less skilled, as opposed to fluent readers, 'lack knowledge about the purposes of reading, lack sensitivity to the need to behave strategically, fail to evaluate the appropriateness of chosen strategies, do not apply strategies spontaneously, and rigidly apply chosen strategies'. In her sensibly practical *The Early Detection of Reading Difficulties* (1981), Clay suggests we ought to give children ways of detecting errors for themselves using syntactic clues such as 'Does it sound right?'; semantic clues such as 'Does it make sense?'; and graphic clues such as 'Does it look right?'

In a recent review article, Reynolds and Wade (1986) warn of unresolved problems in deciding precisely what metacognition is, and in setting up experiments to investigate such difficult questions as whether metacognitive skills learned in one context can be generalized to other situations. Nevertheless, there is enough evidence to suggest that children are often unclear about what is expected of them in school – and a more substantial research literature indicates that in some activities, notably reading, time is well spent in encouraging children to monitor and control their own thinking processes.

Summary This section contains suggestions for extending children's learning – all of which rely explicitly or implicitly on linking children's present knowledge, thinking or skills with new or more advanced levels of performance.

Recent research indicates that more effective learning occurs when the teaching material is pitched at such a level that is demanding but still within the learner's reach.

A frequently recommended way of advancing thinking is to create a cognitive conflict that may force pupils to re-examine their ideas, discover where they are inadequate and, perhaps, become more receptive to new and improved ways of understanding. In the process, children can be encouraged to look for evidence and to search out relationships between variables – abilities critical to developing and defending logical arguments.

Another strategy (meaningful reception learning) again seeks to combine the known with the unknown. Children are expected to work on the information given, to internalize it and, wherever appropriate, to express the new insights gained in their own words.

A further well-used technique, the guiding of children's observations, is based on the realization that existing knowledge determines what is singled out for attention and how the phenomenon is interpreted.

Finally, there is growing interest in making learning more efficient by encouraging children to monitor and control their own thought processes.

SUMMARY AND CONCLUSIONS

In this chapter a framework for using data about conceptual development for teaching purposes was suggested, and this will be used to structure the curriculum chapters that follow. It is based on the proposition that education involves an exchange of ideas between teacher and taught and that the concepts children have acquired informally need to be seriously taken account of in schools.

First, the importance of understanding the nature of academic disciplines in giving a basic form and structure to school learning was underlined. We then examined some of the ways in which children's concepts can be revealed in words, actions and by drawing and painting. In this context, we particularly noted the importance of such probe questions as 'How do you know?' and 'Why do you say that?'

Piaget's and Peel's theories were used in the search for common features in conceptual development. Very roughly, key questions useful to teachers are as follows:

- Is the thinking characterized by tautologies or irrelevancies?
- Are there signs of egocentric thought, centring on perceptual attributes, the inability to reverse a mental operation and the inability to conserve? Conversely, can the children do all these things?
- Can pupils establish relationships between one factor and another?
- To what extent can pupils generalize?
- Can children take account of all the relevant factors and sort out the relationships between them?
- Is attention confined just to the facts provided, or do pupils go beyond the information given and generate independent ideas that govern the solution to the problem?

Finally, we turn to strategies designed to extend children's thinking in various ways: by provoking a cognitive conflict; by structuring meaningful reception learning; by encouraging observation; and by promoting self-monitoring and control of one's own cognitive processes – all of which are based on the principle of matching the learner's level of ability to the new material.

As we have seen, no single teaching method can ever work equally well with all children and for all learning activities. Some things children can find out for themselves, but for others telling is the only option open. Sometimes class and group discussions are appropriate but on other occasions individual tuition is the only way forward. Teaching is not an exact science and so most teachers soon learn to be pragmatic, using the approach that seems to be most effective in each particular situation. I have not tried to cover all the many possibilities reported in the literature, but I would suggest that the techniques described here (all of which derive from the study of conceptual development) make a substantial contribution to the range of options open to teachers.

There is one other point: it is clearly unrealistic to expect teachers to be conversant with the development of all concepts in all curriculum areas. Apart from anything else, the research evidence is incomplete. However, as several investigators have shown, teachers quickly pick up essential information about specific concepts when it is easily accessible. When it is not, a knowledge of basic trends in conceptual development can easily be acquired and used to good effect in making sense of what children say and do and in structuring learning activities.

FURTHER READING

An overview of Piagetian theory is given in Piaget and Inhelder (1969) and general introductions are provided Phillips (1969) and Donaldson (1978), among many others. Gruber and Vonèche (1977) have collected significant extracts from Piaget's writings, which they introduce and appraise. For comments and criticisms of Piaget's theory, see Mogdil and Mogdil (1976), Brainerd (1979, 1983), Brown and Desforges (1979), Ginsburg (1985), Meadows (1983) and Sternberg (1987).

Tomlinson (1981) and Travers (1983) have written comprehensive introductions to educational psychology. Among recent attempts to relate psychological theory to general classroom practice are Bennett *et al.* (1984), Entwistle (1987) and Meadows and Cashdan (1988) and, with respect to mathematics, Hughes (1986).

Sources on teachers' questioning techniques are Galton, Simon and Croll (1980) and Wragg (1984). Reviews of the literature on metacognitive processes are given in Brown and DeLoache (1983) and Robinson (1983).

2
THE LANGUAGE CURRICULUM: WRITTEN EXPRESSION

INTRODUCTION

The high priority given to language in schools comes as no surprise. Language is central to education for, in addition to being studied in its own right, it exercises a powerful influence on learning and teaching in every area of the curriculum.

We cannot possibly cover all of this vast field and so we shall concentrate on written expression that, of the four main strands – listening, speaking, reading and writing – best illustrates the contribution empirical studies can make to the teaching of language.

Before getting down to details, it is instructive to look at how writing was taught in the past. For a very long time, most people thought there was no point in setting children to write until they had a good grounding in grammar, spelling and punctuation. In the late nineteenth century, children in Standard 1 (what would now be the first year of the junior school) could pass the annual HMI inspection simply by copying a line of print. In Standards 2–4, the requirement for a pass – writing from slow dictation – was not all that demanding either. Not until Standard 5 was narrative writing, then called composition, expected. Spencer (1938) who (unusually for an HMI at that time), was a product of the elementary-school system, gives an account of annual examinations he witnessed as a pupil-teacher in the 1890s. He writes (p. 94):

> It is perhaps worth recalling that in Standard V the writing examination took the form of a composition. The inspector read out some trumpery anecdote or one of

Aesop's Fables. It was read twice. Then the class were set to reproduce the story in writing, without too many mistakes in spelling or grammar. In Standard VI the anecdote gave way to a little essay, and the task was to write as least ten lines of original composition on such subjects as 'Ships', or 'All is not gold that glitters', or even an abstract subject like 'Perseverance' or 'Punctuality'.

As the child-centred movement in education gained momentum, the focus shifted dramatically. Writing now became much freer, its range increased and it was much more likely to be based on direct experience. According to this 'personal growth' model, described by Wilkinson *et al.* (1980, p. 7), words are used to understand and to give expression to experiences. In the process, 'the words and structures "come", or are sought out, not provided externally; the "skills" are acquired almost incidentally, though not accidentally, in a context where their need is felt, though not necessarily perceived consciously'.

This short excursion into the past illustrates in extreme form two opposing schools of thought: one where the mechanics of writing are emphasized at the expense of content and where the practical needs of industry and commerce are never far from mind; and the other where written expression is valued mainly as an exploration of experience and where the mechanics of writing are a means to that end. As the national and educational press demonstrate only too clearly, the 'skills versus exploration of experience' controversy is still with us although the alternatives are not always presented in quite such stark terms.

The content and the mechanics of writing are, of course, interdependent. A command of the basic rules of language is necessary to good writing, but correct grammar, punctuation and spelling count for very little unless the writer has something of substance to say. This is why we must be clear about the nature of writing, the uses to which it can be put and its potential for learning. These are the issues to which we turn first.

THE NATURE OF WRITING AND WRITING IN SCHOOL

The Nature of Writing

At a basic level, written language can be defined as a means of expressing and communicating thoughts and feelings through the medium of letter symbols. Writing is a key element in the search for meaning because it allows us to reflect on and to order our encounters with the world and the impact they make upon us. Equally importantly, we write to share thoughts and feelings with others through communications ranging from hastily written notes to formal, carefully argued essays on complex issues.

Another way of appreciating the particular character of writing is to examine the differences between spoken and written language that, in the normal way, we rarely notice. Harpin (1976) sums up their essentials in a few crisp sentences. He writes (p. 32):

> Speech is transient; writing permanent. Speech is immediate: writing premeditated. The writer's audience may be known or unknown, near-at-hand or distant; the speaker ... has his auditors face-to-face. Speech has to be edited, amended, restated in full flow, while writing may be reworked again and again before it reaches an audience.

Summary We define writing as a symbolic activity serving two main purposes: the first is to enhance the development and analysis of thoughts and feelings, and the second is to facilitate communication with other people.

The Nature of Writing in Schools

The basic principles of English-language teaching are clearly and succinctly set out in the DES (1984) publication, *English from 5 to 16*. Part of it (p. 13) reads:

> The teacher must have a clear grasp of the range of purposes for which we need and use language. We need it for the transaction of our everyday lives. We need it for reflecting on and understanding our experiences, for responding to the world about us and for understanding and sharing the experience and insights of others. We use it to resolve problems, to make decisions, to express attitudes.

These principles are reflected in many of the models of written language that have appeared in recent years. Britton *et al.*'s (1975) framework has been particularly influential and it is given prominence here because, for many schools, it has given a refreshingly new impetus to their teaching of written expression.

Although the model is detailed and subtle, its basic proposition is quite simple: we write for a number of different purposes and so at its best, each piece of writing takes on the style appropriate to its particular purpose and the particular audience for whom it is intended. Britton identified three main modes of language use. However, they should not be interpreted as totally separate categories but more as points on a continuum with one form shading into another.

The first of these categories he called the expressive mode. Here we find writing essentially for oneself, such as note-taking or keeping a diary, and it includes the early halting attempts to write – 'After school I went to the park to play on the swings' is a simple example of the expressive mode. It is the first style, out of which grow two, the transactional and the poetic.

Transactional writing is concerned with practical purposes. It is the language people use to get things done, to record, to inform, to persuade and to regulate others. An example of the transactional mode is 'The temperature at noon today was 20°C'.

The poetic mode is something rather different: it exists for its own sake and not for purposes of everyday interaction. Novels, plays and poems are included in this category. Britton (1984) calls this mode the language of the spectator, not least because it gives the writer the chance to test out ideas away from the real world. For Britton (*ibid.*), 'It [literature] is, I suggest, writing in the role of the spectator – spectator of other men's lives, of one's own past or future or might-have-been: writing freed from the participant's need to respond with action or decision'. According to Britton, these characteristics are not confined to formal literature but can also be found in the conversation (especially gossip) and writing of all of us, including young children. Story-telling comes under this heading when it is used as a vehicle for reflecting on and understanding human concerns.

Another feature of this model is the attention it gives to audience. Very briefly, it underlines the common-sense need for writers to adopt a form and style appropriate to the intended reader as well as to the purpose of writing. In the school context, Britton's team identified (1975) the main audiences as 'self', 'the teacher in various guises from trusted adult to examiner', 'a wider known audience such as a peer group' and 'an unknown audience'.

Several other models of language have been constructed, many of which are far too complex to be of much use in primary schools. However, there is one other well-known analysis of writing constructed by Wilkinson *et al.* (1980) that, although too detailed to describe here, is considered in part later in the chapter.

Summary Three main conclusions stand out. First, writing serves many different purposes, some very practical and others of a much more reflective nature. However, a common thread running through this section is the emphasis on writing as an exploration of experience: it is an exercise in thinking, a means of sorting out, redefining and imposing order on ideas and feeling.

Second, we noted that the content and style of each piece of writing is dictated by its particular purpose and the particular audience at whom it is aimed. Third, it is as well to point out once again that, to achieve these ends, children must become proficient in the grammatical conventions of writing. With this background in mind, we can now examine the implications of psychological research to the teaching of writing.

PSYCHOLOGY AND THE TEACHING OF WRITTEN EXPRESSION

Teachers' and Children's Conceptions of Written Expression

As far as I am aware, there are no direct large-scale empirical studies of teachers' objectives in the teaching of written expression. However, there are hints here and there in the literature of the attitudes that inform teachers' work. One indication is the emphasis placed on writing for various purposes. In putting their model to the test in secondary schools, Britton *et al.* (1975) found a heavy concentration on transactional writing and hardly any use of expressive and poetic writing, except in English lessons. Not surprisingly, pupils wrote almost exclusively for their teachers, who read the work largely in their role as examiner.

This is one good practical use of such models of language as Britton's or the Assessment of Performance Unit's (1981a): they provide teachers with simple measures for checking on the range of writing tasks undertaken by their pupils, which, of course, can reveal any obvious imbalances between one type of writing and another.

However, the most telling information often comes not from statistical surveys but from small-scale classroom studies such as the one carried out by Bennett *et al.* (1984). In addition to asking sixteen teachers what they hoped their 6-7-year-old pupils would achieve in written expression, the investigators spent some time observing these same teachers in action. Of 103 tasks assigned, 54 involved topic-writing (usually the reproduction of facts after exposition by teacher or television presentation), 39 creative writing (fiction) and 10 news-writing (a halfway house between fact and fiction). In setting the work, the main aims reported by teachers included motivating children to write, increasing their vocabulary and developing the imaginative content of the writing. But the dominant goal, according to Bennett *et al.*'s (*ibid.* p.101) observations, seemed to be 'to practise writing and to use some aspects of grammar, especially capital letters and full stops as sentence markers'. In practice, the writing sessions followed an unvarying routine. A stimulus was introduced, its main features were discussed using a question-and-answer technique, key words were written on the blackboard and the children set to work. The important point was that the same approach was followed for both topic-writing and creative writing. The emphasis throughout was on neatness, quantity and grammar. Apparently there was no mention of recording the observations children made in topic work, or of exercising the imagination – which is critical to poetic writing. Once the children began to write, we are told, the preoccupation was with spelling.

We now turn to children's ideas about the purposes of writing. Most of the 9-year-old pupils in Broster's (1979) class saw story-writing as a vehicle for exercising the imagination and for improving spelling. Alexis's response is typical. She tells us: 'I do think that there is a purpose in writing a story because it can help you in spelling and opening your mind up and using your imagination'. When asked later on to say how their stories could be improved, the children focused overwhelmingly on good handwriting, neatness, punctuation, grammar, learning new words and, again, accurate spelling. Significantly, it will be noticed, improving the ability to express thoughts and to organize ideas in writing were not mentioned at all.

The study referred to in Chapter 1 (Tamburrini, Willig and Butler, 1984) attempted to quantify children's reasons for writing stories, poems and for recording project work. The sample consisted of 10- and 11-year-old children who were selected by their teachers on the basis of their above-average ability in written expression.

As with Broster, the researchers were told constantly that writing stories 'helps your imagination', which most of them defined quite reasonably as something fantastic, unreal or impossible. But there is another interpretation of imagination that corresponds much more with Britton's (1984) poetic mode. It is concerned with expressing thoughts and feelings about the world through stories of people who are fictional but recognizably human and who, like all of us, are trying to make sense of a complicated world. It is well worth considering imaginative writing in this light, and perhaps giving less emphasis to 'fantastic' writing. More is said on this matter later in the chapter. Another of Tamburrini, Willig and Butler's (1984) findings, and one that now has a familiar ring, was that over half the group looked on story-writing as a vehicle for improving grammar, spelling, punctuation and handwriting.

Most of the very able children interviewed were baffled about the reasons for writing poetry, several of them dismissing it as something for adults only. But when it came to justifying writing in topic work they were again quite definite. Over three-quarters of the sample unhesitatingly told the researchers that project-writing helped them to acquire facts, with the record-keeping and the reference functions coming a close second. The following is a typical comment: 'If you've just learned about it in class by being talked to, after a while you'd probably forget it, but if you've got it down on paper, then you can just look over it again'.

Summary   The main drift emerging from the studies reviewed above is that children as well as teachers were aware of the practical purposes of writing and set great store by mastering its techniques. At the same time, story-writing was approved of and enjoyed as an exercise in imaginative thinking – perhaps because it freed children from some of the constraints associated with transactional writing. However, there were indications that even able boys and girls did not see the relevance of imaginative writing to the real world and overwhelmingly took the view that imagination was about things that could not happen. This led to an undue emphasis on space fiction and stories about witches and the like.

Clearly, we need to know much more about children's impressions of writing, but if the situation suggested here is at all typical, there seems to be a long way to go before pupils understand the varied uses of writing and its potential for exploring experiences.

The Development of Children's Written Expression

To represent research into the very beginnings of children's writing, we begin with an indepth study by Dyson (1983b) that will be of special interest to teachers of young children.

In reviewing later stages in the development of written expression, we shall first consider cognitive and stylistic aspects of writing and then move on to examine research into the ability to spell and to punctuate.

The early stages

In studying the early stages of written expression, Dyson (*ibid*.) did not rely on analysing children's work alone but chose instead to observe how children set about writing in a typical classroom context. She recorded their spontaneous comments and talked with them about their work as it was in progress. Dyson's group consisted of 22 5-year-olds from whom she selected 5 for intensive daily study over a period of three months. Her data included a staggering 500 pieces of writing, records of 36 hours of spontaneous talk and 112 observations, as well as 377 written accounts of visits to the school.

In an effort to impose order on this mass of material, Dyson constructed a model of writing consisting of the following three elements:

1. *Message formulation* – deciding on the message to be written.
2. *Message encoding* – calling to mind the letter symbols needed to write the message.
3 *Mechanical formation* – the actual writing of the letter symbols.

Outside this pattern, there is a fourth element – *message decoding*. This represents a situation where the beginner forms letters but without any particular message in mind and then expects it to be decoded by the reader (an example is given later).

Dyson reasoned that sophisticated writers think of a message (message formation), call to mind the appropriate written symbols (message encoding) and transcribe those symbols on to the page (mechanical formation).

It is important to grasp that young children do not see things in this light at all and, indeed, in the early stage, rarely use all three components in a single piece of work. Sometimes one component is sufficient for their purpose, sometimes two and sometimes three. On rare occasions only, the message-encoding element is added making four elements in all. Further, the components can be combined in various ways to describe particular types of writing. Dyson discovered ten different forms that children's early writing can take, on which she based a tentative scheme for illustrating developmental trends in writing.

At the first stage only the mechanical formation component was involved. All children did here was to produce conventional symbols, such as the alphabet – not to be read but simply to be looked at. For instance, Tracy wrote a long and random string of letters simply for the pleasure of doing so, just 'to make a long one', as she said. Initially, therefore, the focus is not on meaning but on the perceptual – such graphic features of writing as the shape of letters, the form words take, linearity and the direction of words on the page.

At the second stage, two components were involved: mechanical formation and message decoding. The 'message' consisted of some letters and 'words' written at random, but it was quite incomprehensible to the child who wrote it. Nevertheless, Ashley, another of Dyson's group, was confident his work could be read by someone, even if he couldn't do so himself: 'My mama'll read it, and she'll know', he said.

At the third stage, the writing was structured around three components: message formulation, message encoding and mechanical formation. Children now understand that letters and words can be used symbolically to organize phenomena. Dyson noticed an intense interest in labelling or providing captions for objects, persons or events. For example, one girl wrote her apartment number, her mother's name, her brother's name, her own age and the age of her brother all in the same piece of writing.

Finally, children discover that there is more to writing than labelling – speech, too, can be represented and shaped into a particular message for a particular audience.

Clay's (1975, p. 66) investigation produced a very similar developmental scale, which can be summarized as follows: The child

● knows what symbols are;

- knows that writing conveys messages, although his or her own efforts do not;
- can copy a message with some understanding; and
- can independently use familiar sentence patterns.

Clay has also produced a scale for assessing language level that ranges from letters through to words, phrases, sentences and lastly to stories consisting of two or more sentences.

Summary If we take Dyson's and Clay's findings together, they suggest a developmental sequence that goes something like the following. Initially, children construe writing very differently from adults. Their first concern is with writing of symbols for their own sake and with no thought of a message in mind. The realization that writing can be used to communicate comes early on, but children go through a phase in which neither the writer nor anyone else can make sense of what is written. Once the symbolic nature of writing is understood, it is used extensively to label people, things and events that helps to impose system and order on these phenomena.

At the next stage, messages are more or less successfully copied and understood. This leads on to a final stage when children are able to write independent messages that can be followed without difficulty by others.

Classroom applications This research provides teachers with a simple framework for analysing and assessing children's early attempts at writing. The writing itself provides the main clues to achievement. We can see at a glance whether children are just making marks on paper or are using writing for labelling, for copying messages or for independently expressing their own ideas. Sometimes, however, in the very early stage it is necessary to probe a little to discover whether children really do understand that we can communicate with others through writing.

The developmental scale outlined in this section also gives teachers clear aiming points in the teaching of written expression.

Later stages in the development of writing

After the beginning stage, there are several ways of charting the developmental sequence in written expression but, because of the richness and complexity of language and the variety of uses to which it is put, no one theoretical framework can do it justice.

We now turn to Wilkinson *et al.*'s (1980) analysis of writing in schools, which is the most comprehensive to appear so far. It is built around four models of development: the cognitive (which relates to thinking), the affective (which relates to the emotions), the moral and the stylistic - all later tried out in assessing the written language of children aged 7, 10 and

13. As Wilkinson's framework is very detailed, and because we shall be considering moral development in a later chapter, only the cognitive and stylistic models will be reviewed here.

A simplified version of the cognitive model is given in Table 2.1. We could expect most primary children to be at levels 1 and 2 but some children of middle-school age are capable of reaching levels 3 and 4. In collecting material on which this scale is based, Wilkinson and his colleagues asked 7-, 10- and 13-year-olds to describe for someone else how to play any game they knew well. Just consider what this involves for a moment: the writer has to order and classify the information, identify the basic rules and objects of the game and avoid confusing the reader with unnecessary detail.

Table 2.1   Wilkinson's cognitive model

Level	Aspect	Content
1	Describing	labelling, naming, recording, reporting
2	Interpreting	explaining, inferring, deducing
3	Generalizing	abstracting, summarizing, evaluating, concluding, reflecting, classifying
4	Speculating	irrelevant hypothesizing, exploring, projecting, theorizing based on sustained hypotheses

(*Source*: Summarized and adapted from Wilkinson *et al.*, 1980, p. 71–7.)

By and large, the 7-year-olds did not do very well. For example, Wilkinson *et al.* (1980, p. 95) report Sally's explanation of tiddly-winks: 'We all have a number board and a cup in the middle of number board and you flick it in the cup if it land on the number board flick all the count'. In terms of cognitive content, this attempt is at level-1 standard. Some description is there, but very little explanation, and so it is difficult to make much sense of this account. She does name the apparatus needed but she is not at all clear about how to use it; and she is just as vague about the rules of the game. Some of the more able 7-year-olds were able to provide systematic descriptions but over half of this age-group could not satisfactorily explain how to play a game they were very familiar with. As Piaget's theory predicts, egocentric thinking was dominant. Children mainly described what they themselves did and gave scant attention to the part opponents played in the game. Typically, too, only partial information was given, which added to the reader's confusion.

In general, the efforts at explanation of the 10-year-olds were at level 2. Their accounts were much less egocentric than those of 7-year-olds; they avoided the trap of giving only partial information; and they explained the essential function of rules much more clearly. However, children in this age-group were still unable to define clearly and succinctly the object of the game or to give a systematic and complete account of the procedures involved in playing it.

At 13, many children had reached level 3, by which time their powers of explanation and ability to order material were still further improved. They were beginning to generalize about the purpose of the game, and such statements as 'The object of the game is to buy as many property's as possible and to make the appoinint bankrupt' (*ibid*. p. 102) started off the accounts of about a third of this age-group. In addition, children could now methodically identify various aspects of the game, such as its equipment, the main rules and the playing pitch and, most important of all, show how they are interrelated. The authors go into other refinements in some detail for which there is no space here, but it is sufficient to emphasize that the best descriptions, in contrast to a simple chronological account, demonstrated an ability to interpret the rules, to make generalizations about them and to describe how they operate in practice.

This analysis bears the imprint of Piaget's work. There are references to egocentricity, which is replaced by an understanding of writer's audience; to centring on a few details only until, in time, the overall picture is taken into account; and to the initial ignoring of cause and effect relationships until their relevance becomes clear.

Table 2.2 shows Wilkinson's (1980) summary of the stylistic model. It would take too long to describe in detail the application of these scales to examples of children's writing but, briefly, the progression is from writing that is lacking in organization and ignores the reader's needs, to work characterized by careful organization, with syntax and vocabulary adapted to the purpose of the exercise.

Summary   In this section on later stages in the development of written expression we first traced children's growing powers of explanation, where we noted a marked shift from egocentric thinking and simple descriptions of unrelated facts towards ordered explanations of events that took account of all relevant factors and the relationships between them.

The changing features of style are not so easy to analyse, but a growing tendency to adapt syntax and vocabulary to the purposes of the task and the needs of the reader is apparent.

Table 2.2   Wilkinson's stylistic model

Component	Range of ability
Syntax	From simple to complex sentences
Verbal competence	From literal, concrete vocabulary to use of abstract terms and greater discrimination in choice of words
Organization	From little coherent structure to capacity to control ideas and organize structure appropriately
Cohesion	From relatively unrelated components of text to employment of wide range of cohesive devices
Awareness of reader	From assumption that reader understands to sophisticated awareness of viewpoint of reader
Appropriateness	From writing close to speech to a style appropriate to the nature of the writing task

(*Source*: Summarized and adapted from Wilkinson *et al.*, 1980, p. 76–82.)

Classroom applications   The idea of describing how to play a game can be adapted and taken up across the curriculum, for instance, in giving an account of a scientific experiment or in explaining how a model was built. Children's attempts could then form the basis for individual, group and class discussions aimed at encouraging greater precision in writing. Useful questions might be 'Imagine you know nothing at all about this game (or whatever), do you think you'd be able to play it from your description?' or 'How could you improve this explanation?' Better still, children could try to follow each other's descriptions.

Table 2.1 is worth examining for other possibilities. Older children could attempt to summarize their thinking in topic and project work and, as is shown later, it is also possible to use Wilkinson's analysis as a basis for encouraging logical argument.

Research on aspects of writing styles spells out the broad stages of development and guides teachers towards what to look for. The Assessment of Performance Unit's (1981a) language performance survey also contains a breakdown of criteria used in assessing written expression, which serves the same purpose.

Spelling and punctuation

English spelling is erratic but contains more regularities than is commonly supposed. There are countless instances of a straightforward match between sound and letter – as in 'bat' – and very often the pronunciation of a word does provide at least partial clues to its spelling. But the phonic method alone will never get the learner very far: other strategies must be mastered, based not on sound alone but on the meanings of words and how they are organized into sentences. As Read (1986, p. 2) explains, some spellings 'represent morphemes [units of meaning], rather than sounds; thus while "sign" is partly a direct representation of sounds, it also indicates a relationship in meaning and derivation to "signature" and "signify" '.

Stubbs (1980, p. 50) uses a particular morpheme, '-ed', known technically as a past-tense marker, to illustrate the role of meaning in spelling. All experienced users of the language automatically recognize that adding '-ed' to a verb indicates the past tense. However, there are distinct differences in pronouncing '-ed' in 'walked', 'wanted' and 'showed' that in the ordinary way we hardly notice, yet the same symbol suffices because it stands for a common meaning. As Stubbs explains, a strong visual factor is operating so that 'units which look the same, mean the same'. Conversely, he goes on, such words as 'ruff' and 'rough', which are pronounced the same but are unrelated, look very different.

Essentially, English spelling is not so haphazard and illogical as popular myth suggests – it does contain regularities based on correspondences between sound and symbol but, in addition, there are subtler consistencies based on units of meaning.

Clearly, we can no longer simply regard learning to spell as an exercise in memorization. Children will try to make sense of spelling as they do everything else, although the strategies they use may not always be immediately obvious. Take this delightful example from Ferreiro's (1980) account of a 4-year-old Spanish-speaking child's attempts to write the words 'cock', 'hen' and 'chick' (cited by Read, 1986). Ferreiro showed the girl the word 'GALLO' (cock) printed on a card and she then asked her to write 'GALLINO' (hen). The child wrote 'GALL' because she said a hen is smaller than a cock and so needs fewer letters. Following the same line of reasoning, 'POLLITO' (chick) was written as 'GAL' because it is smaller still.

As always, it is the errors in spelling children make that provide a clue to the strategies they are using and, because the same types of errors are consistently found, it is possible to define a developmental sequence of spelling from its crude beginning to the stage when conventional forms are mastered. Gentry (1982) is one of a group of researchers who have identified developmental trends in spelling that he illustrated with material from Bissex's (1980) longitudinal study of the spelling of her own child, Paul. A summary of his scale is given in Table 2.3.

It is also instructive to ask children to explain their own spelling

Table 2.3   Gentry's developmental stages in spelling

Stage	Characteristics	Examples
Precommunicative	Knows that letters and numbers represent a message but does not yet understand the letter–sound relationships so his or her efforts are unreadable	KMLQPR
Semiphonetic	Recognizes that letters have sounds that represent the sounds of words. Spelling is abbreviated in form; words and phrases are not separated	TLEFNBER = telephone number
Phonetic	Can now represent complete surface-sound structure of a word; phonetic spelling is systematic but silent letters are excluded. Words in sentences are now separated	I WEL KOM TO YOR HAWS = I will come to your house
Transitional	Moves from total reliance on phonetic strategy to using morphological and visual spelling	EIGHTEE = eighty TIPE = type HUOSE = house
Correct	Now has a command of the English spelling system and its basic rules covering prefixes, suffixes, contractions and compound words; growing accuracy in using silent consonants; ability to recognize when words do not look right; and mastery of words with irregular spellings	

(*Source*: Adapted from Gentry, 1982.)

strategies, as Radebaugh (1985) did when he analysed how nine good spellers and eight poor ones in the 7–10 age-group tackled various spelling tasks. The core of the experiment centred on children's attempts to spell difficult words and sentences that, they were told, were so hard that they were bound to get the spelling wrong. The pupils were asked to explain what they were thinking as they wrote and why they made the decisions they did.

All the pupils were at Gentry's transitional stage but even so, there were clear differences in the way good and poor spellers set about the task. First, poor spellers mainly sounded out unfamiliar words letter by letter, as in 'koshisle' for cautiously and 'dinusor' for dinosaur. In contrast, good spellers were much more likely to think out possible spellings, bit by bit. Thus we now have 'cociously' for cautiously and 'dinosoar' for dinosaur. Incidentally, the latter version was inspired by the child thinking of 'Dino, my favourite cartoon character, and about pterodactyls soaring through the air, and then I put them together "dinosoar" ' (Radebaugh, 1985).

A second major tactic distinguishing good from poor spellers was the use of visual imagery. Good spellers often reported having pictures in the mind when spelling words. One girl spelled 'squirrel' correctly by visualizing it as she had seen it written on her crayon box earlier in the year; another conjured up an image of the word 'arithmetic' on the blackboard to help her spell it. In contrast, poor spellers made no reference whatsoever to visual imagery.

In essence, learning to spell is a cognitive act based initially on sound-symbol correspondence. Later on when that strategy fails, more sophistic-ated techniques are developed that take account of the meanings of words, how they are arranged in sentences and, quite simply, 'how they look'.

In punctuating, too, children work out their own way of doing things. Cordeiro (1988), who analysed the free writing of 22 6-year-olds and 13 8-year-olds, found clear differences in punctuation errors between the two age-groups. Younger children were prone to make obvious mistakes, such as placing full stops between all the words in a sentence (The.cat.sat.on.the.mat) and at the end of each line or of each page, whether needed or not. Older children, on the other hand, made what Cordeiro calls phrase-structure errors, where they used full stops unnecessarily to split up phrases. Here are some examples: 'I went downtown. with my mother'. 'TV cameras. were at the museum.' 'There were big bottles. and bubbles coming out.' Note however, the significant advance. Children are now making decisions based on their syntactic and semantic knowledge instead of using full stops simply to mark the ends of lines and pages.

In discussing her work, Cordeiro cites other research that suggests that sentences are not a major feature of early oral language, and so, when children come to write, they are dealing with a structure beyond their experience. This finding deserves to be more widely known because it goes a long way towards explaining why writing in sentences is so troublesome to many children.

Summary   In our examination of research into spelling and punctuation, we noted time and time again how children tried to make sense of and use these conventions. Many of the errors children commit are not random but are based on rules they have generated for themselves about how spelling and punctuation operate. In fact, progress in learning to spell, as in so many aspects of school work, consists of constantly forming rules and re-forming rules in the light of increasing understanding.

Classroom applications   We shall be considering the teaching of spelling shortly, but I would advise close study of Table 2.3, which provides a clear structure for leading children through the stages of learning to spell.

Research on punctuation, limited though it is, alerts us to a major problem children have in understanding the function of sentences. The best tactic here is to impress on children the part punctuation plays in making meaning clearer by comparing passages written in sentences with those containing no punctuation at all.

Extending Children's Ability in Written Expression

Before we come to the experimental literature on improving children's written language, there are some preliminary general points we ought to consider. First of all, since writing is a means of clarifying and analysing thoughts and feelings about ourselves, other people and the physical and social world, it follows that writing of real quality can only arise out of significant experiences.

Second, it is probable that good models of writing (and, in particular, literature) positively influence a writer's style, organization of material, vocabulary, spelling and the conventions of written language. Going a step further, good writing also demonstrates to the young learner the power of words to express and to provoke thoughts and feelings on matters the writer cares deeply about.

Extending children's written expression: some implications of research

I shall follow my general plan by turning next to empirical attempts to improve children's written language. Unfortunately, psychology seems to have been little used in this area but, nevertheless, we should not overlook the considerable educational implications of studies reviewed in the last section.

Dixon and Stratta (1986), for instance, give a detailed guide to using the 'argument' aspect of Wilkinson *et al.*'s (1980) model of language, where the stages leading eventually to the construction of a logical argument are set out. I will not give their suggestions in full, but working from Wilkinson's stages the authors urged teachers to watch out for – and encourage indications of a shift away from – unsupported statements, and the assumption that the reader is bound to think in the same way as the writer, towards backing up statements with well-supported evidence, being prepared to qualify generalizations and developing the ability to anticipate the reader's likely problems.

Spelling is the one area that has really caught the attention of psychologists, and in the further-reading section I have listed a number of sources on the teaching of spelling – all of which are based on developmental principles. The research evidence reviewed earlier suggests that pupils at the precommunicative stage need help not only in mastering the alphabet and the direction in which to write but also in grasping the significance of the sound-symbol correspondence. That emphasis carries over into the semiphonetic stage but now the object is to encourage children to expand on the abbreviated forms now commonly used. Semiphonetic spellers, it will be recalled, are content to write BZR for buzzer and so, when the time is ripe, attention is focused on each phoneme in turn, and not just those that seem most important.

A different plan of action yet again is needed for phonetic and transitional spellers, who are now ready to incorporate morphological and visual elements into their spelling strategies. Pupils can now begin to cope with the basic rules of the orthographic system that, for example, governs the spelling of prefixes, suffixes and contractions. They are also ready to begin to analyse the structure of words and to note their similarities and differences. Once there is a good command of the basics, Zutell (n.d.) recommends getting children to sort words into distinct but related words or classes. For instance, words illustrating different pronunciations of the past marker, '-ed', are presented, and children are invited to add further words in each class. Thus

- 'walked' could be followed by 'liked' and 'forked';
- 'played' could be followed by 'showed' and 'blamed'; and
- 'cheated' could be followed by 'started' and 'created'.

Zutell also suggests that what he calls word-webbing can help to familiarize more able children with the meanings of words and relationships between words and their spelling. A 'root' word is given, such as 'native', from which as many words as possible in the same family are derived, such as 'nature', 'natural', 'naturally', 'nation' and 'national'.

The conference and the promotion of revising skills

Two interrelated features of teaching writing have been given prominence by the work of Graves (1983, 1984). The first is the importance attached to conferences, which are, in effect, individual tutorials where teachers and pupils meet to discuss written work face to face; the second is the emphasis on drafting and revising skills.

In this long-term study of twenty children in the 6–8-year-old age-group, Graves and his associates made no direct attempt to control the variables operating in the classroom or to quantify the data. Children were observed routinely at work in the classroom and were encouraged to talk about what they were doing. Although there was a deliberate policy of not trying to influence the teaching, teachers' questions were readily and fully answered. In fact, the schools showed a great deal of interest in the project and, in consequence, as Graves (1984) cheerfully admits, 'we ended up having more influence on the environment than might be expected'.

From these observations and later, more direct involvement in the teaching of written expression, Graves came to a number of conclusions about the teaching of writing. It became clear to him that the initiators of writing ought to be the pupils themselves and not their teachers, who are seen primarily as enablers, not directors. According to this view, the teacher's job is to discover their pupils' purposes, to define the problems likely to be encountered in achieving them and to guide children towards a successful completion of the chosen tasks. As to the selection of topics, Graves is equally unequivocal. Children, he says, should have the chance to write what they know and care about in the full realization that they have something of value to say to teachers, peers and other audiences. Clearly, Graves is much more interested in convincing children that their own lives are worth writing about than in encouraging story- or fantasy-writing. This point is returned to later.

The conference system was developed as follows. In the Graves's study, teachers were asked to hold individual conferences at least once a week. Children were warned in advance to be prepared to talk about their current writing, and the session centred on the pupils' plans – but with the teacher acting in a supporting but, nevertheless, challenging role. Discussion of content had the first priority, leaving problems of form to be dealt with later.

Graves (1983, p. 109) leaves nothing to chance and gives very specific guidance to teachers in how to conduct conferences, right down to the particular questions to ask. For instance, he refers to process questions that are designed to help children put their plans into practice, such as 'What do you think you'll do next?' and 'Where had you thought to start?' In the same careful manner, opening questions, following questions, questions that reveal development and questions that deal with basic structures and questions, are all detailed.

A central purpose of the conference is to develop children's drafting and revising skills that are an essential, yet easily neglected, part of writing. When Tamburrini, Willig and Butler (1984) talked to very able children about their planning and revising strategies, they discovered that (while some children started out with a rough plan in mind), others worked out the story line or description as they went along. When the work was complete, only very rarely was the text re-worked and polished, and even then the corrections made were confined to grammar, spelling, punctuation and vocabulary and never to content.

Graves (1983, p. 152) points out that the changes children make in the text reveal how far they have developed in their understanding of writing. When children first begin to revise, it is spelling they first concentrate on; only many years later do they attempt a really comprehensive revision. The following is the basic developmental sequence Graves describes:

1. Spelling.
2. Motor-aesthetic issues (the mechanics of making revisions neatly and effectively).
3. Conventions (punctuation, capital letters).
4. Topic and information.
5. Major revision (addition and exclusion of information, reorganization).

Basically, Graves's research centres on pupil–teacher interaction (or, as he would call it, the conference), much of it devoted to promoting drafting and revision skills. However, as Barrs (1983) notes, few examples of children's writing are referred to in Graves's (1983) major work; and untypically for a school-based study, neither are data from individual case studies included that might show more clearly the detailed development of writing processes and how they can be enhanced.

While acknowledging the undoubted merits of Graves's approach (and, in particular, its emphasis on freedom to choose topics and the importance of basing the teaching around children's intentions), Barrs criticizes its heavy stress on teaching routines. She also takes Graves to task for, as she sees it, emphasizing writing about personal experience and for information at the expense of story-writing. Finally, Barrs objects to the prominence given in Graves's model to 'publication' (and, by implication, audiences) while at the same time giving only a passing glance to writing as a means of exploring and understanding the world. For my part, to take the last two points first, I am not sure the charges entirely stand up. While Graves undoubtedly harks repeatedly on 'publication', he recognizes that in the early stages writing is highly egocentric in nature and marked by its almost total disregard of audience. Furthermore, I would have thought that exploring and understanding the world would be encouraged by much of the personal writing and writing for information Graves is so insistent on.

The virtual absence of story-telling in Graves's approach is another matter. This issue is really outside the bounds of this book, but I must give support to the claim that, under certain conditions, story-writing has a powerful educational function. There is a good case for imaginative writing made out by Cowie (1984) who, among others, stresses how enjoyable it is in its own right, as well as making it possible for children to explore past experiences and to contemplate future possibilities vicariously. As Cowie (*ibid*. p. 63) says, 'By creating characters, actions and settings they [children] gain insights into real-life happenings'.

Nevertheless, to return to an earlier theme, there is another form of so-called imaginative writing that centres on the literally fantastic and that, unlike the traditional fairy tale or myth, makes no link at all with the reality of children's lives. This is the kind of imaginative writing children mainly focus on. However, it is more difficult to justify educationally because it is often dull and derivative and lacking in the authenticity that comes from real and significant experiences. Perhaps this is why Graves gives story-writing so little attention.

For many, the idea of the conference is the most significant feature of this model. A second, almost equally important, idea is its insistence on teachers taking their cue from the goals children have set themselves. Perhaps there is too much emphasis on the mechanics of writing and publication (apart from the skills of drafting and revising) and an under-emphasis on imaginative writing, but the model is flexible enough to accommodate other objectives teachers give higher priority to.

Summary There are disappointingly few studies demonstrating the application of developmental principles to the teaching of written expression, although general learning principles and allied research in other curriculum subjects testify to their value.

Considered in a wider context, Graves's classroom-based research is important for its emphasis on clarifying intentions and for giving children clear strategies for planning, executing and editing their work.

SUMMARY AND CONCLUSIONS

Language is a difficult part of the curriculum to review from a psychological standpoint, not only because of its broad canvas but also because it is inseparable from practically all other school activities. However, by singling out writing as an example it has been possible to comment in fair detail on some of the implications of psychological studies for the teaching and learning of at least one aspect of the language curriculum that could serve as a model for the whole.

At a basic level, writing serves to represent the phenomena (both concrete and abstract) people encounter as they go about their lives. Written language opens up possibilities for exploring and understanding experience, and also for raising interpersonal communication to a level of efficiency unimaginable without it.

For the last decade or so, it has been impressed on us that there is not just one purpose for writing, but several. A principal endeavour over this period has been to devise models of language for use in analysing the functions and practice of writing in schools. As a result, we are now in a much better position to look for, and to redress where need be, perceived imbalances in the forms of writing children engage in.

Faithful to the principle that clarity of intentions is basic to effective learning, the concepts of writing held by teachers and children were explored. The empirical evidence is not too strong, but it seems that mastering the techniques of writing is a major priority for both teachers and children. Expressive writing is also highly regarded because it exercises the imagination – a concept, however, that is mainly confined to the fantastic as opposed to looking with fresh eyes at 'real-life' experiences. Overall, there is evidence that the basic utilitarian and expressive/aesthetic purposes of writing are understood. However, it is also quite evident that a sharper definition of the objectives of written expression is needed if its full potential is to be realized.

Classroom studies characteristic in this area have a clear advantage over more rigid forms of experimentation often employed elsewhere, mainly because the conclusions offered are derived from studying real children in near-typical situations. Dyson's (1983b) analysis of the early stages of writing is a good example. However, research in this field is uneven so that, for example, we know much more about the development of spelling than we do about the development of style or punctuation. Nevertheless, standard sources such as Wilkinson *et al.* (1980) give a good general perspective of written expression and the stages to be expected along the road to becoming a mature and practised writer. The detail may not always easily be recalled, but the general developmental drift can, which can be used to good effect in the teaching of written expression.

FURTHER READING

A good source on language in general is Bolton (1975). For a critical review of models of language, see Wilkinson *et al.* (1980).

Psychologists have shown intense interest in language acquisition and development, and the relationships between language and thought – subjects beyond the scope of this chapter. Introductory texts in these areas are Greene (1975) and de Villiers and de Villiers (1979).

A general review of the psychology and teaching of spelling is given by Read (1986). Research on aspects of writing not covered in the text include Paramour and Wilkinson's (1985) and Newkirk's (1987) exploration of narrative and non-narrative writing.

General texts on the teaching of written expression are Harpin (1976), Martin (1983), Perera (1984), Wilkinson (1986) and Temple *et al.* (1988). The Bullock Report (1975) and the Kingman Report (1986) – which contains a comprehensive bibliography – include much material of interest to teachers.

3

MATHEMATICAL EDUCATION

INTRODUCTION

Mathematics is generally considered to be, in the current jargon, a 'core subject', but it is not without its controversies. One vocal body of opinion sees mathematics as essentially utilitarian in purpose and emphasizes the learning of number facts, if need be by rote. Others take a contrary view, stressing the fundamental importance of understanding mathematical relationships – not only for their own sake, but also to increase children's awareness of the relevance and meaning of mathematics in their own lives and in the world at large.

A glance at the teaching of mathematics in the past might help to put current controversies in perspective. Two hundred years ago, the teaching of mathematics was certainly geared to the practical. Hawney's (1763) *The Complete Measurer: or, the Whole Art of Measuring* begins with a gentle introduction to the complexities of decimal notation, square and cube roots and the measurement of area. Armed with this basic knowledge, readers were then directed to chapters appropriate to their trade, such as carpentry, bricklaying or masonry. The following is a problem set for plasterers: 'If a Cieling be 59 Feet 9 Inches long, and 24 Feet 6 Inches broad, How many Yards doth that Cieling contain?' And one for 'joyners' reads: 'If a room of Wainſcot be 16 Feet 3 Inches high (being girt over the Mouldings), and the Compaſs on the room 137 Feet 6 Inches; How many Yards are contained therein?' The language might be a little archaic, but the content is not unfamiliar.

Concentration on the utilitarian purposes of mathematics was just as strong early in this century. In Welton's (1909, p. 406) judgement, the content of arithmetic 'should be at least enough ... to make the pupils effective and economical managers of households, whilst still more must be included to render possible an intelligent and critical interest in municipal and national finance'. Later on, he expected mathematics to take on a more practical, vocational slant.

In recent decades, there have been several attempts to improve the quality of mathematics teaching. Included among them, as is described later, was a phenomenon known as 'Modern' or 'New' mathematics that, around the 1960s, appeared to represent a revolutionary alternative to traditional methods. A period of confusion followed but, as is explained later, the situation now seems to have been resolved.

Currently, most educators acknowledge the extrinsic and intrinsic purposes of the discipline, stressing that while mathematics has obvious practical applications, is is also worthy of study in its own right. Under the influence of active theories of learning, a high premium is placed on getting pupils to explore and to strive to make sense of mathematical relationships supported by the active intervention of teachers. However, the tension between learning mathematical facts and skills for largely practical purposes, and the guided-intervention approach with its emphasis on understanding (although blurred at the edges), is still with us.

An appreciation of the nature of mathematics and mathematics education, to which we turn first, puts that controversy in a wider context.

THE NATURE OF MATHEMATICS AND MATHEMATICAL EDUCATION
The Nature of Mathematics

Although it is difficult to convey much of the nature of mathematics in just a few words, it is essential to try to do so if the teaching of mathematics in schools is to make any real impact. From my background reading, where I have drawn particularly on the work of Bergamini (1969), Wilder (1965, 1972), Dieudonné (1978), Steen (1978) and Buxton (1984), I have abstracted five characteristics of the discipline that seem to me to be the most significant. They are:

- its content,
- its search for order,
- its abstract nature,
- its division into pure and applied forms, and
- its concern with proof.

The most obvious distinguishing feature of mathematics is its content, but developments in the discipline have been so complex and so numerous that it is impossible to say much about its various branches and sub-branches (now standing at almost a hundred according to some sources) without considerable over-simplification. Instead, to allow us to move on, it seems preferable to go back to the roots of the discipline and to define mathematics simply and at its most basic level as the study of number and space.

The second characteristic of mathematics is much easier to get across. Mathematicians search for patterns and relationships in number, quantity and space. Above all, they try to impose system and order on mathematical phenomena so as to gain a better understanding of their essential structure.

The third feature that marks out mathematics is its abstract nature. Abstraction is about classifying and generalizing, and it involves sorting out similarities and differences between phenomena. For example, we can abstract the fact that the numbers 15, 25 and 600 share the property of being divisible by 5. We may start with the concrete, but abstraction takes us away from what we see before us and into the realm of new possibilities and ideas. With the extraneous clutter removed, essential relationships between objects can be much more easily detected and understood. This is the main purpose of abstraction.

The fourth characteristic of mathematics (and one shared with science) is that it can be practised in pure and applied forms. In its infancy, mathematics was always used to solve practical problems in the 'real' world. Pure mathematics is different in purpose. It owes its existence to curiosity – arguably the greatest motivating force of all for learning. The founding fathers of pure mathematics, the Greeks, were not content to know that something worked, they wanted to know why it worked: so pure mathematics, in which practical considerations are put aside, was born. At least that was the intention, but in contemporary mathematics the distinction between pure and applied forms has become obscured because, paradoxically, the work of pure mathematicians, which was supposed to be removed from the practical business of living, has proved to be remarkably useful in applied fields.

The fifth characteristic of mathematics, and again one shared with other disciplines, is its concern with 'proof'. We are back again to the problem of tests for 'truth' that, as we shall see in the next chapter, has been so vexing in science. Surprisingly, the situation in mathematics, despite its long dependence on logic, appears to be almost as uncertain. It is not possible go into detail here, but for further information I would advise reading Dieudonné's (1978, p. 550) clear and concise explanation of the problems associated with traditional proofs, part of which reads: 'If we are to believe, like our forefathers, that "God is a mathematician", then we must admit that His ways in using mathematics to build up the Universe are more inscrutable then they ever were'.

The reasons for studying mathematics figure prominently in the literature. Buxton's (1984, Chapter 13) analysis is particularly lucid and comprehensive and is well worth reading in full. The main purposes he lists are briefly set out in Table 3.1 This table demonstrates clearly the wide range of uses for mathematics and no further comment is necessary here.

Table 3.1   The purposes of mathematics

Category	Purpose	Typical activities
Survival mathematics	Coping with the everyday world	Checking change, telling the time
Useful mathematics	Intelligent decision-making	Checking gas bills, interpreting simple statistics
Direct applications	For solving problems peculiar to mathematics	Operational research, linear processing, systems analysis
Mathematics as a language and tool	Instrumental use in serving other disciplines	Applications in physics, geography and psychology
Mathematics for its own sake	Simply to know	Any problem that interests the mathematician

(*Source*: Constructed from Buxton, 1984.)

Summary   Mathematics may be defined simply as the study of number and space. It is an abstract subject, characterized by its attempts to impose system and order on mathematical phenomena. The discipline consists of two forms – pure and applied mathematics – although the division between the two is nothing like as rigid as it once was. Finally, traditional methods of mathematical proof are currently causing philosophical difficulties that appear, as yet, to be unresolved.

The purposes of mathematics may be divided into three broad but overlapping groups. First there is the intrinsic reason for studying mathematics or 'mathematics for mathematics' sake'. Second, mathematics serves instrumental purposes in facilitating the ends of other disciplines. Third, there is another set of purposes associated with the use of mathematics in helping individuals to function effectively in the community.

The Nature of Mathematical Education

As mentioned earlier, around the 1960s many innovative programmes were introduced into mathematics teaching that became known collectively as the 'new' or 'modern' mathematics movement. Unfortunately, there were marked differences among them, which makes it difficult to define precisely the principles on which the new approach was based. However, my reading round the subject (please see the further-reading list for sources) suggests that there was an overriding concern to introduce more up-to-date topics into the curriculum and to bring the teaching of the processes of mathematics in schools more in line with the way academic mathematicians go about their work. A period of upheaval followed, but the dust now seems of have settled. The authoritative Cockcroft Report (1982, p. 82) concluded that 'In our discussions we have not thought in terms of traditional or modern mathematics, nor has the evidence which we have received suggested that it is any longer profitable to do so'. The inclusion of such topics as sets, binary numbers, probability, elementary algebra and geometry in schemes of work is now commonplace but considerable weight is still given to more traditional content.

With that background in mind, we can now turn to current objectives in teaching mathematics to primary-school children. The distinction made earlier between intrinsic and extrinsic reasons is taken up in all the main sources on aims in mathematics education. One of the clearest and most concise statements justifying the inclusion of mathematics in the primary curriculum is contained in the DES's (1978a, p. 4) *Mathematics 5-11: A Handbook of Suggestions*. It reads:

> We teach mathematics in order to help people to understand things better – perhaps to understand the jobs on which they might later be employed, or to understand the creative achievements of the human mind or the behaviour of the natural world. It is the particular power of mathematics that its central ideas help us to do all these things.

In a later document, the Department of Education and Science (1986a) spelt out 22 objectives in the teaching of mathematics grouped around four major dimensions:

1. Facts.
2. Skills.
3. Conceptual strategies.
4. General strategies.

Under the 'facts' heading attention is given to such activities as remembering mathematical terms (for example, shapes and operations) and mastering mathematical notation. Objectives listed under 'skills' include competence in performing basic operations, using a calculator, effectively communicating mathematical ideas and similar abilities. The 'conceptual strategies' are concerned with understanding mathematics, its basic concepts and the relationship between concepts. Objectives under the 'general strategies' component refer to a wide range of matters, such as the ability to estimate, to reason and to generate and test hypotheses.

Summary There are just three points to stress. First, while the new mathematics has introduced new topics into the school curriculum, useful traditional subject-matter has not been discarded and is considered to be as important as it ever was. Second, active methods of learning are compatible with and, indeed, essential to, the spirit of the modern mathematics movement. Third, both intrinsic and extrinsic arguments for teaching mathematics in schools are accepted as valid. However, arguably, the overriding justification for the inclusion of mathematics in the curriculum lies in the unique insights into the world it opens up.

PYSCHOLOGY AND MATHEMATICAL EDUCATION

Teachers' and Children's Conceptions of Mathematics

It is to be expected that children pick up cues about the nature of mathematics from their teachers and for this reason teachers' conceptions of its structure and purposes are beginning to attract attention. Although the evidence is not strong, there is enough to suggest that teachers are disposed to emphasize some aspects of mathematical learning – it might be fact learning or understanding mathematical relationships – and to play down others.

This was the substance of Thompson's (1984) findings from his investigation of conceptions of mathematics held by three teachers, whom he questioned at length and in depth. One of these teachers used discovery methods and gave conceptual understanding a high priority in her teaching. A second teacher regarded mathematics as a 'set of integrated and interrelated topics' that, to her, meant keeping the class on a tight rein so that the material could be presented in an orderly and logical sequence. To the third teacher, mathematical understanding was not much more than a mechanical operation designed to arrive at correct answers, and so her main job (as she saw it) was to drill pupils in the required procedures.

Cobb (1987) went a stage further by directly studying teacher influences on 6-year-old children's approaches to mathematics. He first of all interviewed the five teachers from whose classes they were drawn but, unlike Thompson, he found very little variation in teaching style between them. Essentially, their teaching was textbook dominated and aimed at promoting certain skills and encouraging memorization of certain number facts by constant demonstration and practice. In effect, pupils were geared up to performing routine actions rather than sorting out relationships, and it seems that no real effort was made to discover whether children really understood the processes they were being taught. To give just one example, for these children, the equals sign was interpreted as a trigger to action, and not to express relational equivalence. Given such exercises as 7 + 3 = and 8 − 5 = they knew what had to be done even if they obtained the wrong answer. However, Cobb's group could not puzzle out the meaning of such an expression as 10 = 7 + 3 because it did not suggest a mathematical operation to be performed. As Cobb explains (*ibid.*), most of these children seemed to assume 'that academic arithmetic as represented by the worksheet involves completing a sequence of isolated, unrelated tasks' and has little to do with searching out relationships.

In an earlier study of just two 6-year-olds, Cobb (1985) discovered that children as well as teachers differ among themselves as to the meaning of mathematics and what is involved in doing sums. For one of them, Tyrone, mathematics was about constructing relationships between numbers. Given a series of such problems as 12 + 4, 12 + 5 and 12 + 7 (where the second value was increased or decreased by one or two) he soon spotted a pattern and quickly and accurately arrived at the solutions. In contrast, his classmate, Scenetra, rarely looked for a general principle. Mathematics for her was 'an activity in which one finds unrelated rules for solving unrelated problems' (*ibid.*). Curiously, her mathematical knowledge was quite sound but, for some odd reason, she had the impression that it was naughty, even dishonest, to attempt to relate what she had learnt in one context to another. Unlike Scenetra, whose sole objective was to obtain correct answers, Tyrone wanted to know why answers to mathematical problems turned out as they did because, for him, doing mathematics was basically a search for patterns.

The main theme of this section is reinforced by Bennett *et al.* (1984, p. 211), who write: 'In their desire to obtain praise their life is made much easier if the teacher's demands are specific and concrete. Following procedures to get a row of ticks is easier than puzzling out the precise meaning of place value in tens and units sums'.

Summary Teachers differ in their approaches to mathematics. Some emphasize mechanical learning and others conceptual understanding, although it is reasonable to assume that most teachers come somewhere in the middle of the continuum marked by these two extremes.

Children's approaches to mathematics also vary, influenced in part by what teachers demand of them. Clearly, it needs to be made explicit that there is more to mathematics than doing sums mechanically: it is about understanding mathematical relationships.

The Development of Mathematical Thinking

Piaget and his successors, together with psychologists working in other traditions, have succeeded in building up a mass of data on children's mathematical development that, for once, gives us a problem of selection. Because of its obvious importance, our purposes are best served by concentrating on the concept of number: it has attracted most attention from psychologists, and the research generated has practical implications for the day-to-day work of teachers that goes beyond number and applies to the teaching of mathematics in general.

The concept of number

Piaget's (1952) analysis of the concept of number is long, involved and difficult to summarize. However, it brings home to us better than anything else the mental operations necessary to master it. Numbering, Piaget says, consists essentially of combining two distinct actions: classification (putting things into classes) and seriation (putting things in order).

The essential differences between these two operations become clearer when they are set out side by side, as in Table 3.2. If we count 10 toys – dolls, model cars or whatever – we must first of all concentrate on the main class toys and ignore all other differences in appearance or purpose between them. That is the classification operation.

Table 3.2   Piaget's classification of numbering

Classification	Seriation
Emphasis is on a common class	Emphasis is on differences between objects
Involves cardinal numbers	Involves ordinal numbers

Next we switch attention from the group to each toy in turn so that it can be considered separately, ordered and counted. Piaget and Inhelder (1969, p. 105) say it is the only way 'to tell them apart and not to count the same one twice'. We then begin counting: 1, 2, 3, 4, 5, 6, and so on. In this context, the numbers we use are called ordinal numbers because they represent a position in a series. That is the seriation operation. Finally, we focus once more on the group as a whole, which we now know contains 10 toys. In this context, the number 10 is called a cardinal number. A cardinal number answers the question 'How many?'

This is as succinctly and simply as I can put it. As I hope I have made clear, the classification and seriation elements combine to form a single system with attention switching from what the array of objects has in common to each one separately, and then back to the group again, once the total is determined. All this is a formidable achievement, not possible until the concrete operational stage is reached. At that stage, children can conserve number when they understand, for example, that since $5 + 3 = 8$, $8 - 5 = 3$.

The ability to count

Piaget's abiding interest in basic logico-mathematical structures led him to take a hard line on the concept of number and to ignore the arithmetical achievements of very young children. However, common observation tells us that pupils in the early years of the primary school, not to mention pre-school children, are already counting at some level of competence. Psychologists are now investigating in earnest these earliest encounters with mathematics. This research reveals in sharp relief the surprisingly large number of hurdles children have to negotiate in learning to count. It also demonstrates the remarkable progress many 5-year-olds have made in mastering number operations.

A major investigation of the counting skills of pre-school children was set up by Gelman (1977) and Gelman and Gallistel (1978), a husband and wife team who identified five principles of counting observed among 2–5-year-old children. They are as follows.

The one-to-one principle   In the act of counting, each item is tagged, ticked or given a name that enables the objects that have been counted to be separated out from those that have not. Gelman (1977) stresses that 'one and only one tag is used for each item'.

Nearly all the children, even the 2-year-olds, could make use of the one-to-one principle, but some of the youngest children used their own tag systems, such as '1, 13, 19; 2, 6', or 'A and B'. However, by the age of 3 conventional arithmetic terms were adopted and used in the right order.

The stable-order principle   Essentially, this principle means that the same system of counting, not necessarily the standard form, is used consistently. More than 90 per cent of the 4- and 5-year-olds could negotiate this hurdle although, here too, individual counting systems occurred.

The cardinal principle A cardinal number has special significance because it denotes how many items there are in a set. It is a big step forward as the ability to tag a set as consisting of six items signifies a realization that numbers can represent quantity.

One indication of an understanding of the cardinal principle was the tendency of some children to repeat and emphasize the last tag, thus 'one, two, three. *Three*'. Using this and other criteria, Gelman (*ibid.*) concluded that 'The 3 and 4 year olds did rather well on the smaller set sizes, and most 5 year olds managed to arrive at the cardinal number of set sizes as large as 9'.

The abstraction principle Again, drastically reducing Gelman's (1977) explanation, the abstraction principle denotes the recognition that counting can be applied to any set of objects, whether concrete or abstract, and however different they appear to be.

According to Gelman (*ibid.*) there is a suggestion that 'the young child believes that he cannot apply the how-to-count principles to heterogeneous materials, [and if this is so] we would be loathe to say that he has a full appreciation of number'.

The order-invariance principle Finally, children realize that it does not matter in which order the items are tagged and partitioned. The example Gelman gives is a group consisting of a rabbit, a truck, a dog and a cat arranged from left to right. A point critical to this principle is that it is perfectly proper to count the rabbit as one on the first occasion, and as two on the second – just as it is does not matter if the counting goes from right to left, or even if it is started in the middle of a set.

The Gelman and Gallistel research attracted a good deal of interest and inspired several follow-up studies. Inevitably, some disagreements emerged. For instance, it is difficult to test satisfactorily an understanding of the cardinal principle. Another controversy centres on just how firm children's understanding of the stable-order principle (the rule that numbers must be used in a consistent order over time) really is. This was the focus of Baroody and Price's (1983) research. Their conclusions are based on an observational study of four 3-year-old nursery-school children, carried out over a period of three months. Baroody and Price were particularly interested in knowing whether children's own counting systems remained the same from one counting exercise to another and, just as significantly, whether each tag was used once and once only. It is not enough, of course, to generate a stable-order sequence and to assign one tag to each object. Each tag must be unique – that is to say, not repeatable in the same sequence, even when children's own counting systems are used.

Early on in the testing sessions, one girl's sequences was found to include a beginning stable section and a final non-stable component indelicately described as a 'spew'. Later on, the stable sequence was progressively built up but spewing, containing previously used tags, still continued in contravention of the uniqueness principle.

Two other girls generated different patterns. K.O. and B.H. rarely spewed and, even in counting large numbers, were very sparing in repeating tags. K.O.'s progress over several weeks is interesting. The first attempt to count 20 dots on a pasted card produced the sequence '1 ... 14, 18, 19, 20, 21, 20' (note the error in the teens) (*ibid.*). The next try was as follows: '1 ... 14, 18, 19, 20, 1, 2', but she spontaneously started again. At first she said she couldn't count beyond 20 but, when prodded, she came up with the sequence '1 ... 14, 18, 19, 20, 21, 22, 23'. From then on, although she still got the teens wrong, she always recited the twenties correctly.

Her companion, B.H., began her stable non-standard sequence by repeating the last term of her conventional sequence, so ' ... 13, *13*, 18 ...'. Later on, however, she was careful not to repeat a tag, adopting, instead, a strategy of stopping to count altogether when her conventional sequence dried up.

Summary   These two representative studies show that many pre-school children have already made remarkable strides in learning to count. Once the function of a standard system is understood, and children know that a cardinal number represents quantity, the basic principles of counting are mastered. The remaining abstraction and order-invariance principles are concerned with extensions and refinements of that ability.

Classroom applications   Gelman's model suggests several ways in which mathematics can be made more meaningful to young children. To begin with the 'one-to-one' principle, Baroody and Price believe that while some children may discover the rule for themselves, others might need specific guidance, such as the reminder 'when we count things, we must make sure to use a new number for each thing we point to'.

The stable-order principle suggests that such devices as traditional counting rhymes could serve two purposes. The first is to underline the need to use a consistent method of counting – even when using one's own systems – and the second is to familiarize children with the conventional number system.

Gelman's findings also indicate that young children need a great deal of practice in using the cardinal principle, initially by counting small groups of objects of all kinds, progressing to larger numbers at a later stage. The abstraction principle emphasizes the need to set up activities in which children must count sets of objects made up of very different things.

The order-invariance principle suggests that it would be useful to introduce activities demonstrating the rule that it does not matter which object is chosen to start with or the order in which the other remaining objects are counted. The point to watch out for is that children understand that object A could be counted as 1 on the first attempt to count a set, as 3 on the second try and as 5 on the third attempt, and so on.

The context of addition and subtraction tasks

We now move on to examine early attempts at addition and subtraction in greater depth. As Hughes (1981) reminds us, both Piaget and Gelman studied children's ability to add and subtract only indirectly, and that even now little detail is known about young children's responses to such straightforward questions as 'How many is two bricks and one brick?'

Hughes's experimental tasks incorporate the notion of 'embeddedness' so effectively popularized by Donaldson (1978). She believes that performance is directly related to the degree of embeddedness of the task. Embedded problems are set against a background of things children know well and feel comfortable with and, because they make 'human sense', children are quite successful in solving them. In contrast, disembedded problems are not only outside children's immediate experiences but are also phrased in off-putting formal language. Following her lead, Hughes devised a series of tests reflecting a continuum of 'embeddedness', which were presented in order of difficulty to 60 nursery-school children between the ages of 3 and 5. The tests, labelled T1 to T5 can be quickly and easily described.

T1 box open In this first task, the most embedded of all, the experimenter added to, or subtracted from, a group of bricks already visible to the child. Children were asked how many bricks were finally present.

T2 box closed This time, children could see how many bricks were in the box to start with. The lid was then closed, children could see the number of bricks put in or taken out, but they had to work out how many bricks were now in the box without opening the lid.

T3 hypothetical box The bricks are now no longer in sight. Questions asked took the form of 'If there was one brick in the box and I put two more in, how many would be in the box altogether?'

T4 hypothetical shop A less immediate context was now introduced. The problem set here was 'If there was one child in a sweetshop and two more went in, how many children would be in the sweetshop altogether?'

T5 formal code This, the final form, was intended to be the most disembedded of all. A typical question here was 'What does one and two make?'

One other significant feature of the design ought to be mentioned. Half the tasks involved small numbers (1, 2 and 3); the other half slightly larger numbers (5, 6, 7 and 8).

Now to the findings, looking first at competence with number and ignoring context. A large proportion of these 3–5-year-olds could cope well with simple additions and subtractions. To give just one indication, on the T1 open-box task, 57 of the 60 subjects successfully managed the 1 + 1 and 3 − 2 tasks. However, their performance becomes much worse when large numbers are introduced. Still keeping with T1 box-open form, only 27 of the 60 succeeded with the 6 + 2 task; 25 out of 60 with the 8 − 1 problem.

Next, as predicted, the degree of embeddedness of the problem had a marked effect on performance. As was just mentioned, 56 out of 60 managed the T1 open-box problem. For the T4 hypothetical-shop task, the success rate fell to 44; it then dropped very sharply down to only 22 for the T5 formal-code problem.

These findings are typical of the general trend. Hughes sees the absence of actual, familiar things as the main stumbling block to success in the disembedded problems. However, when problems are set in an everyday context, children have little difficulty in dealing with them because they have something concrete to hold on to.

Hughes goes on to suggest, following Donaldson (1978), that failure on the formal-code tests is not because children cannot manage simple additions and subtractions – their performance in the first four tests is evidence of that. Rather, it is the conventional arithmetic code itself that seems to cause the trouble. Not only are formal code tests context-free, but they are also couched in language unfamiliar to children: a language they only start to learn on entry to school. One 4-year-old questioned in this study had apparently sorted this out for herself. As she explained (Hughes, 1981) she got in a muddle with formal code sums because 'she didn't go to school yet'. It is little wonder then, as Hughes notes, that children become adept at using their own symbols to add and subtract.

Summary   Following the work of Hughes, two major points emerge concerning the early stages in learning number. First, young children could successfully add and subtract small numbers but their performance sharply declined when larger numbers were introduced. Second, children performed better in tasks set in an everyday context than in problems expressed in a formal code and where the material could not be handled or seen.

Classroom applications   Again there are clear messages for teachers in this research. The first and most obvious recommendation is that we should set problems involving small numbers before we introduce large numbers.

Similarly, it is advisable to start with problems that make immediate sense to children and then to increase their degree of 'embeddedness' by gradual stages.

Second, since, according to Hughes (1986, p. 171), young children see little purpose in formal, written arithmetic in school, children's own symbols (using dots, for example) should initially be encouraged in learning to count. Third, and this is something elaborated on later, a sound plan is to build on and develop children's own problem-solving strategies.

Other mathematical concepts

There are several sources dealing with research into other mathematical concepts, which are given in the further-reading list. Many of these experimental studies are based on the work of Piaget, two of which, for illustrative purposes, are now briefly described.

The first example is Wagman's (1975) study of concepts of area, which was modelled on Piaget's original investigation. First of all, she showed the children two sheets of green paper identical in area. A toy cow was placed on each sheet and the children were asked to say if the cows had the same amount of grass to eat. That caused no difficulty, and so she moved on to this next stage. First one house was positioned on each sheet, then two, then three, until eventually there were twelve houses on each sheet. However, there was an essential difference between the two lay-outs. On one sheet the houses were placed adjacent to each other; on the other the houses were scattered all over the field. It was the latter distribution that tricked the youngest children into believing that a cow in the second field would have less grass to eat than a cow in the first field. However, nearly all the 11-year-olds realized that both cows had the same amount to eat – clear evidence that these children could conserve area.

Other researchers have focused on the concept of weight. Hughes (1979) tested this concept using two Russian dolls that were weighed in the presence of the child, who was then asked to confirm that there was no difference in their weight. One of the dolls was then put aside and the other opened up to reveal three smaller dolls inside, which were taken out and arranged in order of height. The child was asked 'Do all these dolls together (the four dolls) weigh the same as this doll (which was put aside unopened) or are they different in weight?' Again, as you would expect, some children were not able to decentre and were deceived into believing that the four dolls weighed more than the unopened one. However, the expected steady increase in the ability to conserve weight was observed as children grew older.

The main educational value of studies identifying developmental trends in mathematical thinking such as these lies, of course, in helping teachers to pitch pupils' work at a more challenging but still manageable level. In other curriculum areas, we have turned to Piaget's stages of cognitive development for general guidance but, as we have already noted, Piaget's analysis of mathematical processes does not cover the earliest stages . As Hiebert and Carpenter (1982) explain, 'Simple skills tasks, routine calculations, or problems that require a straightforward application of a memorized algorithm, may not involve Piagetian abilities', and a great deal of early work in schools fits that description.

In addition to data from experimental studies, there are several diagnostic tests covering the same ground. For example, Denvir and Brown (1986a, 1986b, 1987) constructed a scale consisting of 47 number skills embracing counting, addition, subtraction and place value, arranged in hierarchical order. The scale begins with the simplest operation of all, 'makes 1 to 1 correspondence', and ends up 46 items later with 'mentally carries out two-digit "take away" with regrouping'. This analysis is of great help to teachers of less able pupils as well as to nursery- and infant-school teachers.

Piagetian concepts come into their own at the later stages and are taken into consideration explicitly or implicitly in several schedules designed to assess mathematical ability. One of these, the ILEA (1979) checkpoint scheme, is a particularly comprehensive diagnostic tool that covers development in four areas – underlying concepts, knowledge of facts, performance of skills and applications to problems. Content is divided into sets, numbers, measures and geometry, with further subdivisions where necessary.

With that sketch of the development of number concepts in mind, we turn to experimental studies designed to improve mathematical abilities.

Extending Children's Mathematical Thinking

In this section we shall again concentrate on number. However, the teaching techniques we consider can just as easily be applied to other mathematical concepts.

We first look at problems associated with diagnosing children's errors in mathematics; we then examine the literature on strategies central to the learning and teaching of number relationships that are basic to mathematical education in general.

Diagnosing children's errors and difficulties in mathematics
You might recall Bennett *et al.*'s (1984) study of the match between children's ability and the level of work expected of them by their teachers, referred to in Chapter 1. They reported a satisfactory match in only about

40 per cent of the tasks: roughly a third of the assignments were too difficult and about a quarter too easy. A major cause of this mis-match was the poor or non-existent diagnosis of children's difficulties where, typically, teaching the mechanics of the exercise was stressed at the expense of developing children's conceptual understanding. The main lesson of this study can be summed up in just a few words: the key to successful diagnosis lies in getting children to explain what they are about and to link that information to what we know about cognitive processes.

Many children have particular trouble with written mathematical exercises (often called 'problems'), as distinct from straightforward computation. Clements (1980), in analysing errors children commonly make in attempting problems of this type, produced a breakdown useful to teachers looking for a simple diagnostic procedure. Using a framework devised by Newman (1977), Clements classified 5,158 errors made by 542 10–12-years-olds. Children who gave a wrong answer were asked to try the problem again without help from the interviewer, after which the following instructions were given:

(1) Please read the question to me. If you don't know a word leave it out.
(2) Tell me what the question is asking you to do.
(3) Tell me how you are going to find the answer.
(4) Show me what to do to get the answer. Tell me what you are doing as you work.
(5) Now write down the answer to the question.

This interview schedule reflects Newman's belief that solving written arithmetic problems involves mastering a hierarchy of skills. At the outset, he says, the pupil has to be able to read the problem, to decode the actual, individual words and phrases it contains. The meaning of the problem has then to be teased out and the appropriate mathematical operation selected. Finally, the necessary skills must be applied correctly and the answer expressed in an acceptable form. This hierarchy of skills fits in exactly with the five steps – reading, comprehension, transformation, process skills and encoding – embodied in the instructions given earlier. Mistakes can occur at any of these stages but, in addition, wrong answers can also arise from carelessness or poor motivation.

Clements (1980) discovered that the proportion of reading and comprehension errors was quite small: at least a quarter of all errors in all age-groups were of the transformation type (failure to select the right mathematical procedure); and a minimum of a further quarter were of the process-skills type (incorrect computation). These two categories alone accounted for 50 per cent or more of all mistakes. Writing the answer in the correct form caused little difficulty, but errors due to carelessness or poor motivation were again considerable, amounting to 22 per cent of all errors among 10-years-olds, 28 per cent among among 11-year-olds and 35 per cent in the 12-year-old age-range.

Newman's framework is quick and easy to apply. However, while it reveals the type of error committed, it cannot identify the particular difficulties children experience in making sense of a mathematical problem or completing an arithmetic operation. Only further probing can do that. Alternatively, Newman's hierarchy encourages us to dissect a pupil's thought processes carefully and systematically, which is certainly a preferable procedure to the 'how-to-do-it' attack Bennett *et al.* (1984), among other investigators, tell us is so prevalent.

Summary   We have noted a tendency among teachers to teach and to explain rather than to diagnose. The procedures discussed in this section can contribute to efficient diagnosis of children's errors, which – together with a willingness to listen to what children have to tell us – can lead to genuine and profitable teacher–pupil exchanges in mathematics.

Strategies in learning mathematics

The research evidence discussed next is not difficult to understand but it needs to be described in some detail and studied carefully if its implications for teaching number and other mathematical concepts are to become clear. There is a common thread running through the studies on learning strategies in mathematics we are now about to consider: children already know some number facts – the object of the exercise is to get them to use that knowledge in seeking out further and more complex number relationships.

Let us see how this principle works in practice. The learning of multiplication facts, quite rightly, remains a high priority among parents, members of the public and teachers. Consensus breaks down, however, when we move from ends to means; and in some quarters, it is suspected, the return of drill methods (including table-chanting) would not be greeted with disfavour.

Psychology's contribution to understanding the processes of table-learning is reported by Heege (1985). On drill methods, he says, the weight of psychological evidence is unambiguous: they contribute little if anything to children's understanding of number relationships and, worse still, can even hinder learning if applied to early.

Heege goes on to suggest a three-stage model for learning basic multiplication facts: first, children need ample time to become familiar with problem situations that require a knowledge of multiplication to solve them; second, children are led to discover and to develop their own strategies for multiplication; and, third, the point is reached when basic multiplications are learnt by heart.

Heege (*ibid.*) gives several telling examples of children's self-generated strategies. The following is the record of an encounter with Tommy, an 8-year-old:

> Tommy: '$6 \times 9 = 64$, uh, no, 54'. He explains how he arrived at this answer. 'Because $5 \times 9 = 45$ and then one more 9'. What makes him think like that? Did he learn it by himself? But Tommy hasn't yet finished his explanation: 'And', he continues, '$5 \times 9 = 45$, half of 90'.

In his analysis of that episode, Heege goes straight to the essential point. Obviously, Tommy does not know such arithmetic facts as 6×9 by heart, and so what he does is to fall back on the facts he does know to find the answer.

In another instance, $7 \times 7 = 49$, Tommy does not need to calculate $10 \times 7 = 70$, which is in his existing repertoire of facts, and so he makes this his starting-point. The next step is to halve 70 to obtain 35, which equals 5×7; he then adds 7 to get 42 and another 7 arrive at the correct answer 49.

In addition to his discussions with Tommy, Heege questioned children in the 7–9 age-range about their methods for learning multiplication tables. Significantly, he discovered that a good many children at this age already know most or all of the basic additions up to 20 by heart, which serve as a basis for learning multiplication facts. Thus if $6 + 6 = 12$ is committed to memory, it does not take long for them to realize that $2 \times 6 = 12$.

Heege (*ibid.*) was able to list the following six informal strategies children used in multiplying:

(1) The commutative principle: $6 \times 7 = 7 \times 6$.
(2) Multiplying by 10. This is a support for dealing with problems like $9 \times 8 = 72$ where the children simply subtract 8 from 10×8.
(3) The doubling principle. Children who know $2 \times 7 = 14$ can calculate $4 \times 7 =$ by doubling, a useful device particularly where no carrying is involved.
(4) Halving of familiar multiplications. Thus $5 \times 6 =$ is calculated by halving 10×6.
(5) Increasing a familiar product by adding the multiplicand once. Thus the solution to $6 \times 7 = 42$ is arrived at by using $5 \times 7 = 35$ as a crutch and adding another 7.
(6) Decreasing a familiar product by subtracting the multiplicand once. For instance, $9 \times 7 = 63$ is calculated by working through 10×7 and subtracting 7.

Heege tells us that children opted to use their own methods to solve multiplication problems in preference to the tables they had learnt rote fashion. Nevertheless, 'knowing by heart' was not entirely dispensed with. Heege noticed that in learning the eight-times table, 1×8, 2×8, 8×8 and 10×8 were quickly memorized and used as a basis for other calculations. The distinction between 'working out' and 'knowing by heart' is therefore blurred, but the general message is plain: children can cope much more easily with related facts than isolated ones, and the informal methods they work out for themselves give them a clearer understanding of mathematical relationships than routinely imposed strategies.

Cook and Dossey (1982) went a stage further and deliberately taught techniques for multiplying based on number relationships. This approach proved superior to traditional methods but the really important feature of this study (and my reason for mentioning it) is that it took only two days of in-service education to familiarize the teachers concerned with 'related-facts' strategies that, according to the authors, they later introduced into their classes with the minimum of effort.

In a similar study, Steinberg (1985) aimed at teaching what she called derived-facts strategies (DFSs) for adding and subtracting that are based on, and designed to get pupils to use to the full, relationships between number facts. The DFSs taught to the 23 7-year-old participants in the investigation were of several types. To start off with, Steinberg concentrated on the doubles form $(4+4, 5+5)$ and then on facts that could be related to the doubles form, for example, double $+1$ $(6+7, 7+8)$. Another method involved going through ten. Thus, to solve the problem $8+5=?$, the children (who are given apparatus rather like unifix cubes) were encouraged to make up 10 first (that is, $8+2$), which leaves 3 cubes remaining. Now we have the expression $10+3$ that, it is hoped, is quickly recognized as representing 13.

The general teaching approach was to use apparatus to begin with; later, this was withdrawn and the strategies discussed orally. Children then worked through exercises involving numbers only, and no word problems were set at the teaching stage.

One of the most interesting features of this study concerned children's growing realization that the strategies learnt can be applied in new situations. Several pupils who had mastered the doubles $+1$ process used the principle to solve a doubles -1 problem before that strategy had been taught. In another instance, four children solved the problem $5+9=?$ by using the doubles principle $(5+5+4)$, again without being shown how to do so beforehand. Once children understood that they could use known number facts to find the solution to derive unknown number facts, they were keen to seek out new combinations for themselves.

Steinberg's main objective was to discover whether her teaching had any lasting effect. The final interview results indicated that over the three-months' period of the study, children changed their solution strategies considerably, mainly switching from counting strategies to DFSs. However, she points out that there was by no means a complete conversion to using

DFSs – in fact, counting on and similar strategies were still used by about half the group, despite the overall increase in the adoption of DFSs.

Another general learning strategy takes us back to the 'thinking about thinking' metacognitive processes referred to in Chapter 1 that have been given a great deal of attention in mathematics, although rarely referred to by name. For instance, when Clements (1980) asked children to tell him what the question is asking them to do and how they are going to find the answer, he was encouraging children to use self-monitoring techniques in preference to rushing into computation without prior thought. As Garofalo and Lester (1985) explain, the distinction between cognition and metacognition is really very simple – 'cognition is involved in doing, whereas metacognition is involved in choosing and planning what to do and monitoring what is being done'.

Garofalo and Lester made a special study of cognitive – metacognitive processes within a mathematical setting. Their model is too detailed to report in full here, but it consists of four steps. In tackling a mathematical problem (and particularly one that involves a great deal of reading), it is first of all essential to decide what the problem is. The second stage involves selecting appropriate methods to solve it. During the third stage children begin working out the solution, constantly monitoring their work. Finally, the solution must be verified. Does it seem to make sense? Their plan of action is very similar to the strategy Clements (1980) recommends.

Garofalo and Lester emphasize that teaching mathematics is not only about improving mathematical skills, but it is also about developing self-monitoring techniques that lead children to think more carefully about the rationale of mathematics and to tackle problems more systematically and methodically.

This section ends with a summary of Denvir and Brown's (1986b) account of a teaching session with slow learners, which uses several of the strategies we have considered. Earlier, I refer to the Denvir and Brown (1987) assessment schedule. This was the means of identifying and selecting twelve low-attaining and slow-learning 7–9-year-olds for intensive remedial teaching.

When the experiment began, one of the twelve children, a girl named Je, could manage simple addition and subtraction problems but only by using a 'counting all with models' strategy. 'Counting all' means what it says: thus, in adding 3 and 2, two blocks are counted; then three blocks; the answer 5 is obtained by counting the three and two blocks. This is obviously a laborious process and so the teaching was aimed at developing the next strategy in the hierarchy of skills, called 'counting on'. The 3 + 2 problem is now tackled by counting out three and the total arrived by counting on two more 4, 5.

Working on the 'start-from-the-known principle', the session began with a recapitulation of the 'counting-all' strategy. The new 'counting-on' technique was introduced using a number line such as the following:

> B.D.: Suppose you had 6p and your mum gave you 5p, how would you work out how much you had on the number line?
>
> Je: 6p and 5p? (Counts from one ... 1, 2, 3, 4, 5, 6. (leaves a finger at 6) ... 1, 2, 3, 4, 5... eleven.
>
> B.D   Could you have done 6p and 5p by just putting your fingers at 6p straightaway and going on 5?
>
> Je: Mmm ...   (*Ibid.*)

The counting-on strategy was then reinforced in a number of ways, such as using a number line, covering up the first collection of cubes and then counting on the second collection and doing written sums by counting on using fingers to represent the other number to be added on.

Denvir and Brown (1986b) put Je's success down to three main factors:

1. Her readiness to move on to the next stage.
2. The linking of new skills to the already known.
3. Reinforcing the new technique in a variety of different situations.

Post-test results showed that Je and her eleven companions made very considerable gains over the course of the study and these were maintained long after the intensive teaching sessions had ended.

In addition to adopting the three-pronged course of action just described, the experimenters also impressed on children the need to:

- think about the method of working, not just the answers;
- have confidence in their own way of working;
- realize that there is more than one way of tackling a problem and that it is permissible to vary one's approach;
- try out different methods and consider whether they are equally valid; and
- look for links between different aspects of number.

Summary   Taken together, the studies reviewed in this section reinforce several familiar themes. Most children of school age, including slow learners, have at their command strategies enabling them to solve simple number problems. Starting from that base, pupils can be encouraged to look for further, more complex relationships between numbers.

When the time is judged to be right, new strategies are introduced, again linking the known with the unknown. As mathematical knowledge and skills are constantly built up and practised, more and more mathematical facts are learnt by heart - not by rote methods - but through constant use. As their experience increases, children begin to realize that correct solutions can be arrived at in more than one way. As a consequence, children need guidance and practice in evaluating the processes open to them, and in selecting the most effective techniques for their purposes.

Self-monitoring techniques can be used in every stage of the problem-solving process: in deciding what the problem is, in choosing the best method for its solution, in carrying out the computation involved and in verifying the outcome.

SUMMARY AND CONCLUSIONS

Mathematics education is always in the public eye and, because different people want different things from it, it is more than usually important for teachers to clarify their objectives in this discipline. A tension between learning mathematical facts and skills largely for utilitarian ends and for other purposes not so immediately obvious has alway existed and is as strong today as ever it was.

For professional educators, an understanding of mathematical relationships ranks as a high priority. Due weight is also given to the practical uses of mathematics (which everyone accepts) but particular prominence is given to its role in opening up new perspectives on the world around us.

Potentially at least, psychological research could exercise a powerful influence on the teaching of mathematics. A promising start has been made in identifying developmental trends in mathematical thinking and here – perhaps more than in most curriculum areas – children's problem-solving strategies have been recorded and analysed in fair detail. The main conclusion is clear enough: children have ideas of their own about solving number problems and, given the chance, are prepared to use them. Starting from that promising foundation, children can be guided towards acquiring more refined techniques in their search for mathematical relationships.

The tendency of some teachers to focus excessively on direct teaching rather than attempting to discover children's perspectives of the problem and to sort out where they are going wrong, is also well documented. If nothing else, research in the mathematics area has demonstrated the overriding importance of genuine pupil–teacher dialogue in developing children's mathematical concepts.

FURTHER READING

Buxton (1984) gives a clear account of the nature and purposes of mathematics as well as providing an excellent introduction to the subject, generally written for the lay reader. Critiques of the 'modern-mathematics' movement in education include

Freudenthal (1972), Scott (1972), Creighton-Buck (1978) and Ormell (1980).

Dickson, Brown and Gibson's (1984) review of research into children's learning of mathematics is strongly recommended as a starting-point, while the various Assessment of Performance Unit's publications, for example, Assesment of Performance Unit (1980), detail children's mathematical performance at different ages. The psychology of mathematics is covered by Brown (1979), Collis (1980), Ginsburg (1983) and Hughes (1986).

The Cockcroft Report (1982) is a convenient general source on the teaching of mathematics and, for specific guidance on the teaching of number, see Hughes (1986). Relevant journals are *Educational Studies in Mathematics, International Journal of Mathematical Education, Science and Technology* and *Journal for Reasearch in Mathematical Education.*

4

SCIENCE EDUCATION

INTRODUCTION

For generations of elementary-school pupils, nature study – a subject concentrating almost exclusively on plant and animal life – was the only science taught. The curriculum was not broadened to cover such topics as heat, light and sound until around the late 1950s, when political interest in the contribution of science to the nation at large led to major initiatives by the Nuffield Foundation and the Schools Council, designed to stimulate and improve the quality of science teaching.

For a variety of reasons, not least the uncertain knowledge of science among primary-school teachers, uneven progress had been made in teaching science by the time the DES (1978b) primary survey was published. The report made grim reading: there were criticisms of poor teaching and inadequate resources. However, most serious of all, in nearly a fifth of the schools surveyed, no science whatsoever was taught. A few years later, the companion survey on education in the 5–9 age-group (DES, 1982, p. 88) was more encouraging, reporting that 'in contrast to the findings of the national primary survey, there is more evidence in the first schools of work intended to help children to understand the physical and natural world'. Although it is unwise to generalize about education, it is probable that initial and in-service education courses are beginning to make an impact and, while a sizeable minority of teachers may still not be confident in the subject, there is now more science taught in primary schools – and taught more effectively than ever before.

While this upheaval was taking place in schools, the discipline of science itself was going through a crisis. As we shall see, the cosy image of scientists observing phenomena objectively and, after a series of carefully controlled observations arriving at general laws, has been undermined. The old certainties have been supplanted by new doubts and, of course, the changing conceptions of the nature of science have had major implications for the way it is taught in schools.

From a psychological standpoint, science education is a curriculum area that opens up issues central to education in general. Science educators have written extensively on the problems of perception and observation, as well as giving more attention than most to the phenomenon of 'meaningful reception learning'. In the more general run of research, there are several significant studies of developmental trends in scientific thinking although, in view of the current status of the discipline, there are still surprisingly large gaps in the literature.

We follow the usual plan by first attempting to sort out the nature of the discipline and the objectives of science education.

THE NATURE OF SCIENCE AND SCIENCE EDUCATION

The Nature of Science

Philosophers of science give short shrift to the content of the discipline. However, the field of knowledge it occupies ought to be defined before turning to weightier matters. Among its many areas of concern are the universe, the earth itself and the living organisms that occupy it and mechanics, physics and chemistry. Although there is a blurring at the edges (for instance, are anthropology and economics sciences?), at its centre lies the attempt to bring system and order to the understanding of the physical world.

What really interests philosophers of science is scientific method and the tests for truth it employs. We shall concentrate on two contrasting conceptions of science: the traditional view and the hypothetico-deductive model, which illustrate the current debate particularly well.

The traditional view

According to the traditional view, experiments begin with observation but, it goes on, in the interests of objectivity we should rid our minds of preconceived ideas or prejudices and rely instead entirely on the senses. One observation then follows another and, if the same findings consistently emerge, it is safe to formulate a general law. This description of scientific method (which is known as inductive thinking) seems straightforward enough and probably does not differ much from the lay person's image of dispassionate scientists proceeding systematically towards objective truth. There are, however, serious psychological and logical objections to this procedure.

Take first the idea that statements about observations derive from the direct use of the senses uninfluenced by previous knowledge. This claim is in direct opposition to the basic 'we-see-what-we-know' proposition put forward in Chapter 1, which insists that observations are inescapably linked to previous experiences. We cannot put aside our existing knowledge even if it were desirable to do so – it governs the particular events we focus on and, just as importantly, it shapes the interpretations we put on events.

A second objection to the inductive method is the claim that, when observations of specific instances yield identical results, we can assume a general law to be operating. Again, on the surface this proposition seems to make good sense but perhaps Chalmer's (1976) example of the inductivist turkey based on the Bertrand Russell story might convince you otherwise. On his first morning at the farm, the turkey was fed at 9 a.m. but following faithfully the principle of induction, he kept an open mind and made no assumptions at all about the future. However, as the days went by without variation in the routine, 'his inductivist conscience was satisfied and he carried out an inductive inference to conclude "I am always fed at 9 a.m." ' (*ibid*. p. 13). All went well until Christmas Eve when the turkey had its throat cut.

The hypothetico-deductive model

One alternative to the much-criticized traditional view is the hypothetico-deductive method that Popper (1972, p. 81) characterizes as 'the method of bold conjectures and ingenious and severe attempts to refute them'. As I understand it, Popper's analysis goes something like the following. When a problem is first encountered we may not know how to tackle it. All right then, he would say, let us fall on back on previous experience and generate as many ideas as we can, but let us not worry too much at this early stage as to whether they might work. This allows the imagination to flow freely in an exploratory, untidy fashion until a tentative solution really worth following up emerges.

We then enter the testing stage where the mood changes. Scrupulous attention to experimental method is now demanded, coupled with a cautious and sceptical evaluation of the findings. Popper argues that whatever hypothesis comes out of the chaos of ideas, speculations and hunches must be carefully tested and the conclusions submitted to the most rigorous evaluation. It is at this stage that the falsification principle – a major distinguishing feature of Popper's theory – assumes importance. Every possible attempt is made to detect flaws in the experimental procedures, to falsify and to refute the research findings, and to find other possible and more convincing explanations. If after all that the hypothesis stands up the matter ends there, at least for the moment. If not, then the reasons for failure must be sought to allow the cycle to start all over again. What we end up with is an explanation of phenomena that can be tentatively accepted but only until such a time as new evidence comes along to modify it or to change it completely. All scientific knowledge is therefore provisional.

Popper's and other current theories have been criticized for reasons unnecessary to go into here (see Beveridge, 1980; Harré, 1983). Nevertheless, in stirring things up they have compelled scientists to re-examine and justify their objectives, their experimental methods and their claims for truth, which in the long run can only be good for the discipline.

Summary   We have seen a move in science from a position of certainty to one of uncertainty. The traditional view is now largely discredited because of its insistence on the validity of theory-free observations and its acceptance of the principle that outcomes can be confidently predicted from hitherto consistent findings.

Prominent among the many alternative theories is the hypothetico-deductive method that seeks to combine an active imagination with rigorous methodology. As Gilbert and Watts (1983) point out, the newer theories 'despite many points of disagreement, share a belief in the provisional nature of knowledge; [and] an acceptance of theory ladenness of observations' – and it is those two characteristics primary-school teachers would do well to keep in mind.

The Nature of Science Education

The previous section has important implications for teaching science that the profession is struggling to come to terms with. Ingle and Jennings (1981, p. 81) spell out for us a minimum set of objectives for science education that are to:

(1) equip pupils with a broadly based scientific knowledge;
(2) develop skills in observation, recording and communication;
(3) give an important place to the development of psycho-motor skills, and;
(4) emphasize science as a human activity; as well as;
(5) help children to acquire lively enquiring minds.

The Association for Science Education's (1981) policy statement also underlines the need to understand the relationship between science and society and the contribution science makes to our cultural heritage.

Over the past few years, primary schools have concentrated on the processes of science but the first aim, to 'equip pupils with a broadly based scientific knowledge', is now being seriously considered. The Department and Education and Science (1989) National Curriculum document lists sixteen areas:

The variety of life
Processes of life
Genetics and evolution
Human influences on the earth
Types and uses of materials
Making new materials
Explaining how materials behave
Earth and atmosphere
Forces
Electricity and magnetism
The scientific aspects of information technology including microelectronics
Energy
Sound and music
Using light and electromagnetic radiation
The earth in space
The nature of science.

Teaching the processes of scientific investigation is as important as ever it was. This involves giving guidance in observing, setting up simple experiments, recording the findings, looking for patterns in the results and attempting to explain the data.

Summary This is a particularly difficult area to negotiate but two central points stand out. First, the aims of science education must be considered against the background of changing conceptions of science we have briefly touched on. Second, teachers need to give serious consideration both to the content of science education and to the teaching of the skills of scientific inquiry.

PSYCHOLOGY AND SCIENCE EDUCATION
Teachers' and Children's Conceptions of Science

Teachers' and children's conceptions of science have attracted surprisingly little attention. However, Truscoe's (1983) small-scale study, carried out in middle schools where there is a degree of specialization, is enlightening. He found that a quarter of the twenty teachers in his sample adopted a style of teaching based on the traditional view of science that (as we have seen) is open to serious criticism. For a further 20 per cent, the learning of scientific facts and techniques had high priority. In this group little value was placed on personal observation, and class teaching based on a set scheme of work dominated. Another 20 per cent drew their inspiration from the hypothetico-deductive method. These teachers aimed at encouraging logical thinking, observation and open-mindedness in experimentation, the work was individualized and wide freedom of choice in starting-points was given that could originate either from teacher or pupil.

The diversity of teaching styles Truscoe reports underlines the need for science teachers to understand the nature of their discipline. At first sight, the attempt to discover what science is may appear to be a remote theoretical exercise but it is far from that for, as Truscoe shows, teachers' conceptions of science strongly influence the way in which it is taught.

As a way in to understanding children's conceptions of science, Chambers (1983) asked a huge sample of 4,807 5–11-year-olds to draw a picture of a scientist. From the age of 6 onwards, a stereotype began to emerge that, by 11, had developed into an image of scientists as white-coated, bespectacled, bearded people who used chemical equipment, micro-scopes, telescopes and computers in their work. As a further embellishment, they were sometimes depicted in the act of discovery shouting 'I've done it!' or just 'Wow!' Perhaps significantly, scientists were always shown working indoors (often in a basement) and never exploring nature in the field.

Only further detailed questioning would reveal whether the 'draw-a-scientist' test reveals children's true impressions or whether they are simply falling back on a convenient, conventional stereotype picked up from television or adventure stories. However, at the very least, this exercise opens up opportunities for broadening children's understanding of the work of scientists and of the nature of science itself.

Summary This research speaks for itself and it is only necessary to emphasize how important it is to discuss the objectives of science and its methodology in teacher-education courses.

The Development of Scientific Concepts

Research into the development of scientific reasoning in young children is unsystematic, but children's concepts of life, flotation, gravity and the earth have attracted particular attention and these are the three topics concentrated on next.

Concepts of life

A great deal of time is spent in primary schools teaching children about animal and plant life. It is a far more complicated and long, drawn-out business than it may seem at first sight for it involves putting animals and plants into classes and sub-classes based on the similarities and differences within and between the various groups.

The first study sets the scene well. It was carried out by Looft (1974), who concentrated on just the 7-year-old age-group. He first of all wanted to know how successful children were in distinguishing living from non-living things, and so he got his group to look at eight pictures of each class (see Table 4.1). The pictures were mixed up and each child then had to decide whether or not the subject of the picture was alive or dead.

Table 4.1 Classification of living and non-living things

Living things	Non-living things
Turkey	Car
Tree	Television
Frog	Chair
Turtle	Aeroplane
Fish	Watch
Flower	Camera
Woman	Coffee cup
Honeybee	Gloves

(*Source*: Looft, 1974.)

For most children this caused no problem. Of the 52 participants, 39 correctly classified all 16 objects on the basic living/non-living criterion. Then followed questions about whether the subject of each picture:

● breathes or does not breathe;
● needs food or does not need food; and
● reproduces or does not reproduce.

All these attributes, of course, distinguish the living from the non-living.

This is where the misconceptions really began to show up. Not one child was completely correct in applying the three biological attributes (feeding, breathing, reproducing) across all the 16 objects. The best-understood concept was the need for nutriment, which was understood by about 60 per cent of the group, but only 3 of the 59 pupils made no errors on the breathing criterion and only 4 were totally correct on the reproduction criterion.

Looft attributed this poor showing to confusion about the characteristics of plants (trees and flowers in this case) among most of the children questioned. He also discovered that the more familiar the object, the more likely it was to be correctly classified. Thus, for example, as many as 69 per cent of the group understood that women have a need to eat and breathe and have the ability to reproduce.

What this research demonstrates, and it is representative of much other work in the field, is that many children can successfully differentiate the living from the non-living but at a basic level only. Looft reports that the need for food was better understood than the need to breathe, and that the need to breathe was better understood than the ability to reproduce, which indicates that the build-up to a more complete scientific concept of life takes place gradually and proceeds in a definite order. Finally, these characteristics could be related more successfully to animals than to plants and to familiar rather than to unfamiliar things.

The next investigation, by Dolgin and Behrend (1984), is included because it throws light on age differences in distinguishing living from non-living things, as well as confirming how complex the concepts of life really are. Groups of 3-, 4-, 5-, 7- and 9-year-olds took part in the study, together with an adult control group. Again, children were asked to indicate whether a number of criteria applied to a range of animate and inanimate objects. The 32 objects selected consisted of:

● living and dead beings (for example, a live robin and roast turkey);
● dead and never-living objects (steamed fish and a rock);
● mobile and immobile objects (a cloud and a promontory);
● man-made and naturally occurring objects (a chair and the moon); and
● animates and animate-appearing inanimates (a dog and a girl doll).

No examples of plant life, you will notice, were included as stimuli.

The children were asked to examine four groups of eight photographs in which the 32 objects appeared, and to answer twenty questions about each group. The questions ranged from the obvious, such as 'Which of these grow?' 'Get thirsty?' 'Have mummies and daddies?' to the more obscure, such as 'Might like you?'

The easiest way to present the results is to reproduce some of Dolgin and Behrend's findings in tabular form. Table 4.2 shows the percentage of errors made by each age-group in answer to the twenty questions asked about each object. Let us take the animate category first. As you will see, most 3- and 4-year-olds had no problem in classifying mammals and birds

Table 4.2 'Animate and Inanimate Phenomena' Percentage of errors in each age-group for each category

Category	3	4	5	7	9	Adult
Animate						
Mammals	16	17	6	3	7	4
Birds	20	16	10	6	6	7
Fish	39	27	23	14	22	7
Insects	36	33	22	21	21	10
Inanimate						
Dead animals	13	20	34	7	0	2
Vehicles	9	10	22	3	2	1
Dolls	46	33	45	6	5	1

(*Source*: Adapted from Dolgin and Behrend, 1984.
© 1984 Society for Research in Child Development Inc.)

correctly but they were more uncertain about the standing of fish and insects (so, for that matter, were some of the adults).

Responses to questions about inanimate objects revealed a strong inclination to put dead animals in the 'live' category up to the age of 5 but, from then on, this tendency almost completely fades out. The reaction to dolls is particularly puzzling. It is difficult to know what to make of the large number of errors made by the 3–5-year-olds in attributing life-like qualities to dolls, except to say that, on this evidence, the line between make-believe and reality in this age-group seems to be very thin indeed. You will also notice that the 5-year-olds made more errors on these two categories than did the 3- and 4-year-olds, but their reasons for doing so remains a matter for speculation. Finally, it is clear that dead animals (which have once been alive) cause children more problems than vehicles (which are always inanimate).

Dolgin and Behrend's study confirms that even pre-school children have little difficulty in differentiating between the attributes of such obviously living creatures as dogs and other, just as obviously non-living objects such as crayons. The errors that persist concern the finer distinctions between animate and inanimate objects.

You may have noticed how careful I have been to contrast living with non-living as opposed to other apparent alternatives, such as dead or inanimate. This is because, as Carey (1985) warns, the problems of language cause so much confusion in this field. She discovered that the basic distinction children make is between *alive* and *dead* and not between *alive* and *inanimate*, as many investigators have assumed. If you think about it for a moment you will see the problem: the dead were once alive; the inanimate never were. As a consequence, children are put in a false position when they are asked to apply the living–dead criterion to such objects as clouds, which are neither living nor dead but inanimate. To make matters worse, as Carey explains, young children are at the same time still struggling to come to terms with notions of death. Not only is there a difficulty in understanding that death is final, experimental studies also confirm that both non-existent monsters (which feature so prominently in TV programmes nowadays) and extinct dinosaurs are classed as dead creatures.

Summary At first sight, it may seem easy enough to sort out something as common as children's constructs of living but the more we know about them the more complex they turn out to be. There is no doubt that, early on, children can easily distinguish between the common animals and inanimate objects, and probably their principal reference point in doing so is themselves and what they understand about their own biological processes. From then on, there are two major learning hurdles to negotiate.

The first is to extend the concept of living to all forms of living creatures, vertebrate and invertebrate, and to plants, which young children tend to categorize as non-living objects.

The second hurdle, and it is complementary to the first, centres on the characteristics of living organisms. Children must eventually learn that there are some basic attributes possessed by all animals. Looft's (1974) findings suggest a uniform sequence in the development of that knowledge where the need for food is better understood than the need to breathe and the need to breathe is better understood than the ability to reproduce. In addition to understanding these universal attributes, children also have to realize that there are other properties, such as flying, possessed by some creatures but not by others. Added to this are problems of sorting out where inanimate objects, dead animals and fantasy creatures fit into the scheme.

Classroom applications This research has considerable potential for teaching. It provides examples of both open and closed questions and suggests a whole range of comparisons that might be invited between living and non-living things. More than anything else, it suggests a developmental sequence the teacher might bear in mind when dealing with the many characteristics of animal and plant life. We examine specific attempts to teach this topic later in the chapter.

The concept of flotation

You will find 'floating and sinking' recommended as a suitable science topic in nearly all the practical guides to infant-school teaching. However, it is as necessary to remind ourselves at the outset of an obvious fact: although young children find it quite easy to decide which objects float and which do not, it is well into the secondary school before most pupils finally understand why some objects float and others sink.

Inhelder and Piaget's (1958) classic work on this topic aroused a great deal of interest. It traced the progression of children's ideas about floating bodies through a series of stages from the most elementary right up to the mastery of Archimedes' principle, which is normally achieved around adolescence.

The concept of flotation is complex. Archimedes' law states that a body immersed in water loses as much in weight as the weight of an equal volume of water. Flotation, therefore, depends on the ratio of weight to volume. If an object weighs less than an equivalent volume of water it floats; if it doesn't, it sinks. Phillips (1969) gives the formula

$$\frac{Wo}{Vo} = d,$$

where Wo is the weight of the object, Vo is the volume of the object and d is the density of the object. If we assume that the object is 'solid' it will float if

$$\frac{Wo}{Vo} < \frac{Ww}{Vw}.$$

Finally, to express the same idea a little differently, if the upward thrust of the water is greater than that of the object pushing down on it, the object will float. If the upwards thrust is less, the object sinks.

It is necessary to be able to conserve both weight and volume before flotation can be properly understood. In Chapter 1 we examine Piaget's experiment in which a child is shown two balls of clay the same size, one of which is distorted into a sausage shape as the child watches. If the child says there is still the same amount of clay in both balls, he or she can conserve – he or she now recognizes that the quantity of material remains the same whatever happens to its shape.

The same principle applies to the conservation of weight. However, this time (Beard, 1963) two balls of clay identical in appearance are placed on a balance to demonstrate that they are equal in weight. One ball is then flattened and the child has to say whether he or she thinks it still weighs the same as the other ball. Beard also had a test for conservation of volume in which the experimenter put a ball of Plasticine into a glass of water, which made the water level rise. The other ball was flattened into a biscuit-like shape, and the child was asked if hé or she thought the water would rise to the same level when placed in the glass. A 'yes' response is taken as evidence of the ability to conserve volume.

With that in mind, we can now turn to Inhelder and Piaget's (1958, p. 20ff.) experiment. Their testing took the usual form: various objects were shown to the children who were asked to say which would float and which would sink and then to give reasons for their judgements. They were also given a chance to test out their ideas by putting the objects in a bucket of water, after which they were invited to summarize their observations in the form of a general proposition or law.

At the pre-operational level (up to about the age of 7), children are not short of answers but what they say lacks generality and is full of inconsistencies. For instance, one 4-year-old who was shown two metal needles of identical appearance thought that one would sink and the other one float. Contradictions did not bother him. He seemed to be looking for explanations that satisfied specific cases instead of a general law.

Early on in the concrete operational stage, children discover that small objects are not always lighter than large ones. One 8-year-old's rule seemed to be 'Light objects (e.g. wood, matches and paper) float; heavy objects (e.g. keys, pebbles and nails) sink; and other objects come in between'.

At around 9 years of age, children begin to conserve weight but are still unable to conserve volume consistently. In consequence, as Inhelder and Piaget (*ibid*. p. 32) explain, 'in comparing the weights of specific bodies to the weight of water (which begins at this stage), the child does not relate the object's weight to that of an equal volume of water but rather to the water contained in the entire receptacle'. It is not unusual, therefore, for children at this stage to believe that the same piece of wood will float in one bucket but not in another.

At the final stage there is no suggestion of relating the weight of the objects to the weight of all the water in the pail. One 12-year-old boy immediately compared the weight of the object to an equivalent volume of water. The principle was quite clear in his mind. He said, 'You take the quantity of water for the size of the object; you take the same amount of water. If it were the same quantity of cork, it would float because the cork is less heavy than the same quantity of water' (*ibid*. p. 38).

Summary   Judging whether or not an object can float is a complicated matter, for there is no way in which the ratio of weight to the volume of the object or the ratio of weight to the volume of the displaced water can be directly observed.

Inhelder and Piaget have traced a developmental pattern that has been largely confirmed by later investigators (see, in particular, Halford, Brown and Thompson, 1986). At the outset, children's ideas are unstable and inconsistent but they settle down to focus on perceptual characteristics commonly associated with weight (such as size) to explain why some things float and others do not. With the onset of concrete operational thinking children learn to conserve weight and with it comes the realization that small objects are not always lighter than large ones. This is a significant step forward but children around 9 years of age still cannot conserve volume and, as a consequence, the weight of objects is related not to an equal volume of water displaced but to all the water in the bucket. Even with the advent of conservation of volume, the principle of flotation still eludes them. That final stage is only reached when children become formal operational thinkers and are able to compare mentally the ratio of weight to the volume of the displaced water. Archimedes' law is now understood.

Classroom applications Later on we shall be looking at deliberate attempts to teach the flotation principle but there are two general points arising from this experiment we ought to note immediately. First, it demonstrates better than most what a long, drawn-out business the acquisition of advanced concepts is. We must return again and again to the same topic and set realistic objectives at each stage in the process.

Second, getting children to state a general rule (as Inhelder and Piaget did) forces children to express the new knowledge in their own terms and to put their personal stamp on it.

Concepts of gravity and the earth

Selman *et al.* (1982) investigated developmental conceptions of gravity based on interviews with pre-school, kindergarten and first-grade children (making the age-range roughly between 4 and 7). The particular aspect we shall consider centres on the principle that all bodies, irrespective of shape, size and weight, fall at the same rate (apart from the effects of air resistance). Helpfully, the authors give details of their interview schedule together with typical responses from children who had reached the first and second levels on a scale of scientific thinking. Their findings are shown in Table 4.3. Selman and his team related their findings on gravity to a general developmental scheme consisting of four levels of scientific thought.

At level 1, children (typically in the 3–7 age-range) focus on observed cause-and-effect relationships. They can describe accurately what they see but they do not grasp that unseen forces are at work. A typical response is 'The edge of the table makes things fall'.

Table 4.3   The development of concepts of gravity

Question	Level 1	Level 2
What makes things fall to the ground?	You let them go. They hit the ground. They were too close to the edge	The weight of them. (Probe.) The heaviness pulls them down. The earth pulls them
If we drop these (unequal weights) will they hit at the same time? (Why or why not?)	Yes, cause you drop them. No, cause one is bigger. (Probe.) Cause it will hit first.	Yes, because they are both pulled down by something to the ground. No, because that one is heavier and it gets pulled more
(After dropping them.) Why did they both hit at the same time?	Cause you let them go at the same time. They are both big. You held them close together.	The weight must not make a difference in how fast they fall. The pull must be the same.

(*Source*: Selman *et al.*, 1982
© 1982 John Wiley and Sons Inc.)

At level 2, where the age span is 5–9, children now offer explanations based on unseen forces, but only one such force is considered at a time and it is always defined by its overt effects. Thus we hear 'Gravity always makes things go down'. The possibility that two gravitational forces may be operating on a single object is not considered.

Results from another phase of the investigation enabled Selman to complete the developmental pattern. Level 3 covers a very wide age-range from 7 to 15 that overlaps with the previous level. The salient feature now is that conceptions take account of more than one unseen force. For example, the response 'One planet is pulling it this way and the other is pulling it that way' clearly takes account of competing gravitational pulls. The interaction of these two factors is, however, still not completely understood – this is the final step achieved at level 4, where the reported age-range is 12–18. Balanced relationships between the various unseen forces are now suggested, as in the response 'The force of gravity is stronger the closer you get to the earth'.

Much of Selman and his associates' analysis will be familiar. In fact, they go on to relate their levels of scientific reasoning to Piaget's stages. Level 1 reflects cognitive abilities at the pre-operational stage; levels 2 and 3 broadly follow the pattern of concrete operational thinking; while level 4 represents formal operational thought. It also has much in common with Peel's (1971) model of conceptual development.

Let us now extend the discussion to include children's ideas about the earth. Nussbaum and Novak (1976) studied both the concepts of gravity and of the earth held by 7-8-year-old children. Essentially, they were asked to describe the shape of the earth and to give reasons for their answers. In the process, many supplementary and probe questions were put to them involving their understanding of space, force and gravity – all of which contribute to children's ideas about the earth.

Even within this narrowly restricted age-range, five distinct concepts of the earth were discovered. The first principle children hold can be summed up in just a few words: 'The earth we live on is flat'. Although children begin by asserting the earth is round, their reasons for doing so soon reveal how mixed up they really are. Although they have been told the earth is round and, as evidence, they see photographs of it taken from space and represented by globes in school, some children believe they have to look up to the sky to see the earth. It is as if two earths exist, one they live on (which is flat) and the other a kind of planet in the sky, which is round. At the other extreme, some of the children had a concept of the earth as a spherical planet: they know it is positioned in space, and that dropped objects fall to its centre.

In a follow-up investigation among 9–14-year-old children, Sneider and Pulos (1983) drew on Nussbaum and Novak's work and Nussbaum's (1979) refinements of it but separated out the concepts of gravity and the earth. These scales are shown in Figure 4.1.

One of the tests that helped to identify ideas about the earth's shape was simple and effective. Following instructions, the child drew a picture of him or herself standing on the ground. Next, the child drew the earth in space together with the sun, moon and stars. The experimenter then asked: 'Why did you draw the ground flat here and earth round here? If you refer to Figure 4.1 you will see that some children believed that people live on the flat bit in the middle of the earth or on top of a ball-shaped world. The 'shape-of-the-earth' scale itself is self-explanatory.

The 'gravity' scale and the testing on which it is based needs a little explanation. In one test, a globe represents the earth and a figure is placed at the North Pole carrying an open bottle of water. The child is invited to draw what happens to the water when it is taken from the North to the South Pole. If the person carrying the bottle is drawn upside down in the

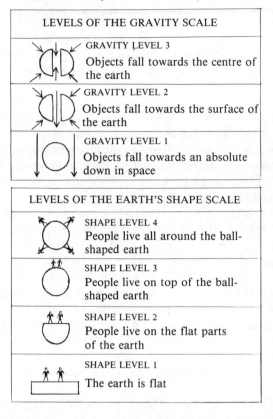

Figure 4.1   The earth's shape scale and the gravity scale
(*Source*: Sneider and Pulos, 1983 © John Wiley and Sons Inc.)

southern hemisphere with the water flowing out into space, then the child is judged to be at level 1.

More advanced reasoning is tested in another way. The child is shown a styrofoam ball with a tunnel gouged out that goes from one pole to the other. The child is then asked to draw what would happen to a rock dropped at the North Pole. If the rock is thought to go right through the earth and out into space beyond, the child's thinking is categorized at level 2; if it is thought to stop at the centre of the earth then the child's thinking is judged to be at level 3.

Sneider and Pulos reported a wide range of understanding within most age-groups although, of course, far more younger children were at earth-shape levels 1 and 2 than were older children while, for the most part, only 13- and 14-year-olds reached gravity level 3.

Summary There is no need to dwell on Selman's and Sneider and Pulos's scales (which reflect the general course of cognitive development), but the research on concepts of the earth's shape reminds us that what children say is not always an inaccurate reflection of what they know. Nearly all Sneider and Pulos's group said the earth was round but when put to the test, their true understanding of the earth's shape was very different.

Classroom applications These two topics open up fascinating areas for discussion and exploration based on the experiments just reported, which can easily be adapted and extended for teaching purposes.

Extending Children's Scientific Thinking

In the previous section we saw examples of children's thinking in science that could never have been the result of formal teaching. By some means or other, children have picked up knowledge of a scientific nature from any number of sources, such as parents, television and books, and they have processed it in sometimes quite curious ways.

In a very useful analysis, Osborne, Bell and Gilbert (1983) spelt out the essential differences between what is sometimes called children's science and formal science. First, they point out, children's views of the world are 'human-centred' and anchored in everyday experiences, whereas scientists use abstract reasoning. Second, children focus on the specific in contrast to scientists, who are always looking for general explanations. Third, the everyday language children apply to scientific objects and events clashes with the strict and precise definitions scientists use. Nevertheless, successful science teaching depends on respecting children's ideas – whatever their limitations – and building on that foundation.

We begin by examining empirical studies designed to advance children's concepts of living and flotation. Then, to remind you of the three methods for promoting learning discussed in Chapter 1, we examine the cognitive-conflict principle, meaningful reception learning and observation in the context of science education.

Concepts of living and flotation

Several studies demonstrate the effect direct teaching can have on children's scientific thinking. They are experimental and, therefore, to some extent artificial, but they are of interest to teachers not only because they set out a progression in the teaching of a concept but also because they show what concentrated teaching can achieve.

In one study that links up with the empirical work reported in the previous section, Wolfinger (1982) arranged for 4½-7-year-olds to be taught about the characteristics of living organisms for five half-hour teaching sessions. The topics covered were the significance of movement in distinguishing the living from the non-living; the need for food and drink; the ability to reproduce; the ability to grow and change; and the processes of respiration and excretion.

An active approach to learning was adopted. For example, to illustrate the difference between living and non-living things, the movement of live mice was compared with the static nature of a box of crayons. In lesson 3, reproduction was considered using living plants, a litter of mice and a range of visual material.

The results of Wolfinger's study were certainly encouraging. Children who went through the programme improved their understanding of basic characteristics of living organisms considerably as compared with their counterparts in the control group. Wolfinger stopped at the point in the development scale that is comfortably within the competence of pre-operational thinkers of this age. However, as we saw in the last section, there are many further obstacles to overcome before an understanding of life is complete. Children may still get muddled about the status of dead animals or teddy bears and remain totally unaware of the lesser-known characteristics of living things – not to mention the elaborate systems used to classify them.

Just as fortunately for us, Wolfinger also decided to study the effects of direct teaching on children's concepts of flotation. Again the teaching sequence was divided into five sessions:

1. Children placed objects in water and classified them according to whether they floated or sank, nothing more.
2. The focus was on heavy objects. The experiences planned were designed to show that objects heavy for their size (e.g. a penny) would sink.
3. The emphasis switched to demonstrating that objects light in weight for their size (e.g. styrofoam blocks) would float.
4. Objects of the same volume but of different weights were experimented with to encourage comparison of the weight of the object with the weight of an equal volume of water.
5. Children were invited to mould a piece of Plasticine to a shape that would float. The area of Plasticine in relation to the amount of water has to be taken into account.

You will see that this time a direct attempt was made to teach the principle of flotation not normally understood until adolescence to children none of whom were over 7. Not surprisingly, Wolfinger's teaching programme made no difference to the quality of thinking of pre-operational children but concrete operational thinkers did make some progress – although not enough to achieve a complete understanding of the flotation principle.

To put it baldly, the teaching programme on living things was much more successful than the one on flotation (and for obvious reasons). As Wolfinger explains, it is a relatively simple matter to concentrate one at a time on such factors as the need for food and the ability to reproduce. In contrast, an understanding of floating and sinking is dependent on the ability to conserve weight and volume and deal with abstract relationships. Primary-school children can be helped towards an understanding of floating but it falls short of reaching the ultimate goal.

As it happens, there is another study on flotation that bears out these findings. It is included here because it gives a fair deal of detail about the teaching techniques used. A group of Italians, Dentici *et al.* (1984) were particularly interested in finding out the effects on children's thinking of a strategy that combines adult intervention, opportunities for active learning and peer-group discussion. Thirty-five children between the ages of 6 and 8 took part.

Initially, a pre-test was given to determine the level of children's concepts of flotation. Groups of three children were then formed that first had to predict whether an object would float in water; they were then encouraged to put the hypothesis to the test; finally, they were asked to comment on the outcome.

Details of the experiment are set out in Table 4.4. Experiments 1 and 2 focus on the upward thrust of water. Experiments 3 and 4 bring in the weight factor. Experiments 5 and 6 draw attention to shape as well as to the material the object is made of. Experiment 7 demonstrates conservation of volume.

In the results, nearly all these 6–8-year-olds shifted in their thinking. There was a particularly sharp decline in pre-operational responses that at first sight seems to go against Wolfinger's (1982) findings looked at earlier. However, the discrepancy is due to the age difference between the two samples. Many of Wolfingers 4–7-year-olds were not yet ready to make the transition to concrete operational thinking, whereas many of Dentici *et al.*'s 6–8-year-olds clearly were. In the Dentici study also, children at the concrete operational level made good progress within that stage but only a very few exceptionally able pupils were able to go much further.

Summary The three studies we have just considered are admittedly

Table 4.4   Sequence of experiments and related questions

Experiment	Questions
1. One wooden block and one Plasticine cube (having the same dimension – (2 cm) are put in water	Why do you think the Plasticine has sunk? Why do you think the wooden block floats? Can you make the wooden block stay under water? How? Why?
2. The wooden block is pushed by hand so that it is completely submerged in water	Is it the water then that pushes the wooden block up? Why do you think (child's answer)? Does the water push the Plasticine up too? Why do you think (child's answer)?
3. The Plasticine and the wooden block are attached to a spring in succession	Why does the spring's length increase when the block is hung from it? Has it become longer with the Plasticine or the wooden block? Why has it become longer with the Plasticine?
4. Experiment 3 is repeated with the Plasticine only and the length of the spring is marked on a stick. The Plasticine is put in water and the length is observed again	Has the spring become as long as before? Why do you think it is shorter now?
5. The floating experiment is carried out again with the Plasticine	Could we make it float? How?
6. The Plasticine is shaped into a concave form and placed in water	What have I done to the Plasticine? Why does the same Plasticine now float?
7. The shaped Plasticine is attached to the same spring as in 3. The fact that it now has the same length as with the Plasticine in the cube shape is pointed out	

(*Source*: Dentici *et al.*, 1984. © Taylor and Francis Ltd.)

artificial but, taken together, they illustrate some basic teaching strategies not only in science education but also for teaching in general. Typically, the object of the assignment is clearly set out, and all three studies, explicitly or implicitly, recognize the importance of discovering children's existing scientific concepts. We saw examples of the cognitive-conflict strategy in operation, notably in Dentici *et al.*'s study, where things that happened caused children to doubt their existing ideas and to re-fashion them in the light of that experience. In common with many studies reported in the literature, children were encouraged to try out their predictions, to reflect on what they saw and did and to provide explanations for what happened. However, that in itself was not enough. Teacher intervention was also necessary to challenge the conclusions reached and to force children to re-think their position.

These three studies also demonstrate that such advanced concepts as the principle of flotation need to be visited and re-visited right throughout the primary school and beyond.

Cognitive conflict

In Chapter 1, cognitive conflict was suggested as one way of helping children to learn. Although it is not referred to by name, something like it was clearly in the minds of Osborne, Bell and Gilbert (1983), who write of the need to arrange 'well chosen learning experiences which will highlight to the child the inadequacies in a present view'. This principle was put to the test in an experiment designed to correct children's notions of current flow in a simple electrical circuit where one wire leads from a battery to a bulb and a second wire leads from the bulb back to the battery.

The teaching began with a diagnostic stage where children offered their first thoughts about the flow of the current. For instance, one group decided that there was current in the outward wire only and that it stopped short at the bulb. A second group thought that two currents flowed outwards from the battery along both wires that met, or rather clashed, when they reached the bulb. In addition, yet another group of children hit on the 'correct' interpretation, explaining that the current flowed from the battery to the bulb and then back to the battery through the second wire.

The pupils were then invited to test their ideas using an ammeter. This was followed by a phase of intensive teacher questioning and class discussion intended to reveal the range and quality of solutions offered and to get children to reflect on their ideas and to change them if flawed.

One of the most significant points the authors make (*ibid.*) is 'that where no pupil puts forward the accepted scientific viewpoint as a possibility, this alternative might be introduced by the teacher for pupils to consider'. This suggestion is sensibly cautious because, plainly, while the formal scientific view may make sense to some children, for others it will be way beyond their understanding. In another paper, Osborne (1985) implies that there is no sure way of knowing when and how the accepted scientific explanation should be put before children. In that case common sense dictates that if a teacher suspects children might be at a transitional stage and ready for new knowledge, then they should be exposed to it without delay. It is a risk worth taking even if it does not come off.

Meaningful reception learning

There is a link between Osborne's (1985) argument and Ausubel's (1968) principle of meaningful reception learning, which is also described in Chapter 1. Ausubel makes a distinction between rote and reception learning, which is taken up and elaborated by Summers (1982) in his comparison of reception learning and discovery methods in schools. He points out that the former is criticized because it is wrongly equated with rote learning, whereas discovery methods draw a much more enthusiastic response because they are always assumed to promote meaningful learning. However, as Summers (*ibid.*) explains, unless the learner already possesses relevant knowledge to which the new material can be assimilated in a meaningful way, 'then rote learning will result, independently of whether reception or discovery methods are used. Discovery methods can be as disastrous as didactic teaching, conversely both can be equally effective'.

Ausubel attaches much importance to what he calls advance organizers, which are essentially a means of alerting the learner to the link between new material and existing knowledge. McClelland (1982b) gives several examples of advance organizers, one of which concerns the concept of living we have been considering. The key statements he gives under the headings of 'adaptation' are as follows: 'Plants and animals have to solve three problems: (1) How to get food. (2) How to avoid being eaten. (3) How to breed'. Others could be added, of course.

An advance organizer can help the learner to make sense of the exercise in hand, although whether a tightly worded key statement should always be given before children have had a chance to sort out their own ideas is open to question. Nevertheless, at some stage the scientific principles expressed in advanced organizers can usefully guide children's explorations and give their conclusions a generality they would not otherwise have.

Observation in science education

We now return to a central principle – that what we see is dependent on what we know. Observation is a selective process by which existing knowledge exercises a controlling influence on what is attended to and on the interpretation of incoming information. Earlier in this chapter we touched on a closely related matter – the flurry caused by misgivings about observational methods based on the now-discredited theory of induction. It is unnecessary to rehearse the powerful arguments against that position, but it does no harm to emphasize that good science depends on a conjunction of theory and observation that allows observations to refine theory and theory to refine observations.

It is at the secondary level where the pitfalls in observing are becoming more widely recognized and where, if the journals for specialist teachers of the subject are a reliable guide, this changing view of science is beginning to make some impact. In the primary sector, too, a few recent publications – notably Harlen's (1985) – are opening up the issues involved to a wider professional audience. One major difficulty is that new developments in science education might appear to run counter to discovery methods, and the emphasis on developing children's powers of observation through first-hand experience. That would be a mis-reading of the situation, but there is no doubt that (in the light of new knowledge about the processes of perception and an awareness of how complex it really is) there is an obvious need to re-examine what we are about when we encourage children to observe.

Fortunately, there are three main sources – Driver (1983), Harlen and Symington (1985) and Hodson (1986a) – that bring clarity and common sense to the issue. Hodson (1986a) states the problem precisely in three short sentences: '(1) Observations do not provide a secure basis of fact. (2) Observations do not constitute the starting point for science. (3) Observations cannot be theory independent'.

The other side of the coin is that children are not the proficient, eagle-eyed observers we may sometimes assume them to be. Harlen and Symington (1985), citing data from the Assessment of Performance Unit (1981b), point out that the 11-year-olds tested tended to focus on gross features rather than the finer details, and were inclined to notice differences much more easily than similarities. Further, in observing a sequence of events it was the result that remained uppermost in children's minds, not the events leading up to it. When asked to identify a pattern in the events shown to them, only about one in fifteen could do so. One general finding is particularly instructive: even where children made a good attempt at grouping objects or at detecting a pattern in observations, many found it difficult to put their thoughts into words and explain the reasons for their actions or conclusions.

In the face of all these difficulties, what action should we take? Initially, there is a strong case for allowing children to explore something new without restriction, to discover what interests them and what they say about it. Left to themselves, children will always make something of the phenomena before them and, even where their observations are well wide of the mark, these can still serve as a pointer to the next step forward. In science education this often means deliberately directing children's attention towards significant features of the object and away from the peripheral in order to encourage more relevant and disciplined observation and interpretation.

Driver (1983) gives an example of what this means in practice. She reports an incident in a class of 11-year-olds where children were making drawings of a woodlouse with the creature in front of them. In analysing their work, the teacher concentrated on the number of legs represented in the drawings. 'He counts the legs on one drawing, then those on another. "Seven, eight, ten ... are you all looking at the same woodlouse? How many legs does it have?" ... They repeated their drawings, this time not simply looking *at* the woodlouse, but looking *for* specific features' (*ibid.* p. 13).

Similarly, Harlen and Symington (1985) touch on the need for teacher guidance in helping children to detect relevant similarities and differences between objects, and to discount the irrelevant. To illustrate the point, they describe the attempts of a group of children to distinguish between cooked and uncooked eggs. Differences in the movement of eggs were recorded, in the sounds they made when tapped and in many other ways. However, the fact that the shells were different in texture or that one was labelled red and the other blue had nothing to do with the cooked or uncooked state of the eggs and so it was necessary to make explicit the distinction between relevant and irrelevant differences.

The same authors also point out that children can be led to notice similarities between things, which in many ways is even more important than picking out differences. The trouble is that objects within the same category often look nothing like each other and, as we saw with the concept of life, many children and even some adults become tangled up with the various attributes and sub-categories. Again, a complete mastery of the classes and sub-classes of more complex concepts comes only slowly and over a long period of time.

From the outset, children need help and encouragement in formulating their conclusions and in justifying them. Harlen and Symington (*ibid.*) tell of one group that, after investigating the strengths of different kinds of threads, concluded that the thickness of the thread made no difference to its strength. When asked to substantiate their findings they explained that when they hung the 600-gram weight on the thick one it broke, and that the same thing happened with the thin one. This is a case of back to the drawing-board, helped by a 'What would happen if ..?' type of question from the teacher. However, the main point about the episode is that children, just like scientists, have to be initiated into the practice of questioning their own results and looking for alternative explanations.

To digress slightly, among the tests for determining the validity of knowledge is the repeatability criterion. 'Do you think the same thing will happen again?' becomes a standard question in the science teacher's repertoire and with young children who are still egocentric thinkers it would be just as well to ask 'If George did what you did, would the same thing happen?' This is the beginning of the process leading to an understanding of what it means to be a scientist. Eventually, as Hodson (1986a) reminds us, 'only observational evidence which achieves consensus within the community is admitted to the corpus of scientific knowledge. By analogy, only that which achieves consensus within the class should be regarded as legitimate by the children'. The implications are obvious: group- and teacher-led discussions have as weighty a contribution to make in developing children's observational powers as they have in advancing learning generally.

But to return to the theory dependence of observations as it affects learning, if we conceive theory as being the ideas about science children already hold, then in that sense we have discussed little else in this chapter. The central thrust of the argument is quite clear: the starting-point is children's existing knowledge. That knowledge is challenged and children are forced to re-examine the phenomenon in a more focused and disciplined way, so that finally (if all goes well), children's ideas are extended and refined. Eventually, we hope, children will come to understand that existing expectations influence the observations they make; that these expectations can change in the light of new experiences; and that, in consequence, future observations will take on a different pattern.

Summary In ending this section, I can do no better than to summarize Harlen and Symington's (1985) guidelines for developing observation and promoting its role in learning:

1. Children should have enough time to make observations on their own account before teacher intervention occurs.
2. After the initial observation, appropriate guidance should be given and a definite goal set.
3. Materials selected should give opportunities to detect similarities and differences, and involve a sequence of events that allows a conclusion to be drawn.

4. Group work is recommended together with class discussions where results of experiments by individuals and groups can be described and critically appraised.
5. Care needs to be exercised in posing questions. Broadly focused questions allow children to decide what to observe; narrowly focused ones come into their own where children are ignoring a significant feature.

SUMMARY AND CONCLUSIONS

The days are gone when science was looked upon as the only discipline producing solidly 'objective' data. Traditional methods of scientific inquiry have been undermined by the growing realization of the tentative status of knowledge and the influence of theory in determining the focus of observations and abstracting meaning from what is observed.

There has been a corresponding reappraisal of science education but, because of the time lag in communicating new trends in the discipline to schools, its full effects have yet to be felt. As far as can be judged, the emphasis is still on a process model of science education – partly because it appears to correspond most nearly with children's 'natural' modes of learning, and partly because it matches up well with the experimental methods of science. Process methods will rightly continue to find favour in primary schools although more attention is bound to be given in the future to the content of science teaching.

Psychology has a contribution to make in the current re-assessment of science education. However, it is only recently that the significance of children's thinking in science is getting through to a wider professional audience. The steadily growing research literature on developmental stages in children's scientific concepts can help in selecting appropriate content, in devising graded teaching sequences and in judging children's readiness for further learning experiences. Similar purposes are served by experimental studies designed to promote learning that also provide useful models of questioning techniques and other devices designed to get children to reflect on and to revise their constructs of the physical world.

Empirical studies have also caused us to reconsider the role of observation in science education and the part teachers can play in drawing children's attention to significant aspects of the environment and away from the irrelevant.

Psychology has also struck a chord with science educators in the matter of reception learning. Ausubel and his followers make a good case for identifying and spelling out in statement form the principles governing a learning experience. While it may not always be advisable to give the principle at the outset, it could be a significant aid at some point in the learning process and, most of all, in summarizing and interpreting the findings of the exercise. There is a time to guide and a time to tell, and an explanation showing how new knowledge relates to the old and how to make sense of it must be helpful to the learner.

FURTHER READING

Clear and readable accounts of scientific theory and method are given by Medawar (1967) and Chalmers (1976). Hodson (1985, 1986a, 1986b) deals with the same issues but from an educational perspective.

Extensive and detailed summaries of research into science education are given in Lawson, Costenson and Cisneros (1986), Shymansky and Kyle (1986) and Gallagher (1987). Other sources are Driver (1981, 1983), Osborne, Bell and Gilbert (1983), Osborne and Wittrock (1983), Osborne (1983, 1985) and Hodson (1985, 1986a, 1986b).

On the specific issue of concepts of living, Piaget's (1929) original research and studies by Carey (1985) and Trowbridge and Mintzes (1985) are recommended.

General texts on the teaching of science include Harlen (1985), who deals specifically with the primary years of schooling, Driver (1983) and Osborne and Freyberg (1985).

Relevant psychological journals are the *International Journal of Science Education, Research in Science and Technological Education, Science Education* and *Studies in Science Education*.

5

EDUCATION IN HISTORY

INTRODUCTION

History is another of those fields of study, such as geography, that was slow to become established as a serious academic discipline in its own right. In fact, because of its original strong connection with story-telling, history was often reduced to being a branch of literature and, even as late as 1889, the chairs of History and English at Owen's College, Manchester, were still combined (Marwick, 1970, p. 48).

According to Welton (1909, p. 221), history was practically unknown in elementary schools before 1875 and, by 1899, was taught in only a quarter of the schools. Not long after the beginning of this century, history at last became a compulsory part of the curriculum. However, as most teachers were untrained in the subject, the teaching consisted largely of memorizing little-understood historical facts and long lists of dates from textbooks.

In the pupil-teacher centres and training colleges of the time, the instrumental purposes of history – and particularly the patriotic and moral values it was meant to inspire – were very much to the fore. Garlick (1901, p. 258), in his manual for teachers, writes: 'History calls forth feelings of patriotism. It stimulates the national pride, promotes a love of virtue, gives powerful object lessons against vice, and tends, rightly taught, to make good citizens. This ought to be its prime aim'.

With the advent of the child-centred movement, the teaching of history took on a different character. Children's interests were taken more fully into account, the teaching was frequently based on the local environment and attempts were made at genuine historical enquiry. This movement gained pace in the decades immediately after the Second World War, when the first serious efforts were made to balance the subject-matter and methods of history as an academic pursuit against what was known about child psychology.

Today, history is frequently taught as part of a general topic where insights from a number of different disciplines are brought to bear on the study of a particular theme. This approach has wide support among primary-school teachers but it is often quite loose in its structure and adds to the difficulties in planning history teaching in primary schools. The Department of Education and Science (1978b, p. 72) criticized the superficial and fragmented nature of the work inspectors saw in a clear majority of schools visited. According to a more recent survey carried out in the north west of England by Swift and Jackson (1987), the situation is still much the same. They, too, found that the teaching of history was often 'superficial, characterised by a lack of uniformity of subject matter and a lack of sequence and progression in the selection and development of historical themes'. Their report also indicates a need for primary-school teachers, who are mainly non-specialists, to be clear about the purposes of history (our first concern in this chapter) and the strategies most appropriate to teaching young children about the past.

THE NATURE OF HISTORY AND THE NATURE OF EDUCATION IN HISTORY

The Nature of History

Historians carefully distinguish between history and the past. In its strict sense, history represents a systematic attempt to describe and to explain the past and, in common with other academic disciplines, it has its own concepts, methodology and tests for truth.

The term 'the past' has a much less specialized meaning and stands for something very different. As the historian sees it,

> Man from the earliest days of recorded time, has used the past in a variety of ways: to explain the origins and purpose of human life, to sanctify institutions of government, to give validity to class structure, to provide moral example, ... to interpret the future, to invest both the individual human life or a nation's with a sense of destiny.

> (Plumb, 1973, p. 11)

The past, then, was used, and not infrequently exploited, for social and political purposes. However, this was not the only problem. At one time many historians were so concerned with literary effect that the 'facts' of history became subordinate to telling a good story. Others, as we have noted, saw history as a means of imparting moral values rather than as a genuine means of discovering what happened and why it happened in the way it did.

It is in the works of von Ranke (who lived from 1795 to 1886 and who, incidentally, with touching optimism, embarked on writing a history of the universe in his eighties) that we find the first significant break from the literary and moralizing schools of historical writing. In tune with the spirit of the age, his objective was 'simply to show how it really was' by introducing scientific methods to the study of history. The strategy appeared to be foolproof. First, search out the facts by going straight to primary sources, for example, original official documents, diaries and eye-witness accounts. Second, allow the facts to speak for themselves. Third, arrive at conclusions drawn from that data, and from that data only.

With hindsight, we know that this conception of scientific method is untenable. Earlier on, when discussing observation in science, the principle that what is 'seen' is dependent on what is known was explained. Observation is a selective process where existing knowledge determines not only the focus of observation but also how the incoming information is interpreted. Carr (1964), writing from a historian's perspective, takes exactly the same position. He writes (p. 11): 'The facts speak only when the historian calls on them: it is he who decides to which facts to give the floor, and in what order or context'.

Since absolute objectivity in historical writing is an unattainable ideal, we must settle for second best – just as we have to do in every other discipline. But second best does not mean third rate. Throughout a long apprenticeship, the historian learns to draw not only on original written sources but also, where necessary, on insights from related disciplines, such as archaeology, sociology and economics. However, the material painstakingly amassed cannot speak for itself: it demands a disciplined imagination to interpret it, the ability to set aside modern perspectives and to see events as they might have appeared to people living in the past. Only in this way can a reasoned and coherent account of past events be produced.

I would not want to give the impression that there is a comfortable consensus among historians about the practice of their craft – there is not. Nevertheless, they are united on many issues, not least in their reluctance to claim too much for their discipline, particularly in the matter of predicting the future on the basis of past events. True, historians do look for common patterns in events and they can make, at a very general level, some forecast about how things might turn out. However, such is the complexity of historical events that one incident in the past is never precisely the same as another and, indeed, far more often than we imagine, what appear to be roughly comparable circumstances lead to widely differing outcomes. The historian, Carr (*ibid.* p. 69) tells us, 'is bound to generalise; and in so doing, he provides guides for future action which, though not specific predictions, are both valid and useful. But he cannot predict specific events, because the specific is unique and because the element of accident enters into it'. What history can do, however, is to make the lay public more sensitive to social change and the forces to which it is subject.

This is perhaps the main answer to the question, 'What is the use of history?' Of course, history is interesting in its own right but as Howard (1981) powerfully argues,

> a knowledge of the past is requisite to an understanding of the present. ... To know the way in which our society came to be formed, to have some understanding of the conflicting forces that created it and are still at work within it, is not only an advantage in the conduct and understanding of affairs: it is indispensable.

Summary History is an attempt to describe and to explain the past by applying a disciplined imagination to historical sources. A principal justification for the study of history lies in its power to help us to make sense of the present through an understanding of the past.

The Nature of Education in History

All manner of claims have been made for studying history in schools. Some say it is supposed to discipline the mind; others to encourage a sense of curiosity; others to act as a spur to creativity or to promote general study and reference skills. However, many disciplines, geography for one, advance similar claims and we must therefore look further for the particular contribution history makes to the curriculum. To this end I have turned for guidance to the recent DES (1985b) statement on history teaching, the ILEA (1980) history guidelines, together with more general sources, such as Dickinson and Lee (1978) and Portal (1987).

First of all, and following on from the last section, the main justification for teaching history in primary schools is not only because the past is a matter of intrinsic interest for most children but also because it throws light on the present. What is happening now has its roots in the past and a historical perspective contributes to understanding the world of today.

History is essentially about change and continuity. At the simplest level, children can grasp that a past existed that is different from the present in some ways and yet similar to it in others. Initially, therefore, the common-sense approach is to concentrate on similarities and differences between then and now, and move on from there when the time is ripe to begin to explore the reasons for change and to look for cause-and-effect relationships. At this point we are approaching the heart of history that, as I hope is now clear, is an effort after meaning rather than a routine matter of recording and describing events.

Valid explanations for historical change are based on respect for evidence, which ranges from written documents and artefacts of all kinds to the testimony of living witnesses. The critical question in history, as in all other disciplines, is 'How do we know?' It follows, therefore, that a central objective must be to encourage pupils to weigh up evidence and to use it in making historical judgements.

A sense of empathy is a second indispensable condition for understanding the past. For the moment it is enough to define empathy in the historical context as the ability to imagine the thoughts and feelings of people living in previous times. As we shall see later, this concept is a subtle and complex one but, again, at a simple level, children can have some grasp of what it must have been like to live as their forebears did. Finally, we ought not to forget that history tells gripping stories about real people that have an immediate appeal to adults and children alike.

Summary   The objectives peculiar to the teaching of history are reasonably clear and can be summed up fairly concisely. Essentially, we want children to develop a bond with people living long ago, to cultivate an interest in the past and to understand its relationship to the present. We hope that, eventually, children will be able to describe and to interpret historical change and, to this end, the development of two essential skills needs to be encouraged. The first is the ability to collate and evaluate evidence in determining causal relationships in history; the second is the capacity to shed present conceptions and prejudices and to enter into the thoughts and feelings of people who lived in the past.

PSYCHOLOGY AND THE TEACHING OF HISTORY
Children's Conceptions of History

I have tracked down only one study that deals seriously and at length with children's understanding of the nature of history. Levstik and Pappas (1987) faced 24 middle-class children – four boys and four girls in each of the age-groups 7, 9 and 11 – with the question, 'What is history?' With a little prompting even the youngest age-group could say what they thought history was and, by the age of 11, children were giving quite sophisticated answers.

First of all, and without exception, history was firmly linked with time. The younger children referred to history as 'the past', 'long ago' and 'before a long time ago', while some of the older children gave more specific definitions, such as describing history as 'events that happened in time, dates and times'.

The second major theme running through many of the children's responses was the view of history as being about the significant past as distinct from everything, and especially trivial incidents, that had happened in times gone by. The two youngest age-groups frequently mentioned death, tragedy and brutality as events qualifying as history (perhaps because they knew about the assassinations of Abraham Lincoln and Martin Luther King) but, again, the 11-year-olds were more precise in their thinking. Typical responses at this age were 'an important event in the past' and 'famous happenings', while one particularly sharp child suggested (*ibid.*) that events that 'made a change in the world or country or something' were the stuff of history.

The third major characteristic emerging from children's explanations of history concerns what Levstik and Pappas call the ambiguity of history, revealed as much as anything by children's confusions about the exact meaning of the term 'past'. For most of the 7-year-olds, the past was generally construed as a long time ago. By the age of 9, about half the age-group had moved on to thinking of the past as 'any time ago', which one boy neatly defined (*ibid.*) as 'five years ago, yesterday, two minutes or just a little bit past'. The definition 'a long time ago' still persisted without qualification among some 11-year-olds, but about half this age-group had progressed to believing that history embraced significant events in the immediate past including those that took place in their own lifetime – for example, the Challenger space-shuttle disaster.

Summary   If these findings are typical, it seems that, unlike so many other curriculum areas, children have a fair grasp of the subject-matter of history. All age-groups understood that history was concerned with the past and was about important as opposed to trivial happenings, while some older pupils added the rider that history embraced the immediate as well as the distant past.

In brief, it seems that towards the end of the primary school many children can grapple with the distinctions between time and history with surprising subtlety and insight.

The Development of Historical Thinking

Until recently, efforts to understand children's thinking in history have been confined to the secondary-school sector. However, a small but growing body of research of interest to teachers of young children is now available, much of it reported by Blyth (1988).

We begin by considering children's concepts of time – research on children's political concepts is reviewed next. The concept of empathy, now a highly topical issue in the teaching of history, is then considered, followed lastly by a brief comment on the relevance of moral reasoning to learning history.

Concepts of historical time

Levstik and Pappas's (1987) study convincingly demonstrates that children as young as 7 realize that history is about the past. Unfortunately, that does not tell us anything about their sense of time, often seen as a major stumbling block to learning history. At the outset it is necessary to make an important conceptual distinction between personal time – the hours, days and weeks children actually experience – and historical time, which covers the entire period from the remote past to the near present.

Psychologists have concentrated on personal time. Reviews by Partington (1980) and Patriarca and Alleman (1987), among others, tell us that around the age of 5, children can use such terms as 'yesterday', 'today' and 'tomorrow' with understanding and, as they progress through the primary school, pupils learn to tell the time and become familiar with conventional units, for example, hours, days and weeks, the seasons of the year, and so on.

However, we are interested in historical time where, unfortunately, the evidence is much thinner and more difficult to interpret. The early and now classic investigation by Oakden and Sturt (1922) suggests that children cannot easily distinguish between one historical age and another. For instance, they discovered that even children who had studied the Stuart period for a term still thought that mud huts and Roman idols were around at that time – it is difficult to be more confused than that.

The simplest way of approaching historical time is through sequence because then we do not have to bother about the duration of events – only the order in which they occurred. In Bone's (1984) study of sequence, 7-, 9- and 11-year-old children were asked to arrange in chronological order sets of pictures of British monarchs, famous people who lived in the past, historical events and various artefacts, such as buses, homes and rooms. The following are some examples of her material:

- *Famous people*   Robin Hood, Guy Fawkes, Captain Cook, Nelson and Churchill.
- *Historical events*   The building of Stonehenge, the Roman invasion of

Britain, the Battle of Hastings, the Great Fire of London and the Battle of Trafalgar.
- *Homes* A Roman villa, a Saxon village, a thirteenth-century castle, an Elizabethan house, a Jacobean house, a Regency crescent, a Victorian house and a modern dwelling.

As expected, the sucess rate varied according to age. In general, the differences between the scores of the 7- and 9-year-olds were not all that great but by 11 there was a marked increase in correct sortings. Children had least trouble in sequencing such artefacts as buses and aircraft, and most difficulty in putting major historical events and rooms furnished in the styles of different periods in order of age.

Bone's results reveal a muddle in the minds of some children about the relation of one historical age to another but, nevertheless, there is a more positive side to the findings we ought not to ignore. To cope with the sequencing tasks as well as they did means that even if children could not accurately locate events on a time scale, they had managed to acquire a fair knowledge of the past.

Let us now move on from sequencing, where no attempt is made to estimate the interval of time between one event and another, to historical dating, which does. Typically, as in Bradley's (1947) work with 8–12-year-olds, children are asked to arrange names and dates in chronological order, as in the following examples:

- Attila lived in Hungary in AD 438.
- Philip lived in Spain in AD 1585.
- Nero lived in Rome in AD 50.

Only about a third of the 8-year-olds and 62 per cent of 10-year-olds could do so without error. In contrast to this poor showing, the success rate of the 12-year-olds was 85 per cent, by which age it appears most children had mastered the basics of the chronological system.

Bone (1984) included a similar test in her study. She got her group to order a set of dates (300 BC, 50 BC, AD 1482, AD 1879, AD 1903, AD 1945) 'starting with the one furthest in the past, or longest ago, and ending with the one nearest our time'. This proved too much for the 7-year-olds, apart from one child who had quite clearly hit on the correct order by chance. As expected the BC dates caused a great deal of confusion but, more surprisingly, only five of the ten questioned gave 1945 as the most recent date. However, the 9-year-old group did much better. Two were completely correct and seven made only one error, falling into the trap of putting 50 BC before 300 BC. Five of the 11-year-olds made the same mistake but the remaining five completed the exercise successfully.

The Bradley and Bone studies are not directly comparable but, taking into account Bone's inclusion of BC dates that made her task more difficult, there is a hint that children of today have a better grasp of the system of dating events that their counterparts forty years earlier.

Useful though it is to be able to arrange historical dates in their correct order, it is another matter altogether to conceptualize the duration of time indicated by conventional units, such as century, decade and generation. Here we are dealing with vague abstractions difficult enough for adults to master and so it comes as no surprise to learn that such a problem as 'Robin Hood lived in 1187. Would your grandmother be alive then?' was not correctly solved by most children before the age of 9 (Bradley, 1947).

Summary   Although children soon learn to link history firmly with the past, their concepts of historical time are uncertain and develop only very slowly. Initially, children cope better with sequencing where duration of time between events is ignored, than with arranging historical incidents in chronological order using conventional units of time.

Classroom applications   We will return to this area later in the chapter but, before moving on, we ought briefly to consider the classroom applications of the research on sequence. Other subjects for sorting might include various forms of transport, exteriors of buildings, paintings and sculpture. In the first instance it might be advisable for children to order in sequence only two pictures or artefacts, gradually extending the number as children become more proficient. This activity is dependent on accurate observation of detail and, as always, it is useful in discussion to determine which factors children attend to in making their judgements and which they ignore.

Children's political concepts

Perhaps the easiest introduction to children's understanding of history is through the meanings they attach to such political terms as 'parliament', 'laws' and 'freedom'. Wood (1967) asked his subjects, aged 9–19, to define these and other concepts, one of which, 'kingship', provides a striking indication of developmental trends in political thinking.

At the most basic level, we receive irrelevant responses, such as 'the king lives in a castle far away', which tells us nothing of consequence. At the next stage, concrete attributes, such as the importance of kings or their wealth, are uppermost in children's minds. At the third level there are references to kings actually ruling over their countries that, although it is a step forward because it puts kingship in a political context, is still a long way from the final stage where the ability to think in the abstract leads to such definitions as 'a king is a person who may rule his country by himself, may rule it in co-ordination with advisers or a government, may simply be a figurehead'.

Using a similar approach, Stevens (1982) asked children to write about what the queen did as part of a wider investigation into the political awareness of primary-school pupils aged 7, 9 and 11. In this study also, the most elementary responses were either irrelevant or concentrated on outward appearances only. There were references to the queen riding a horse, sitting on the throne, giving out medals, writing letters to 'people who are a hundred', doing her paperwork, making speeches and visiting many places (free of charge, as one girl noted). As children passed through the primary school there were increasing references to the queen ruling the country and looking after it but, in this part of the study, there was as yet no hint that children were beginning to appreciate the formal role of the monarch in the political system of the country.

Stevens also asked children to write down their impressions of politics in general. These showed a surprising depth of knowledge. Even the 7-year-olds knew that politics is about voting, political parties, parliament and making laws. By 9 years of age, children had a clearer idea of the purpose of voting and its organization, and there were a few references to economic matters as well – a theme particularly taken up by the 11-year-olds, who frequently talked about such matters as wages, prices and taxes.

In addition to the written questionnaire, children met in groups to explore such issues as what governing the country entails and the role the monarch, the prime minister and political parties play in the process. Many of these fascinating discussions are reported at length and helpfully interpreted in the light of developmental theory. Stevens concludes that at 7, many children had crude but fairly recognizable ideas about the nature of political activity, which they were eager to discuss. By 9, concepts such as democracy, leadership and accountability in government could be understood at a basic level but, from then on, the pace of learning accelerated so that 11-year-old children had already worked out that political parties represent different ideologies and recognized that such issues as conservation, women's rights and economics involve moral judgements.

Summary   Children's political understanding follows the standard pattern. Children's first political ideas are hazy and unco-ordinated. They then progress to concentrating on familiar and concrete attributes of government before reaching the final stage when the abstract nature of politics is understood.

Stevens was clearly impressed with the knowledge and understanding of political matters that children had acquired by the end of the primary school, and is seems that in this aspect of history at least, teachers have a solid base on which to work.

Classroom applications   The classroom applications of this research are easy to see: it alerts teachers to the necessity of discovering the meanings children give to such terms as parliament, law, taxes, republic and democracy. History abounds in such specialist terms as these that, by the end of the primary-school period, ought to be explored, preferably in the context in which they arose.

Children's thinking in history in general

Results from the first widely publicized research into children's thinking in history were far from encouraging. Hallam (1967) asked a sample of 100 children (drawn from all age-groups attending a comprehensive school) to read a passage about William the Conqueror's laying waste to the north of England and then to answer questions about his motivations and the morality of his actions. Hallam's analysis of the responses showed that Piaget's concrete operational stage was not reached until about the surprisingly late age of 12, and the formal operational stage not until around the age of 16, which caused some gloom among history teachers.

One reason for this poor showing might be that, twenty years ago, when this study was carried out, the accent was on exposition and memorization rather than on getting pupils to solve historical problems for themselves. As a consequence, most pupils would have been unprepared for such a test as Hallam's, where independent thinking is demanded rather than a reproduction of stock answers parrot-fashion. Later research by Booth (1978), Jurd (1978) and Shemilt (1978) bears this out. Booth documents the high level of thinking in history possible among fourth-year secondary-school children who were taught by open-ended, enquiry methods, while Shemilt (*ibid.*) concludes that 'Whatever caveats we may wish to make about the limitations of adolescent intelligence, the fact remains that adolescents are capable of far more than is customarily demanded by content-orientated O-level and CSE courses'.

Summary   The evidence on children's thinking in history has come mainly from secondary-school sources but, inevitably, it has had some impact on the work of the primary schoool. The original Hallam (1967) study cast doubts on the viability of teaching history in depth until the sixth form; therefore, so the argument ran, little of substance can be achieved at primary-school level. We have now passed through that stage of doubt. Evidence from other primary-school-based research (which is more conveniently examined in the final section of this chapter) justifies the current optimism about the level of historical thinking young children can reach.

Concept of empathy

Developing a sense of empathy is now a firmly established objective in the teaching of history. Quite obviously, we cannot understand the pattern of historical events unless we are able to go some way towards entering into the minds of men and women who lived in the past.

We are once again dealing with a slippery and over-used construct, but Portal's (1987) definition of empathy as 'an exercise in imagination, a harnessing of all we have learnt about the behaviour of people as individuals and in society to the understanding of the past' makes the concept more manageable. Empathy, in this historical sense, is rather like an inspired but well-informed guess – a feeling that this is the way things must have been. As Portal sees it, empathy is an act of the imagination that points to likely directions to explore and the right questions to ask. But that is only part of the operation. Scholarship then takes over, harnessing the professional knowledge and skills of the historian to the testing of hypotheses and arriving at reasoned judgements, in a process very similar to that of scientific discovery. As a Department of Education and Science (1985b, p. 3) publication explains, 'Empathizing is not the same as identifying with, still less sympathizing with, people in the past; it is simply a word used to describe the imagination working on evidence, attempting to enter into a past experience while at the same time remaining outside it'.

Let us now consider empathy from a psychological standpoint. The ability to take on the point of view of others is firmly linked to the shift from egocentric to sociocentric thinking – a basic mental process we have noted time and time again in all curriculum areas. It is particularly marked in moral development and, in Chapter 8, is an analysis of the growing awareness of the perspectives of others that is relevant to the present discussion.

One dimension of empathy is an understanding of other people's motives. In Hallam's (1967) study discussed earlier, secondary-school children had to decide whether William I was cruel to lay waste to the north. The quality of the motives ascribed by Hallam's group were quite clearly governed by the pupils' cognitive ability. At the highest level, children produced (*ibid.*) sophisticated and well-argued responses such as 'It depends what you mean by cruel. If the definition of cruel is to kill and ravish and burn for any purpose whatever, William was cruel. On the other hand if one is prepared to accept political necessity, William's cruelty was justified'. This 14-year-old boy can take detached view: he is able to identify the relevant factors and to balance one against another. He does not dismiss cruelty out of hand but tries to see the situation as it was then and in all in its harshness rather than from the moral perspective of the twentieth century.

This leads on to a second, equally important condition governing the ability to empathize in history – namely, historical knowledge. The psychological evidence suggests that primary-school children can see a situation from the point of view of people living in other times that can be worked on and developed. However – and this is a critical point – the more history the children know, the more effective their powers of empathy will be. This view is reinforced by Dickinson and Lee's (1978) finding that children's understanding of Jellicoe's strategy at the Battle of Jutland was seriously handicapped by a lack of historical knowledge and, as a result, only 'conventional and conceptually stereotyped views' were possible.

Summary   Essentially then, as we have seen, the ability to appreciate the thoughts and feelings of people living in the past is, in part, a function of the stage of cognitive development children have reached and, in part, dependent on historical knowledge. Therefore, as far as young children are concerned, the major classroom application of this research is to formulate suitably modest and realistic objectives that take account of these two essential factors.

Moral issues and the study of history

In the introduction to this chapter, the role of history in Victorian times was described as a means of learning the moral values acceptable to the establishment at that time. This is a mis-use of history but, nevertheless, historians cannot avoid making moral judgements about the actions of men and women who have significantly influenced the course of events. For example, it is one of the duties of professional political biographers to give disinterested and objective verdicts on the morality of the political conduct of their subjects.

Cockburn (1981) investigated judgements of the morality of Henry VIII's treatment of Thomas More among 123 children in the 8–13 age-group. The moral issue involved was simple enough: a conflict existed between the principle of the king's authority and the principle of justice for the individual.

A sizeable majority of the 8-year-olds equated authority with the obligation to obedience. In their eyes, Thomas More was wrong because he owed allegiance to his king and kings must be obeyed. However, about a third of this same group took a contrary position – they saw no reason why More should not have taken an independent stand and they took a poor view of his execution.

The older the age-group, the more common this view became until, around 12-years-old (but not before), other, more sophisticated judgements began to appear. A significant minority of adolescents took a broader view. Some wanted to know what the law said and others thought the king and More ought to have met to argue the matter out. As Cockburn comments, this progression parallels the changing conceptions of morality reported by Piaget (1932).

Summary The developmental trend is clear: children began by equating morality with the dictates of authority; then a concern for justice became the main moral criterion; and, finally, a genuine conflict between two moral principles was recognized that necessitated taking all relevant circumstances into account in making moral judgements.

Classroom applications Cockburn (1981) makes a telling point when he says that, although primary-school children cannot appreciate the full complexity of such incidents as the dispute between Henry VIII and Thomas More, they are able to grasp that issues of right and wrong are involved. By judging the moral actions of people in the past, he argues (*ibid.*), 'the history will register with them, interest them, and enhance their motives to explore further'. At the same time, of course, children's general moral education benefits.

It is hardly necessary to add that moral issues abound in history. Initially, children will judge the problem in the light of their own experiences but gradually they will come to realize that different circumstances dictate different decisions. This is where a knowledge of the past makes a significant contribution, and encourages children to begin to think in the manner of a historian.

Extending Children's Historical Thinking

Although there are only a few strictly controlled experimental studies in this area, there are other sources that provide useful pointers for classroom practice – particularly in respect to helping children to acquire a better sense of historical time and to think seriously about the past in general.

Concepts of time

Evidence discussed earlier suggests that older primary-school children can sequence historical events with a fair degree of accuracy although they still have trouble with conventional units of measuring historical time, such as 'decade' and 'generation', and the troublesome AD and BC distinction.

Classroom-based studies on facilitating historical-time concepts are sparse, but there is an interesting investigation by Vikainen (1965) in which a subtle technique was used to improve children's sense of historical time.

Vikainen rejected a direct approach preferring, instead, to teach a class of 11-year-olds in such a way that the historical period the class was dealing with was clearly identified and related to other periods in the context of material the children were studying, rather than as an isolated concept. The chronological pattern of events was not over-emphasized and no dates were given. Apparently, this strategy worked well, resulting in the class being given special treatment out-performing a control group in tests measuring both time concepts and general historical knowledge.

The Vikainen approach is in line with Patriarca and Alleman's (1987) recommendations, which suggest that – whatever topic is studied – pupils' consciousness of time ought to be deliberately heightened. For instance, in studying D-Day in the Second World War, suitable questions would be 'How many centuries ago did this event take place?' 'How many decades ago did this event occur?' and so on. Similarly, it is advisable to introduce such terms as 'generation' and 'decade' and the vaguer 'age' and 'era' in context, thus linking the central idea to be conveyed to existing knowledge. Patriarca and Alleman suggest that if the word 'decade' crops up in discussion, the concept is better understood if it is related to something personal, for example, the number of decades they and other members of their family have lived.

As far as I am aware, there are no empirical studies demonstrating the effectiveness of the long-established but, nevertheless, controversial practice of using time charts. Jahoda (1963) was sceptical about their value on two main grounds: first, because the weight of the research evidence shows that it is well into adolescence before children achieve a real grasp of historical time; and, second, because he suggests that in any event it might make more sense to work backwards in time, starting with parents and grandparents.

Recent opinion is much more pragmatic. Partington (1980) favours starting off with very simple time charts. For instance, a time scale representing just three generations might help to fix the idea of a century; similarly, a chart with basic divisions that ignores the time element can give young children a rough idea of the sequence in which such groups as the Romans, Saxons and Normans came to prominence. Dates and exact representations of the duration of various periods can come later when children have a firmer and deeper understanding of historical time.

Summary Although there is very little direct evidence on improving children's understanding of historical time, the literature has two clear classroom applications. One is that time concepts are most effectively acquired as an integral part of studying history and not as something separate or just tagged on. The other is that sequence scales and time charts should be graded according to difficulty and matched to the children's level of understanding.

Children's historical concepts in general

The disappointing performance of children in tests of historical understanding reported by Hallam (1967) may have given the misleading impression that history is too abstract a subject to be studied seriously in secondary schools – let alone primary schools. However, recent research is more reassuring. Even 6-year-olds, it appears, are capable of thinking seriously about the past when open-ended inquiry methods of teaching are used.

Some years after his original research, this was exactly the approach Hallam (1978, 1979) himself used in attempting to improve logical thinking in history. In one part of the experiment, Hallam taught a class of 9–10-year-olds for an hour a week for the best part of an academic year. The teaching emphasis was on encouraging pupils to be critical, to evaluate, to 'go beyond the information given' and to be on the look out for bias. At the end of the experiment the attainment in history of this class was superior to that of a second class acting as a control, which was taught by more traditional methods where the emphasis was on listening and copying.

Hallam's latest work successfully demonstrates the effectiveness of an active approach to teaching history in the primary school, and it is also significant for the meticulous way in which the logical processes identified by Piaget were related to historical material. Some of the questions about family relationships, such as 'What is the relationship of Elizabeth I to Henry VIII?' were designed to test the ability to classify using a family tree. Other questions, such as 'Do you think Mary had anything to do with the murder of Darnley?' were much more probing and more directly related to history. They also revealed the depth of children's understanding of cause-and-effect relationships in history.

Apart from formal testing, there are other more practical ways of examining children's understanding of history, for example, those pioneered by West (1978, 1981, 1982). One approach he tried was to ask children between the ages of 6 and 10 to examine a wide range of objects (mainly borrowed from a museum collection) that included an antique phonograph, prehistoric stone tools, First World War medals and a medieval charter.

West (1978) gave teachers a number of criteria to help them informally but systematically to assess children's reactions to the objects, which included the following:

1. The quality of vocabulary used, for example, in responding to pre-historic tools.
2. The identification of the object and its uses.
3. The extent of associated background knowledge, for example, 'these people (also) made cave paintings'.
4. Signs of deductive powers, manifested, for instance, in deducing that a shaft could be inserted in a stone to make a hammer.
5. Evidence of empathy and a sense of time.

Overall, the children's performance was impressive. Teachers co-operating in the project were surprised at the careful way in which children examined each object in their search to uncover clues that would help them to date the artefact and to discover its purpose.

If you are interested in trying something similar with your own classes, Blyth (1988) has a very good section on the use of objects in teaching history to young children. She cites the work of Forrest (1983), who gives a clear example of the sort of deductions that handling things from the past can lead to. For instance, children had to work out how a flat iron was heated. It did not take them long to realize how slow and laborious the old-fashioned method was in comparison with modern appliances.

West (1981) also asked children to study historical narrative pictures that included an excerpt from the Bayeux Tapestry, a nineteenth-century painting of a mail coach in a snowdrift and a museum postcard of an Edwardian street. West was mainly interested in pupils' judgements of the authenticity of each picture and its age, but his research also throws interesting light on children's interpretations of pictures generally. His group, he reports (*ibid.*), 'fell into two categories: the observant majority and those who seemed unable to see clearly and even to "see" things that were not there'. Some children saw men walking in the fire in a painting of the Great Fire of London, while the Victory's gun-deck was variously interpreted as a factory, a bakery, a gasworks and a supermarket. West rightly points out that the skill of looking at pictures, which is particularly important in history, ought to be taught deliberately and practised and, with this in mind, he recommends leading pupils to examine pictures from top to bottom, from side to side and from corner to corner.

Still on this point, Gunning, Gunning and Wilson (1981) offer a framework for observing pictures specifically designed to develop the intellectual skills of interpretation, classification, extrapolation and evaluation in social studies. Briefly, the object of interpretation questions is to force children to concentrate on what is being communicated in the picture. This goes beyond simply asking what is happening in the painting.

Children are expected to recognize and to interpret symbols, to look for clues indicating who is a slave and who is a free person, to note the height of castle walls, to explain why they were built so high, and so on.

Classification questions, as the name implies, are framed to focus attention on characteristics shared by groups of people or obejcts, for example, 'Are the people in the picture soldiers or civilians?' followed by the inevitable supplementary, 'How do you know?' Evaluation questions encourage children to make judgements and to express opinions they must then justify, for example, 'Would you like to be an attacker or defender of the castle?' Finally, there are extrapolation questions that are extremely stretching because they go well beyond the given information and prod children into contemplating the implications of what is shown. A common lead in is to ask 'What do you think will happen next in the picture?'

The work of Gunning and her co-authors is outside the general run of studies reviewed in this book in that it does not contain an empirical component or attempt to identify developmental stages in interpreting pictures. Nevertheless, their framework for questioning by teachers (and later, we hope, by children) provides an extremely useful general guide for teaching, and it deserves detailed consideration.

To return to West's (1981) study, although he points out deficiencies in children's analyses of historical narrative pictures, there is a much brighter side to his findings. Many children picked out such details as a barely visible flock of birds in the mail-coach picture that would be missed by most adults. Not only did children observe closely, they also thought carefully about what they were seeing. One child could distinguish between equipment used by German soldiers in the two great world wars, pointing (*ibid.*) out that 'modern soldiers' packs are smaller and smoother'. Many of these pupils had built up a rich store of historical knowledge from television (a main source), war games and toys, and the memories of the past recounted by parents and grandparents.

Summary Using the little research evidence available, I have sketched out some of the practical techniques used in teaching logical thinking in Fistory. As West (1978) illustrates, when close observation and scrutiny of evidence are encouraged, it is not long before children can generate and test simple hypotheses. West's criteria for examining artefacts and Gunning, Gunning and Wilson's guidelines for interpreting pictures give teachers keen to try these approaches a helpful plan to work to.

Although it has not been studied directly, another obvious strategy is to encourage children to look for, and to explain, any differences observed between then and now.

SUMMARY AND CONCLUSIONS

History is about people and the main function of teaching history in schools is to describe and to explain what happened to people in the past. In the process we hope to develop a concern for evidence in identifying cause-and-effect relationships in history, and in tracing the continuities and discontinuities between past and present.

As we have seen, psychology has a part to play in achieving these objectives. There is evidence to suggest that, by the age of 9, children understand that history is concerned with significant events in the past and, long before even that age, children have often acquired a foundation of historical knowledge informally from television and many other sources. That knowledge, however unsystematic and inaccurate it might be, is the starting-point for introducing children to the discipline of history.

At the outset we try to discover concepts children already hold about the historical topics we are dealing with and place them roughly at some point along a developmental scale. At first, as Peel (1971, p. 143) explains, young children find it difficult to make sense of historical material but this initial confusion is replaced by a tendency to build their explanations around one piece of circumstantial evidence, and one piece only, to the exclusion of any other facts that might be operating. Following that stage there is a growing ability to take two or more factors into account, to suggest several possible explanations and to choose between them on the basis of evidence and logic.

All the standard techniques are used in extending children's ability to think logically in history and, in particular, there is an emphasis on close and systematic observation of artefacts of all kinds and on giving reasoned justifications for the conclusions reached. However, it is as well to remind ourselves that observation is only as good as our existing knowledge allows it to be and there comes a time – when analysing a picture, for instance – when giving information takes priority over trying to elicit information from children. Similarly, historical knowledge is a precondition for pursuing the entirely proper objective of helping children to understand the thoughts and feelings of people who lived before us.

Psychologists have begun to map out the general course of children's thinking in history but this is still a surprisingly under-researched area. Decisions about the content of history are not the concern of psychology, but what it can do is to investigate children's understanding of the themes chosen – and perhaps this will become its most significant and practical contribution to the teaching of history in the future.

FURTHER READING

Clear and authoritative explanations of the nature of history are given in Carr (1964), Marwick (1970) and Plumb (1973).

There is a, by now, classic review of the psychology of history teaching by Peel (1967). More recent sources include Dickinson and Lee (1978), Shemilt (1978) and Ashby and Lee (1987). Jurd's (1978) theoretical account of concrete and formal operational thinking in history makes demands on the reader but repays careful study.

ILEA's (1980) guidelines for teaching history in primary schools gives a lucid, concise overview of the field and another good general introduction is the Department of Education and Science's (1985b) publication on history in the primary and secondary years. Blyth (1988) deals clearly and systematically with the practical problems of teaching history to young children.

The Historical Association regularly issues short publications of interest to teachers of young children. A relevant journal is *Teaching History*.

6

GEOGRAPHICAL EDUCATION

INTRODUCTION

The place of geography in the school curriculum has never been secure. In the early 1900s, Gonner (1903) complained of the continuing dominance of classical education in the secondary-school curriculum and (*ibid.*) of 'old fashioned prejudices against subjects' like geography 'which could be put to immediate uses'. In the universities the situation was no better. The first chair in the subject was not established until as late as 1917 and in the early 1920s there were still only five professors of geography in British universities (Proctor, 1987).

The teaching of geography in elementary schools consisted largely of memorizing isolated facts. Spencer (1938, p. 52) recalls learning such technical definitions as 'an island is a piece of land surrounded by water' and 'a peninsula is a piece of land nearly surrounded by water' when he was only 8 years of age. However, the *Century Geographical Readers: Reader VI, The British Colonies and Dependencies* (1890) suggests that there must have been serious attempts to teach geography more meaningfully to senior classes in elementary schools. This textbook was published towards the end of Queen Victoria's reign when the British Empire was at its height. The various chapters contain informative and interesting accounts of the physical, economic and social features of the constituent lands of the Empire but, to the modern reader, it also includes much that jars. For instance, there is a curiously inconsistent description of the Bushmen of South Africa, who are rated as 'amongst the lowest and most degraded members of the human race. Short in stature, of slight though wiry build, these wretched people live in holes and caves like wild animals. ... Attempts to civilize them have met with little success' (*ibid.*). But then it goes on (*ibid.*) 'An interesting feature in this savage race is that they are very fond of music; and they also show some skill in making rough drawings of animals and men with which they decorate the walls of their caves'. Although not as extreme as this, textbooks contained inaccurate or stereotyped portraits of inhabitants of other lands until well into the 1930s.

After the Second World War, the teaching of geography in primary schools slowly changed and became much less textbook dominated. The study of geographical phenomena at first hand became more and more common and serious efforts were made to link what children knew about their own environment with the physical geography of other countries and the life-styles of their peoples.

However, as Morgan and Storm (1989, p. 29) point out, 'It remains extraordinarily difficult to generalize about geographical education in primary schools – its extent, its quality, or even its existence'. For this reason it is all the more important to understand the nature of the discipline and its specific contribution to the school curriculum, the starting-point for this chapter.

THE NATURE OF GEOGRAPHY AND GEOGRAPHICAL EDUCATION

The Nature of Geography

Let us begin with a useful general description of the field put forward by Lewthwaite (1986), who defines geography as dealing 'with the areal, or spatial variations and relationships of everything on the earth's surface, from rocks and rainfall to people and places'. Now this definition makes two things immediately clear: first, geography covers a remarkably wide field of study; and, second, despite its diffuse nature, geography is essentially about the earth – the physical environment of humanity.

Most of us will recall from our own schooldays that there is not one geography but many. The most obvious distinction is between the physical and human sides of the discipline. Physical geography concentrates on the study of landscapes and the processes by which they emerged; the central concern of human geography is with the interplay between human beings and the physical world – the influence of the environment on humanity and humanity on the environment. To round off matters, there is one other, less well-known strand that ought to be mentioned – biogeography, which looks to botany and zoology to help explain certain features of the environment.

The various divisions and sub-divisions of geography, following Quam and Freeman (1980), Bailey (1986) and Lewthwaite (1986) among others, can be represented in diagrammatic form as in Figure 6.1. This is the basic structure of the discipline. I do not intend to comment on the subject-matter of each of these sub-divisions – the titles themselves give a good enough clue to their content.

There is another way of describing the activities of geographers that makes use of the terms 'systematic' and 'regional'. No one person could possibly study in depth all the sub-divisions of the field just described and so geographers are compelled to specialize. All the separate specialisms included in Figure 6.1, for example, climatology, plant geography and political geography, are subsumed under the general heading of systematic geography.

Regional geography, on the other hand, is something altogether different. Its purpose is to bring to bear the relevant knowledge and understanding contributed by systematic geographers to the study of a particular region. It is an act of synthesis, an interdisciplinary exercise

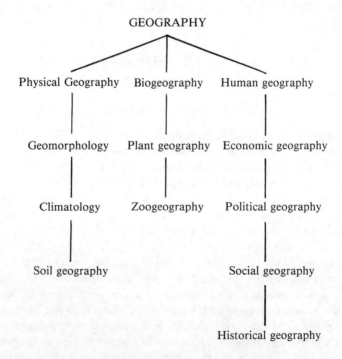

Figure 6.1: The Field of Geography

concerned not with the separate elements but with all the forces that combine to make a region what it is. The regional geographer operates as a co-ordinator who brings together insights from the various branches of the discipline that are used to construct as comprehensive a picture of the locality as possible.

Finally, to return to and to underline a point made earlier, geography covers a surprisingly wide range of activities embracing both the sciences and the humanities. As a consequence, geography is usually classed as a interdisciplinary field of study rather than a form of knowledge in its right. Perhaps this makes it a little clearer why it is so difficult to define the nature of geography and to mark out exactly where it stands on the map of knowledge.

Summary Geography is an interdisciplinary study that offers yet another perspective of the world, and earns its place in the curriculum because of its concern 'to promote an understanding of the nature of the earth's surface and, more particularly, the character of places, the complex nature of people's relationships and interactions with their environment and the importance in human affairs of location and the spatial organisation of human activities' (DES, 1985a).

The Nature of Geographical Education

The most recent Department of Education and Science (1986b) publication on teaching geography appears in the *Curriculum Matters* series under the title, *Geography from 5 to 16*, and – as it is a particularly influential document – I shall quote from it at length.

Paragraph 10 sets out fifteen objectives for teaching geography in the early primary years that are later extended and elaborated on in a further list of ten objectives for the later primary-school years. To avoid unnecessary repetition it is the latter group we shall concentrate on. I have noted in brackets the aspects of geography each objective covers.

Paragraph 24 states that the curriculum, for the later primary years, should enable pupils to:

(1) investigate at first-hand features of their local environment: its weather; its surface features; and some of the activities of its inhabitants, especially those aspects that involve spatial and environmental relationships; [physical; human]
(2) study some aspects of life and conditions in a number of other small areas in Britain and abroad, which provide comparisons with their own locality. From such studies pupils should gain knowledge and understanding of some of the ways in which people have used, modified and cared for their surroundings, and

of the influence of environmental conditions, culture and technology on the activities and ways of life of the present inhabitants; [regional]

(3) develop an appreciation of the many life styles in Britain and abroad, which reflect a variety of cultures, and develop positive attitudes towards different communities and societies, counter-acting racial and cultural stereotyping and prejudice; [offshoot of regional studies]

(4) have some understanding of changes taking place in their own locality and in other areas studied, including some appreciation of the ways in which human decisions influence these changes; [human]

(5) gain some appreciation of the importance of location in human affairs and some understanding of such concepts as distance, direction, spatial distribution and spatial links (especially the movements of people and goods between places), having applied these ideas in appropriate contexts; [physical; human]

(6) become acquainted with a variety of maps, including large scale maps of their own neighbourhood, and be able to apply simple techniques of map reading and interpretation; [physical]

(7) acquire familiarity with globes and with atlas maps and be able to identify such features as the continents and oceans, countries, cities, highland and lowland, coasts and rivers; [physical]

As objectives 8 to 10 mainly cover more general considerations, for example, continuing to develop language and mathematical skills through studies in geography, they are not included here.

Summary School geography takes it cue directly from the parent discipline and, in the interests of a balanced programme, there is much to be said for making clear links between the many faces of geography and the demanding curriculum objectives set out for primary schools to achieve.

The emphasis throughout is on describing and explaining the influence of place on human life, together with examining the effects of natural and human forces on the earth's surface. The study of geography lends itself to inquiry methods and begins with first-hand experiences of the local environment before branching out to consider other areas at home and abroad.

PSYCHOLOGY AND GEOGRAPHICAL EDUCATION

The Development of Geographical Thinking

The contribution of psychology to understanding the development of geographical thinking has been uneven. There is a very strong literature on map interpretation that we shall examine under two headings: cognitive mapping and children's interpretations of maps. We then move on to consider what research there is into other, more general geographical concepts. Lastly, we turn to the area of prejudice and stereotyping where again there is particularly extensive psychological literature, much of which has a bearing on the work of geography teachers.

Cognitive mapping

Cognitive mapping is a flourishing current research interest. It is about the mental maps of the spatial environment we carry around with us in the memory store, access to which tells us a great deal about children's developing concepts of space and their understanding of the relationship between one location and another.

The most direct way of discovering children's 'maps in the mind' is to ask them to draw a map of a route they know well, for example, from home to school. An alternative method used by Matthews (1984) was to ask 172 pupils aged between 6 and 11 to imagine that

> I [the investigator] was staying at your home and you were going to show me around the area around your home. Please would you draw me a map of the area around to show me some of the things I might see nearby. Name any of these features that come to mind.

Figure 6.2 shows some of the children's efforts numbered in ascending order of complexity. It is unnecessary to dwell on the obvious developmental sequence represented here, but there are two major features of the children's maps – the landmarks chosen and the attempts to indicate relationships between one location and another – that we ought to consider in a little more detail.

You may have noticed that in map 2, the garages in particular were focused on while, in map 4, the home, school and shop were picked out as important reference points. Allen *et al.* (1979) are among the many investigators who have made a special study of landmarks such as these, which are essential to finding our way about. Their principal interest was in knowing which environmental features were singled out as landmarks, and whether children and adults made roughly similar choices. Briefly, the experimental set-up was as follows. Primary-school children and college students were shown 52 colour slides representing a winding walk through a commercial neighbourhood unknown to them, after which they were asked to select nine scenes (landmarks) that would most help them to remember the various points along the route. As expected, the college students picked out slides representing critical points in the journey, such as where the direction changed or where roads were crossed. The 7-year-olds' choices were very different. They selected colourful awnings and eye-catching window displays as reference points – things of little use as landmarks because they could not easily be distinguished from many others like them.

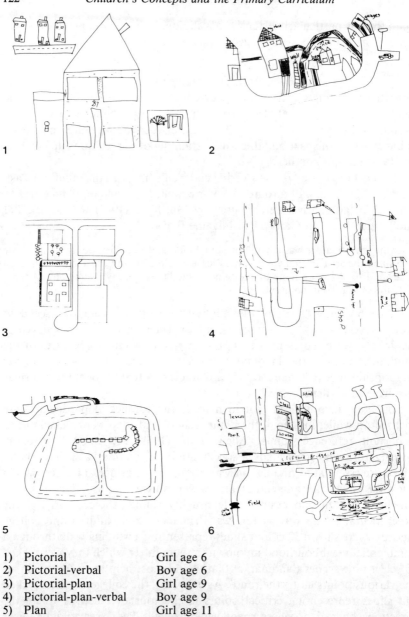

1) Pictorial   Girl age 6
2) Pictorial-verbal   Boy age 6
3) Pictorial-plan   Girl age 9
4) Pictorial-plan-verbal   Boy age 9
5) Plan   Girl age 11
6) Plan-verbal   Boy age 11

Figure 6.2   Grades of mapping ability
(*Source*: Matthews, 1984.)

Some of the 10-year-olds also made poor decisions by picking out shopfronts that could easily be recognized close up but not from a distance.

Quite clearly then, children need help not only in understanding the purpose of landmarks but also in choosing suitable features to act as reference points. The other aspect of children's maps that has been studied extensively is how one location is related to another. This involves the skills of orientation and perspective-taking.

Anooshian and Young's (1981) study is typical of the field. It is not easy to summarize, but the gist of it is as follows. The experiment took place in a neighbourhood very familiar to the twenty boys and girls in the 7–8, 9–11 and 13–14 age bands taking part in the study. Three landmarks – a recreation area, a playground and a 'fast-service store' – located at the main entrance to the housing development were selected as target points. These are marked by an 'x' in Figure 6.3. In addition, four reference sites were chosen, labelled A, B, C and D in the figure.

Each child was walked individually around the area. A halt was made at each reference point where the child was instructed to point a telescope (which couldn't be seen through) at the recreation area, the playground and the store in turn. Figure 6.3 shows the set up. To make the diagram easier to read, I have represented a sighting from point D only to the recreation ground. The dotted line from D represents a correct pointing, the line composed of dots and dashes an incorrect pointing. The difference in degrees between the correct and incorrect sighting was used as a measure of the ability to orientate.

It is not necessary to give the full detail of the findings but all the children taking part, even the youngest group, had a good idea of the relative

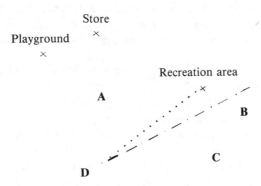

Figure 6.3 Map of the neighbourhood area with landmarks, reference sites (*Source*: Adapted from Anooshian and Young, 1981 © Society for Research in Child Development Inc.)

positions of the various landmarks. The greatest improvement occurred between the youngest and intermediate age levels and from then on there was generally slower progress.

In the next part of the experiment, each child was taken back to his or her own home where sightings from several imagined positions were made. An example will make the procedure clearer. In one part of the test, children were encouraged to 'try real hard to picture in your mind that you are standing at the front door of the store. Pretend that I am the door, and the telescope is set up right in front of it. The store is behind me, and the parking lot is right here' (*ibid.*). From that imagined position, pupils had also to indicate the direction of the other two landmarks. This is a test for egocentric thinking not unlike Piaget's 'mountains problem' reported in Chapter 1. I will not comment on the findings except to say that, as expected, all but the oldest children found this exercise in decentring quite difficult.

This study is very detailed and there is only space to sketch out the essential findings. However, the main point to keep in mind is that all the children involved in this study, irrespective of age, had managed to achieve informally a fair understanding of spatial relationships in a territory they knew well.

As well as investigating children's knowledge of direction, Allen *et al.* (1979) and Herman, Blomquist and Klein (1987) went on to inquire into how successful their subjects were in judging distance. Herman and his colleagues' method was to show children a 100-ft long wall and to impress on them that its length represented one unit. The pupils then had to tell the experimenter how far away in 100-ft units they estimated several target objects to be. In brief, the ability to judge distance improved with age but, for reasons that are unclear, the 19-year-olds tended to over-estimate distance while the 8- and 11-year-olds tended to under-estimate distance.

Summary First, young children vary considerably in their ability to draw maps from memory and, in particular, they need help in selecting landmarks that are sufficiently distinctive to fulfil their purpose as reference points. Second, even children around the age of 8 appear to be reasonably accurate in their compass bearings of landmarks taken from a number of different positions in an area well known to them. However, many children in the 10-year-old age-range were still poor at perspective-taking – that is to say, they were unable to imagine themselves standing at one landmark and pointing with reasonable accuracy in the direction of another.

Third, children's estimates of bearing become more accurate as their knowledge of particular environments increases. Fourth, although judgements of distance improve with age, there is some evidence to suggest that children, as opposed to adults, have a tendency to under-estimate distances.

Classroom applications   There are many practical activities suggested by the research we have considered so far. The opportunities for mental mapping are considerable and could include making maps of parts of the school itself, and well-known and not so well-known local areas. The effectiveness of the maps could be discussed, noting particularly the landmarks selected and the accuracy of orientation and scale. By adapting Anooshian and Young's methodology, practice in orientation and judging distances in the field is also possible.

Children's interpretations of maps

We now pass on from cognitive mapping (children's own mental maps of the physical environment) to the other side of the coin – children's understanding of maps drawn by other people. Muir and Frazee (1986) identify eight skills integral to map interpretation:

1. Interpreting symbols.
2. Envisioning perspective.
3. Locating places.
4. Determining direction.
5. Computing distance.
6. Understanding scale.
7. Imagining relief.
8. Understanding elevation.

Although the empirical evidence is incomplete, it is worth touching just briefly on those skills not covered in the discussion on cognitive mapping so that we can build up a more rounded picture of the intellectual demands made by map reading we take so much for granted.

Interpreting symbols   Every single feature of a map is symbolic. However, some symbols are much easier to interpret than others. The pictorial signs for churches, lighthouses and sites of battle, and the convention of using initial letters to represent post offices, telephones or the National Trust give little trouble. However, as we shall see later, other symbols, such as the latitude and longitude system, contour lines and scale, represent abstract ideas and are not usually understood until children reach secondary-school age.

Locating places   According to Bartz (1970), most children master the simple letter–number co-ordinate system for finding places on a street map relatively easily. However, latitude and longitude co-ordinates make much heavier demands and are not properly understood until the secondary-school years are reached.

Determining direction   Muir's (1985) assessment of the literature leads her to propose a three-stage progression in the development of perceptions of direction:

1. Children first use environmental terms, for example, 'over', 'under' and 'behind', to indicate direction.
2. Next come such terms as 'forward' and 'front' and their opposites. (Presumably, the expressions 'right' and 'left' could also be included in this stage.)
3. Finally come the global directions: north, south, east and west.

In Muir's experience, schools often go straight to teaching the compass points ignoring altogether the environmental and personal expressions children characteristically use.

Understanding scale   Piaget and Inhelder (1956, p. 445) once set up an experiment where children drew a plan of a model village that was later used to reconstruct the model after it had been dismantled. When asked about their method of working, successful pupils offered explanations such as 'you have to measure the bigger distances in the same proportion' (*ibid.*) that show they have grasped that a correct use of scale is dependent on understanding the principle of proportionality. If you are interested, Piaget and Inhelder (*ibid.*) studied this concept in depth, and detailed the stages children go through before culminating in the recognition that the difference between the length and the height of an object to be scaled up or down is a constant ratio.

The ability to apply the principles of ratio and scale are accomplishments only met with at Piaget's formal operational stage and it is, therefore, little wonder that the concept of scale is so troublesome to primary-school children. Bartz (1970) discovered that primary-school children find statements such as 'one inch to 340 miles' confusing and, even when one particular scale has been mastered, they cannot apply the same principle to a different scale, for example, 'one inch to 680 miles'.

Imagining relief and understanding elevation   These are skills that await detailed investigation, but the experimental literature suggests that the ability to interpret contour lines is a late acquisition beyond the competence of most primary-school children.

Summary   Blades and Spencer (1987) demonstrated that nursery-school children as young as 4 could navigate their way through a maze set up in the playground with the help of a simple map but, of course, much more advanced skills are needed to read Ordnance Survey maps with understanding. Piaget and Inhelder (1956) believe that it is not until around the age of 12 that children can read maps at this level of difficulty – which, they say, depends on being able to

1. take an aerial perspective;
2. co-ordinate position and distance; and
3. understand the principle of proportionality, which in turn is essential to understanding scale.

There have been several attempts at devising a sequence of teaching graphicacy skills based roughly on the kind of research described here. The relevant sources are given later in the chapter.

Classroom applications   Even the outline of research given here suggests a number of classroom applications. For instance, it is an interesting exercise to see what children make of the variety of symbols from concrete to abstract used in Ordnance Survey maps.

The Muir (1985) three-stage sequence in perceptions of direction could also quite easily be used for teaching purposes by asking children to describe the direction of various objects or reference points in the classroom, playground and the local district.

Geographical concepts in general

There is very little research directly concerned with the development of children's geographical concepts at the primary-school stage. However, there are three studies that provide useful indications of progress in children's thinking in this area of learning. The first, by Rhys (1972), is not so much concerned with particular concepts as with the developing pattern of thinking within a geographical context; the second study, by Jahoda (1984), deals with the advent of young children's understanding of the economic system and it, too, is firmly within a developmental tradition. Finally, I shall describe a study by Milburn (1972), in which pupils' interpretations of common geographical terms is examined.

The processes of geographical thinking   Rhys (1972) analysed developmental stages in children's understanding in geography. He set 9–14-year-old children a number of problems including one about prairie farming in Canada. A map of the Canadian farming regions and a set of oblique aerial photographs showing the main features of the local economy provided the data they were expected to interpret.

One of the questions (*ibid.*) was 'Why has this small town grown up just here, where the main road and railway cross each other?' that, although it seems to be simple enough, stretched even the ablest pupils. The youngest children, around 9 years of age, were unable to interpret and interrelate the information given in a single photograph let alone collate and organize data from a series of photographs. The best they could do was to offer such explanations as 'Because the land is flat and they build on flat land usually' that could apply equally well to any number of locations.

At 11, pupils could sort out some of the relationships involved but only from the perspective taken by the camera. As they could not yet decentre, we receive such suggestions as 'It [the town] would be situated in the middle and have the same amount of land on either side'.

At 12, there was a shift away from the perspective of the camera and it was now understood that the town was a centre for all the farmers in the area. Responses were now of this order: 'Because you can get the wheat here by road and rail, and seeing as how the railway goes straight through it can pick up all the wheat from the farms'.

Around the age of 13, children had acquired an even wider perspective. Explanations now frequently referred to the Great Lakes, the St Lawrence River, ocean transport and overseas' markets. Finally, pupils aged around 14 and above understood the local context, were able to relate the prairie area to Canada as a whole and beyond that to the world at large.

Rhys's (1972) analysis of responses owes a great deal to the developmental scale constructed by Peel (1971), which was referred to briefly in Chapter 1.

Development of thinking about socio-economic systems   The economic activities of humanity profoundly affect the use of the earth's surface and, inevitably, a specialism has grown up within the discipline known as economic geography. Before children can begin to understand the cause-and-effect relationships between economic activities and the physical environment, they must have some understanding of trade and commerce. Jahoda (1984) therefore decided to investigate the most common economic system of all – the shop – that, although it is well within children's experience, is far from simple in operation and is imperfectly understood well into the primary school.

Jahoda divided shopping transactions into three main elements:

1. Customer-shop (retail sale).
2. Shop-supplier (wholesale purchase).
3. Shop-sales staff (wage system).

Scottish working-class children and, subsequently, Scottish middle-class and Dutch children of varying socio-economic status were questioned about shops and how they operated. The findings are of unusual interest.

The 6-year-olds looked upon buying and selling as a kind of game. Most thought that goods were given automatically to the shopkeeper when the supply ran out and, because many of the youngest children interviewed did not look upon selling as a job, the problem of paying assistants did not arise.

A little later on children begin to recognize that after selling something the shopkeeper ends up with more money and fewer goods but this was as far as they could go. When they were asked what happened to the money the shopkeeper had taken, their ideas were very vague. Some suggested that it might be given to charity and others seemed to have the idea that it somehow just went out of circulation.

With the onset of the concrete operational stage around the age of 7, respondents began to realize that working in a shop is a proper job that has to be paid for; and it also dawned on them that shopkeepers have to pay for goods they subsequently re-sell. Oddly, however, most children in this group thought that the price charged by the wholesaler was the same as that charged by the shop and, as a consequence, could only guess where the money came from to pay the shop assistant. One child suggested that the mint might be the source; another thought bank interest might be the answer. Perhaps the most ingenious response of all came from a 10-year-old who thought that the shopkeeper could get the necessary surplus cash by cutting his or her retail prices, which would entice more people to buy from that shop.

The following is a transcript of an interview with a 10-year-old who had successfully puzzled out how the operation works but, as the dialogue between the interviewer and the subject reported below shows, he is still not sure he has got it right:

I [Interviewer]: What happens to the money at the end of the day?
S [Subject]: I think it gets counted out. I don't think they give it out till the end of the week.
I: Who do they give it out to?
S: They pay the people who've been serving.
I: Do they give it all out?
S: They keep some to buy more stuff for the shop.
I: Does the shop pay the same for the things?
S: I think they get them cheaper. If they got them at the same price they wouldn't be making anything.

(Jahoda, 1984)

Jahoda makes the interesting observation that most of the children were not repeating something they had been told but were trying to piece together the scraps of information they had picked up incidentally. This is why, as Jahoda makes clear, progress in understanding the three elements of the shop as an economic sub-system – the retail transaction, the wholesale transaction and the wages principle – was slow and halting and, often, completely off-track.

Language and children's geographical thinking   Milburn (1972) started out from the premiss that children's understanding of geographical terms provides a strong clue to the quality of their thinking. In following this line of investigation, he collected a number of commonly used geographical terms that he asked 500 primary-school children to define, prompted by such questions as 'What does this word mean to you?' and 'Tell me something about this word'.

As usual, it is the children's confusions that are most revealing. Take homonyms, for instance – quite understandably, it is the everyday meaning children go for so that 'cape' is defined as an article of clothing, 'ford' is a car and a 'peak' is something 'on your cap'.

However, despite these misapprehensions (which, incidentally, may be due to presenting isolated words out of context) many children were beginning to grasp the concept of river at an early age. One 7-year-old defined a river (*ibid.*) as 'a long pathway full of water'; by 8, the notion of flow had appeared although, as the definition of a river (*ibid.*) as 'a line of water leading in from the sea' indicates, the direction of flow was sometimes confused.

In contrast, the notion of a valley caused great problems. Although there were some acceptable definitions, such as 'a dip between two hills' and the rather poetic 'a river-chiselled ditch,' other much hazier descriptions, such as 'a low village' and 'lots of houses', were also reported.

Although not in any real sense technical, there were many examples of perfectly satisfactory working definitions offered by primary-school pupils. We have a beach defined as 'the edge of the land near the sea', a coast as 'the edge round the land' and a cliff as 'a hill with a flat front'.

Milburn (1972) rightly warns of the danger of using terms such as beach, hill and river without further exploring how they are understood. However, there is a corresponding danger that in our anxiety to put things right children may be burdened with formal and confusing definitions long before they are ready for them. As always, there is a delicate balance to be struck between the imperfect (but perhaps adequate for the time being) knowledge of children and the more precise, disciplined knowledge of teachers.

Summary   Each of these three studies in its different way illustrates the trend of children's thinking in geography and shows how it mirrors cognitive development in general. From idiosyncratic and wide-of-the-mark responses, children progress to concentrating on concrete features of the problem before finally taking account of all relevant factors and the relationships between them in reaching a considered conclusion.

Of the three investigations summarized, perhaps Jahoda's is the most revealing. He takes something as apparently simple as a shop and uses it to reveal the true complexities of trade and commerce. He then goes on to show that, although children pick up impressions about buying and selling quite incidentally, these impressions are rarely reflected on or properly organized. In consequence, many of their ideas about trade (a basic concept in geography) remain flawed well into the primary school.

Classroom applications Again, these are easy to see. The Rhys (1972) study suggests a number of possibilities for considering how the environment came to be as it is. We might ask, 'Why are there six supermarkets in the High Street and only a general store in the adjoining village?' 'Why is the cinema closed?' 'Why are there fewer bus routes now than ten years ago?' 'Why are some schools closing down?' 'Why is there a new road around the town?' These issues could well lead on to wider questions of value concerned with the environment.

The Milburn (1972) research parallels the investigation into children's political concepts we looked at in the last chapter. The point of it all is that teaching is in part an exchange of meanings between teacher and taught and an essential part of this process must be to bring children's present understanding of concepts into the open and to develop the dialogue from there.

Jahoda's (1984) work suggests several topics that could be followed up with older children. The siting of local industry is one; the import and export trade and the question of wages in times of labour surplus and shortage are others.

Children's concepts of national groups

One of the Department of Education and Science's (1986b) objectives in teaching geography refers specifically to the need to 'develop an appreciation of the many life styles in Britain and abroad, which reflect a variety of cultures, and to develop positive attitudes towards different communities and societies, counter-acting racial and cultural stereotyping and prejudice'.

This is an area where social psychology (a discipline that sets out to describe and explain the behaviour of individuals in a social context) can make a substantial contribution. Social psychologists have always given a high priority to studying the influences that determine and shape human attitudes but, sadly, the outcome of all this research effort is not encouraging. The overwhelming conclusion is that prejudice is easily learnt, quickly established and difficult to shift.

Stereotyping and prejudice, along with attitudes, constructs, concepts and schemas, are terms used to denote attempts to make sense of the physical and social world. Stereotyping has a positive side in that it helps us to cope with new situations. The impressions we have of other national or ethnic groups gives us something to fall back on in the early stages of an encounter, however rudimentary they might be. Our stereotype might include such characteristics as friendly, generous, energetic, thrusting, socially demanding and jingoistic – a mixture of positive and negative evaluations typical of stereotyping. At first we respond to the individual as a member of the group to which he or she belongs because that is all the information we have to go on. However, as the relationship develops, many of us learn to set aside the stereotype and to make up our own minds about the individual as a person in his or her own right, irrespective of the group to which he or she belongs. If that cannot be done, the stereotype persists in the ossified form we call prejudice. This is formally defined by Gergen and Gergen (1981, p. 121) as 'a readiness to respond to a person in an unfavourable manner on the basis of his or her class or category membership'.

How curious, even bizarre, some of these stereotypes can be is borne out in Wickert's (1984, p. 45) informal survey of American, Soviet and British secondary-school pupils' views of each other. According to the American group, Russians are 'ugly, fat with fur coats, unhappy, unemotional, sturdy, hard-working, peasants, unfriendly and Commies'. The British view was much the same but one positive characteristic 'friendly' was added.

The British children gave the Americans a mixed reception, describing them as 'friendly, loud-mouthed, unhealthy, grey-haired, sporty and inventive'. The Russian view was more critical. The characteristics listed included 'wore casual dress, hot-tempered, lazy, cheerful, money minded and generation gap'.

The British came out of the exercise quite well. The main themes identified in the American responses were 'civilized, cultural, classy, well-spoken, dry sense of humour and peaceful', not very different from the Russian view, where the British were characterized as 'polite, neatly dressed, use a walking stick, have a sense of humour, tall, fair-haired and clerks'.

Tajfel (1981) conducted a formal and tightly controlled study of children's preferences for various national groups in which he enlisted the help of nearly a hundred British children in the 7-, 9- and 11-year-old age bands. Ten dolls, identical in appearance except for a name label, were used to represent Australia, China, England, France, Germany, India, Italy,

Japan, Russia and the USA respectively. First, participants were asked to place each doll on one of three platforms marked 'like', 'neither like nor dislike' and 'dislike', after which they were called on to make more refined judgements by standing each doll in turn at the appropriate point along a 40-inch stick marked 'like very much indeed' at one pole and 'dislike very much indeed' at the other extreme. This 40-point scale gave a numerical liking/disliking score for each nation.

As expected, countries were more clearly discriminated by the older groups but even the 7-year-olds ranked England highest and Russia lowest in terms of preference. For the whole sample, the order of liking was as follows: England, Australia, France, USA, Italy, China, Japan, India, Germany and Russia.

Tajfel went on to find out how much children actually knew about the countries concerned that, as it happens, was not much. For instance, only about 60 per cent of the total sample realized that the French and the Italians were not English-speaking while over 30 per cent thought that the Germans were non-white. Even so, Tajfel's group knew most of all about the countries they liked; next in order of extent of knowledge came the countries disliked; and least of all was known about countries children had no strong feelings about one way or the other.

There is a related issue – pupils' perceptions of ethnic-minority groups they meet at school or in the community at large – that is of even more general interest. We cannot pursue this matter here but, for interested readers, a number of sources on inter-group contact is listed in the further-reading section.

Summary   The main findings from these sources, from Milner (1984), and studies referred to in the further reading, indicate that the present state of knowledge about children's ethnic attitudes is essentially as follows. First, there is a tendency for children to evaluate favourably their own national group and, by implication, to look down on other nationalities. Second, children very quickly pick up information about national and ethnic groups from such sources as the family, the peer group and the media. Third, there is a suggestion that when an ethnic group is highly represented in a school, but is not a majority, fewer cross–group friendships occur than in a situation where its numbers are small.

Fourth, while there is a marked, ethnic, in-group preference, the majority of children do choose some friends from ethnic groups other than their own. Fifth, there appears to have been some improvement in children's racial attitudes and behaviour over the last twenty years or so.

We will discuss the implications of this research for teaching geography shortly.

Extending Children's Geographical Thinking

This section will be a short one because there is little empirical research directly addressed to the problem of advancing geographical thinking. However, there are some excellent texts on the teaching of geography that take note of the experimental evidence (see the further-reading list) and, of course, we can always turn to general learning principles for guidance.

Developing children's graphicacy skills

A small-scale study directly relevant to the classroom was conducted by Dunn (1984), who drew on research into children's understanding of maps in his attempt to improve the mapping skills of 9–10-year-old children. Initially, he asked them to draw a map for a person new to the district who had to find his way from the nearby County Hall to the school. This map (together with a questionnaire assessing eight mapping abilities) provided the pre-test for the investigation. Dunn then embarked on an intensive teaching programme consisting of six sessions.

Session 2, for example, covered direction and orientation. The following is an extract illustrating the techniques used:

> Preliminary activities centred around identifying the location of objects and part of the building in terms of left and right. The children were set a task in which they had to devise for a partner, a route through the buildings to a particular destination, using appropriate terminology such as straight on, turn left, turn right, etc. The notion of quarter turn and the need to have a complete turn upon arrival at the point of destination was emphasized. Routes were written out and used by the children's partners to attempt to reach the appropriate destinations. Difficulties were discussed when the whole group re-assembled. The greatest difficulty had been in the preparation of the route for the return, which indicated the degree of confusion on the part of the children to re-orientate themselves.

In a similar manner, the group was led through the intricacies of scale, co-ordinates, symbols and the interpretation of maps generally.

The post-test showed that, for the most part, children's map-reading and map-making skills improved considerably over the period of the study. Dunn is not claiming that the concepts of scale or location were perfectly understood. However, the results did indicate that within the period of the few weeks devoted to this study, there was a conspicuous improvement in children's ability to understand maps. It is possible, of course, that the significant increase in scores can be put down to children's limited knowledge of maps in the first place and, quite possibly too, progress will be much slower once the slack is taken up. However, this study shows the value of systematically teaching mapping skills especially where, as in this instance, it is based on the immediate environment.

Although there is a lack of empirical work on improving primary-school children's graphicacy skills, there are several graded schemes on map interpretation now available roughly based on the psychological research described earlier. There is an American programme (Anderson, 1985), which sets out map activities appropriate to each year group from kindergarten to sixth grade (which roughly corresponds to the age-range of UK primary schools), and ILEA (1981) has produced an excellent scheme suggesting map activities suitable for lower, middle and upper primary-school children.

Boardman's (1983, 1985) analysis of graphicacy skills is particularly thorough. He lists a series of achievements relating to the concepts of direction, location, scale and symbolism normally within the competence, respectively, of children aged 5-7, 7-9 and 9-11. For instance, the youngest age-group is eventually expected to be able to 'follow directions using left, right, forward, in a circle, etc.'; the middle group should be able to plot the 'cardinal points NESW'; while the oldest group ought eventually to manage to 'plot the sixteen points of the compass'.

Catling (1981) outlines an even more detailed plan. He specifies activities for children aged 5, 7, 9, 11 and 13 centred on the topics of position/orientation, symbols, scale, perspective, purpose, style, drawing, map reading and map interpretation.

Summary There is little to add except to point out that there are now several sources available that give teachers excellent guidance in developing children's mapping skills.

Counteracting inter-group prejudice

Earlier in this chapter, a recent Department of Education and Science (1986b) curriculum document was quoted that underlines the role of schools in the matter of counteracting racial and cultural prejudices. As Milner (1984) reminds us, 'There is a great deal of highly evaluative information about national and ethnic groups "in the air" in a form readily accessible to children'. Consciously or unconsciously, young people pick up this information, make it their own and frequently never question its truth.

Many people believe that bringing hostile groups together and giving them the chance to rub shoulders with each other will inevitably reduce prejudice. The literature (see, for example, Stephan and Rosenfield, 1978) does not always bear out this optimistic assumption. The general consensus seems to be that there are at least two conditions to be satisfied if inter-group contact is to be instrumental in reducing prejudice. First, all groups should be accorded equal status whatever their differences, and this means that formal institutions setting out to lessen prejudice have a clear responsibility to create an environment conducive to treating everyone on equal terms. Second, the setting of goals that are in the interests of everyone to achieve can facilitate good relationships between previously hostile groups. Research shows that differences can be more easily put aside when co-operation is the only means of achieving mutually desired objectives.

The psychological background provides useful general guidelines to follow in changing attitudes but, as far as schools are concerned, there is also much to be said for bringing the reduction of racial prejudice firmly within the orbit of moral education. After all, treating people on the basis of their ethnic-group membership alone is unjust and violates the basic moral principle of respect for persons (I would suggest reading the chapter on moral education from this perspective – there I describe the well-tried discussion technique where children are forced to face up to the implications of their views on moral issues and, it is hoped, to revise them when they do not stand up to scrutiny). In Chapter 8, reference is made to role-playing, a technique intended to encourage sensitivity to the thoughts and the feelings of others that has been extensively used in attempting to modify negative stereotypes.

Summary   The role of geography in teaching about people of different national groups has changed. Not so long ago geography textbooks concentrated on the exotic and emphasized differences among the various nationalities rather than the common characteristics of humankind. Nowadays teachers are not only expected to provide balanced and accurate information about distant peoples and places but also to take an active part in changing prejudiced attitudes. To this end, the lessons of social psychological research, together with the techniques now developed in moral education, are of help to teachers embarking on the demanding and difficult task of modifying negative and inaccurate perceptions of national and ethnic groups.

SUMMARY AND CONCLUSIONS

To the outsider, geography may seem to be outside the main stream of the school curriculum. This is because it is a wide-ranging, interdisciplinary field of study rather than an area of learning contained within the neat boundaries of a distinct subject-matter. In the early part of the century, geographers were compelled to fighi hard for recognition in the university world. Even quite recently, the status of geography as a separate element in the curriculum was seriously questioned although, in the end, it did appear as a separate entity in the national school curriculum.

In pursuit of its prime objective to describe and explain the impact of natural and human forces on the earth's surface, geography necessarily looks to other disciplines – but it is none the worse for that. Geographers collate material from diverse sources, put their own peculiar stamp on it and, in the process, provide us with yet another unique angle on the world and its inhabitants.

Psychologists (and geographers with an interest in psychology) have made a useful start in identifying the changing character of children's geographical thinking. A reasonably clear picture is emerging of the origin and development of the many skills necessary to map making and interpretation and there is a handful of studies bearing on the growth of problem-solving abilities in geography and on children's perceptions of rivers, mountains and other common geographical phenomena. However, there is scope for a much more concerted and systematic effort to investigate the characteristics of children's geographical concepts at various ages in the primary school.

In the meantime, we can do two things. The first is to follow developments in psychological research in related disciplines, such as science, economics and mathematics, and incorporate the lessons of that research into the teaching of geography. The second is to take account of general learning principles in this curriculum area and, in particular, to use children's existing knowledge, imperfect though it is, in advancing geographical thinking.

FURTHER READING

Johnston (1985a, 1985b) writes on the nature of geography as an academic discipline, while Bennetts (1985), Bailey (1986) and Proctor (1987) examine the place of geography in the school curriculum.

General reviews of research into thinking in geography are given by Slater (1973) and Graves (1980). Piaget and Inhelder's (1956) work on the understanding of spatial relationships is also relevant reading.

Further sources on cognitive mapping are Anooshian and Kromer (1986) and Presson (1987). Texts on improving mapping skills include Boardman (1985), Matthews (1985) and Muir (1985).

An account of the implications of research into children's understanding of economics is given by Schug (1987), while Stepans and Kuehn's (1985) investigation is one of the few devoted to children's concepts of weather.

The dynamics of attitude change are covered in all the standard texts on social psychology, for example, Kelvin (1969) and Gergen and Gergen (1981). Sociometric studies of interaction between members of different racial or ethnic groups include Davey (1983) and Denscombe (1983). Walford (1986) writes on multi-ethnic considerations and the teaching of geography.

General sources on teaching geography in primary schools include ILEA (1981), Mills (1981) and Bale (1987).

7

ART EDUCATION

INTRODUCTION

At its core, art education, in common with all other curriculum areas, is about constructing and understanding meanings. Through the medium of visual symbols, the activity of art enables children to heighten their awareness of, and to express their thoughts and feelings about, people, objects and events of significance in their lives. At the same time, from a teacher's perspective, children's art offers another glimpse of their conceptions of the world, expressed not in language but in visual form.

Over the years, the teaching of art has been subject to particularly violent changes of fashion. In the first years of the century, Landon (1902) wanted children to draw repeatedly from actual objects and so did Welton (1909), who went further and called for a virtual ban on 'design' or original work that, he said, was fancy drawing that needed no training whatsoever and was therefore without educational value.

Twenty years or so later there was much talk of freedom of expression in child art. Supporters of progressive education, many of whom took Freud's strictures about repression very seriously, cautioned teachers to stand back for fear of stunting children's creative flow.

There is no way of knowing how much their advice was heeded but, by the time the Department of Education and Science (1978b, pp. 63–5) survey appeared there were criticisms of insufficient guidance in the use of appropriate techniques and of the practice of passing on quickly from one medium to another and mastering none. The current view is that nothing of quality can be created unless children possess the necessary skills. These are best acquired not in isolation but when they are needed – to give expression to the imagination and to represent experiences of the world.

As a first step towards marking out the specific contribution art makes to the school curriculum, we first of all examine the nature of art itself. To that end, I have drawn particularly on the work of Aldrich (1963), Langer (1963, 1970), Reimer (1970), R. A. Smith (1982) and Reid (1983).

THE NATURE OF ART AND ART EDUCATION
The Nature of Art

In attempting to outline the nature of art it might make matters just a little easier if I confine my comments mainly to painting. Artists paint pictures for many different reasons. They may want to record an outstanding event; to make better sense of their ideas and feelings about something that has attracted their attention; to convey their impressions and emotions to other people; or to create pleasing and colourful shapes. And so we could go on. You will appreciate how difficult it is to generalize about this art form but I must start somewhere. Hence I offer a definition that, although not comprehensive, tries to capture the essence of painting as an aesthetic activity.

As I understand the literature, a painting can be defined as a visual, symbolic representation, possessing both form and style, of an artist's thoughts and feelings about an experience of significance to him or her. It allows the artist to reflect on that experience and to communicate the ideas and emotions it provokes to other people.

Four generalizations about painting are embedded in that definition. Painting

- involves thinking;
- is predominantly concerned with feelings;
- is a symbolic activity; and
- has form and style.

The first generalization we can venture is that painting necessarily involves thought: an artist's choice of subject is not random but is governed by a desire to deliberate on, and to understand more deeply, particular aspects of the physical and emotional world.

The second generalization we can make is that painting is an affective activity; that is to say, it is concerned centrally with feelings. To the psychologist, thinking and feeling are bound together but not necessarily in the same relative strengths. Nevertheless, art stands out primarily because it gives full weight to the expression, refinement and understanding of human emotions and it is this major defining characteristic that distinguishes it from all other disciplines.

The third generalization is that painting is a symbolic activity. The visual symbols artists use convey meanings that cannot be directly expressed in words. Indeed, if words were adequate for the purpose, painting as we know it would not exist. Their elements, for example, light and shade, as Langer (1963) points out, have no standard meanings. Separately they mean nothing but when the various elements are brought together, as in portrait, Langer (*ibid.* p. 94) believes, 'an incredible wealth and detail of information is conveyed' conjuring up feelings and thoughts that cannot be expressed in words.

The fourth generalization is concerned with form and style. Both are slippery concepts difficult to pin down. R. A. Smith (1982) sees form as 'a work's web of relations' and Langer (1970) as 'the sense and wider shape of a thing ... the way it is put together'. Form gives a work its aesthetic dimension, its distinctive stamp. Let us take a simple illustration. If we translate a poem we know well into ordinary, everyday language its impact is lost because in the aesthetic domain it is not enough to have something of significance to say – it is the manner in which it is said that matters and makes the communication art.

The idea of style is even more difficult to explain, partly because it has much in common with form. Briefly, when we talk about style we are referring to particular features that characterize the work of an artist or a school of artists. It is a sort of thumb print that gives a work a personal and recognizable identity and makes it different from any other – a Lowry painting, for example.

Summary   The position we have reached is that there is some agreement in the literature that art is a particular form of knowing, which embraces thinking but which is especially concerned with feelings. A work of art is a visual medium possessing form and style and having the capacity to convey meaning to people prepared to look for it. Its message is rarely spelt out directly and, for this reason, Reimer (1970) suggests that we should look to art not for information but for insights.

The Nature of Art Education

Art education, no less than other curriculum areas, enables meanings to be constructed and understood. The symbols used in art are independent of language and can be used to give children those unique insights into their physical and social worlds open to no other discipline. That, in essence, is the case for art education in schools.

Let us now be a little more specific and try to discover why drawing and painting are made so much of in schools. Briefly, in the act of painting, children not only represent visually what they know and feel, but they also organize that knowledge and make it more explicit. Painting is not an easy option at any age because it involves hard thinking on at least two different levels: first, it is necessary to think about the subject-matter itself; and, second, there are problems of representation to be overcome that necessitate experimenting with new techniques and making considered judgements about their effects. In fact, Goodnow's (1977) description of painting as, in part, a problem-solving activity is no exaggeration.

Centrally, art is about feelings but, as Reid (1983) makes clear, 'If it [art] were just self expression of emotions there would be little place for education in art. A "self" grows by what it feeds on, and it must be given nourishment outside itself. Young children, and all children have to learn as well as to express themselves'. Broudy (1966) makes much the same point in distinguishing between what he calls the 'popular' arts and 'serious' art. The popular arts, he argues, are picked up in the culture and need no training. In contrast, serious art makes heavy demands not only in its creation but also in developing sensitivity towards art in general. For most of us, such an initiation is possible only through the systematic and disciplined opportunities offered in schools.

Art serves many purposes – to entertain, to instruct, to record, to tell a story or to move – and different strategies are needed to meet these ends. If we probe a little deeper, we come to the conclusion that some drawings are aesthetic creations and others are not. To be properly called a work of art a drawing should conform to the criteria of expressiveness previously laid down but, clearly, not all drawings meet these conditions and there is no reason why they should. A sketch to represent what happened in a science experiment does not need an affective dimension: its primary object is to record as clearly as possible how the experiment was set up and conducted and what the conclusions were. True, fine judgements often have to be made between what is aesthetic and what is not but the essential point is that while drawing can be an activity executed for its own sake (for purely intrinsic purposes), it can also serve legitimate extrinsic ends in recording children's experiences and making them more vivid right across the curriculum.

Soon after writing the last passage, I came across a Schools Council Art Committee's (1978) discussion document that takes the same line. Four different purposes for drawing – recording, analysis, communication and expression – are identified but, obviously, some overlap between them is inevitable. The application of a model of child art analogous to Britton *et al.*'s (1975) analysis of written expression described in Chapter 2 could help to make the different purposes of drawing and painting more explicit to teachers, and to give art education a clearer sense of direction. It could also expose obvious imbalances in the uses to which painting is put.

There is one further aspect of art education I want to touch on briefly, and that is the appreciation of art, which more and more primary schools are taking seriously. According to Feldman (1983), few people can be competent practitioners of art and fewer still can make a substantial contribution to its development. However, that is no justification for not guiding children towards an understanding and appreciation of art in the attempt to reveal what it can do to enrich the lives of people prepared to make the effort.

Summary First, the intrinsic function of art remains paramount in the education of young children. In this 'art-for-art's-sake' context, a drawing is a personal statement of the artist's thoughts and feelings about things that excite, interest and concern him or her.

Second, art serves other important and legitimate educational ends in practically all other curriculum areas where, although feelings may still be involved, drawing primarily for recording, analysing and communicating information takes precedence.

Third, the appreciation of art is an integral part of education of young children and, as is described later, this dimension is, happily, steadily attracting the attention it deserves. In essence, then, art is a particular means of constructing and understanding meanings through visual symbols – an essential element in a rounded education.

PSYCHOLOGY AND ART EDUCATION
Children's Conceptions of Art

Children's ideas about art were studied by Johnson (1982), who asked 251 pupils aged between 5 and 17 the question, 'In your opinion what is art?' or one similarly phrased, such as 'What do you think art is?' Her inquiry was carried out informally during art classes where, apparently, she went up to individual children as they were working, put the question and tape-recorded their responses.

No statistical data are give for fear (perhaps unnecessarily) that coding might distort meanings, but it was possible to make some generalizations about developmental trends. First of all, up to the age of about 6, art was often referred to as something that happens at a specific time and place: thus, 'Art is right now' or was seen as something you make or do, leading to such responses as 'You make' and 'You paint'. Several children of this age thought art was fun. According to one boy, 'art gives you something to do' and, to another, the main point was that art was not made by a machine. Around the age of 11, children began to talk in more abstract terms and the emphasis changed from making and doing to creating and expressing. Now the content of art, Johnson says (*ibid.*) 'was more often designated as pictures, things, and what you feel and your feelings'. By the age of 15, responses such as 'art is each person's way of expressing themselves', 'something you know of yourself' and 'something you make that pleases you' became more common.

We see here a familiar move from the concrete to the abstract but what struck Johnson most was that so many children assumed art to be a personally determined subject 'devoid of social consequences and import' (*ibid.*). A second, apparently common, assumption she uncovered was that art is an essentially making and doing activity in which thinking and decision-making play only a minor part. In the same vein, works by artists past and present were not referred to and children seemed to be unaware that art could be observed, talked about and enjoyed for its own sake. More direct probing on these issues might have revealed less rigid views but on the basis of the evidence available from children's spontaneous responses, Johnson rightly suggests that time ought to be set aside to talk with children about what art means to them and to progress from there to widen and refine their understanding of the range and purposes or art. She wondered, too, about the conceptions of art held by teachers and the impressions of art they were conveying, not only by what they said but also through the experiences they were offering their classes. These are good questions that, once again, underline the critical role of intentions as a precondition of effective learning and teaching.

The Development of Artistic Abilities

The broad developmental sequence in the ability to draw is now well documented, as is the link between drawing and basic cognitive abilities. However, the study of the power to express feeling, which after all is central to art, is still in its infancy.

On a more optimistic note, there is a steadily growing interest in children's preferences for paintings and this can be put to good use in helping pupils to respond sensitively to what Copple, Sigel and Saunders (1979, p. 57) call the 'nontranslatable messages in paintings, statues, photographs, etc.'

Sequential stages in children's art

Classic studies by Eng (1931) and Kellogg (1969), together with a growing number of contributions from other sources, allow the general course of children's art to be defined with reasonable confidence. Various classifications of stages have been devised that, although differing in emphasis and detail, reveal roughly the same pattern. Of these, Lowenfeld and Brittain's (1987, pp. 474–9) analysis is among the better known, and I shall use their framework to set the scene. It is apparently based on an amalgam of observation and experimental studies and it gives in great detail the characteristics to look for at various stages in a child's artistic development. An abbreviated version of their framework concentrating on the drawing of human figures is set out in Table 7.1. Lowenfeld and Brittain's (1987) analysis provides a useful backcloth to the experimental studies next described.

Art and cognition

Since art is indisputably a cognitive activity, there is every reason to anticipate a correspondence between the progression in child art and Piagetian stages of cognitive development. Schirrmacher (1980) is one of those who has attempted to make that link. He listed the major characteristics of the sensori-motor, pre-operational, concrete operational and formal operational stages and set them against the corresponding levels of artistic expression. For example, at the pre-operational stage, he suggests that egocentricism (taking one's own viewpoint to the exclusion of others) is associated with lack of naturalistic spatial representation and 'X-ray' drawing (a technique I shall explain later). Similarly, centration (where attention is firmly fixed on one feature and other elements minimized) can be related to distortion, exaggeration, omission and random spatial organization. Operational thinking brings with it a greater naturalism and, in like fashion, the onset of the ability to conserve is linked to linear perspective.

As we have seen so often, a key characteristic distinguishing pre-operational from operational thinking is egocentricism, and there are plenty of examples from young children's art that strikingly reveal their tendency to adopt a very personal view of the world. Children appear to work on the principle that what is important to them is included in the drawing, even exaggerated, and what isn't is omitted – and not always for lack of technique. Lowenfeld and Brittain (1987, p. 237) reproduce an excellent example of this characteristic in which a child conveyed the experience of walking barefoot on the grass after rain by sketching his toes disproportionately large, and by representing himself suspended several

Table 7.1   Sequential stages in children's art

Stage	Characteristics
Scribbling (2–4 years)	Random marks gradually become more organized and controlled. No attempt is made to draw recognizable objects
Preschematic (4–7 years)	First attempts at representation of people and objects appear. A typical depiction of a person is a 'head–foot' configuration but other strategies emerge. Objects drawn are placed randomly on paper and not in proportion one with another
Schematic (7–9 years)	Definite form concepts developed – thus the scheme for people is repeated constantly with only minor variations. Characteristically, objects are drawn in a straight line across the bottom of the page
Dawning realism (9–12 years)	The rigid scheme for drawing a person is dropped but figures have a 'stiff' appearance. Items of clothing are drawn separately and the work is generally more detailed. The 'bottom-of-the-page' tendency disappears coupled with the emergence of the plane
Pseudo-naturalistic (12–14 years)	Human-figure representation is drawing closer to correct proportions. There is continued attention to detail. There is also a greater awareness of differences, for example, sex characteristics are over-emphasized. Drawings are no longer spontaneous
Period of decision (14–17 years)	Naturalistic attempts at human-figure drawing now appear. There is an awareness of proportion and perspective drawing is acquired by some. A conscious development of artistic skills is also evident

(*Source*: Adapted from Lowenfeld and Brittain, 1987. Reprinted with permission of Macmillan Publishing Co.)

inches off the ground. The exaggeration of the toes directs the eye to the feature he wanted to emphasize and, at the same time, little attention is given to what is regarded as subordinate detail.

'X-ray' pictures, referred to by Schirrmacher (1980), are the other side of the coin. Exaggeration and omission now give way to wanting to show what is known, whether it can be 'seen' or not. For example, both the outside and the inside of a house may be drawn, with representations of the occupants and possessions out of view somehow manoeuvred into the same picture, giving it a stage-set-like effect.

X-ray paintings have been investigated experimentally in a study by Mann and Lehman (1976), who looked for developmental trends in transparency drawing – their term for the technique – among 91 4–9-year-old children. First of all, children were asked to draw two pictures, one of a lady and, after being diverted on an irrelevant intervening task, a second lady, this time 'all dressed up to go to a party with a long skirt on' (*ibid.*). Transparencies represented about a third of all second drawings and appeared in more than one form. The usual procedure was to draw the body first and to add the clothing afterwards. According to the investigators, non-transparent drawing involves holding the two ideas of body and clothes simultaneously in mind. The 'transparent' drawer falls back on the one-at-a-time ploy and so evades the more difficult task of coping with two things at once. However, it does seem that some of these children were not too happy about the end product. One 8-year-old, who had a suspicion that something was not quite right, suggested that the lady had 'bought a size too large'. I suspect further probing might have shown that some children know fairly well that an object in front generally blocks the view of one at the back, but what bothers them is how to translate that knowledge into two-dimensional form.

Figure 7.1 gives another example of X-ray drawing. This is a typical X-ray effect. No attempt is made to omit the part of the spade hidden by the opaque bucket.

Perhaps the most common phenomenon of all in young children's drawings frequently commented on by teachers is the manner in which

Figure 7.1 X-ray drawing

objects – usually a house – are drawn on a hillside. A 5-year-old's attempt to do so is shown in Figure 7.2. What children do is to position the house perpendicularly to the hillside but at right angles to the base of the hill itself. It is not the hill as a whole that captures the attention and becomes the base line, but the side of the hill that acts as the major reference point for locating the house. Piaget and Inhelder (1956) investigated this same phenomenon in detail and conclude that there is a very slow shift in children's ideas about spatial ideas – concepts that obviously influence the capacity to draw.

Experimental studies continue to examine the proposition first put forward by Luquet (1927) that children begin by drawing what they know before 'visual realism' is achieved. On the whole that principle stands up well to empirical verification at a general level but, as Light (1983) points out, 'the young child does not represent in his drawings all that he knows about the objects drawn nor does the older child draw all that he sees'. It could well be that children do not bother to include features they know are there because they are not important to the idea they are trying to express.

Summary   There is really only one point to make: there is an established link between children's thinking and their artistic expression and, as we have just seen, there is broad but qualified support to the generalization that children draw what they know.

Figure 7.2   Representation of houses on hillsides

Classroom applications   Above all, the analysis of the thinking behind children's drawings enables teachers to make better sense of the art their pupils produce. It would be easy to dismiss 'egocentric'-type paintings or houses drawn perpendicularly to hillsides as 'inaccurate' copies of reality. But once we know that these representations are consistent with the developmental pattern of children's thinking we can relate to children's art with greater understanding.

As there is always the possibility that children deliberately exaggerate physical features because that is the way they want to represent them, direct teacher intervention in this respect and at this stage may be inadvisable. As we shall see shortly, there are other more appropriate ways in which teachers can guide children's artistic expression.

Art and feeling

The only reason for separating out feeling from thinking is that it is sometimes necessary in the interests of balance to focus directly on the emotions – an area that tends to be on the fringe of studies in developmental psychology. Even in art (where expressiveness is such a dominant characteristic) not much is known about the development of the ability to represent feelings in drawing and painting. The explanation for this gap in research is obvious enough: the conceptual and methodological problems are formidable and, so far, only very tentative attempts have been made to tackle them.

Carothers and Gardner (1979) reinforce an important point when they say that, while all drawing occurs in an artistic medium, not all drawings are works of art because of the omission of the necessary aesthetic dimension. In their empirical study they went on to determine the development of this dimension in the artwork of 11 boys and 11 girls in each of the age-groups, 7, 10 and 12.

In one of their tests (the perception task), participants were asked to complete pictures by selecting from two versions of a missing piece the one that better fitted the style of an unfinished drawing. Thus, in investigating awareness of happy and sad feelings, one of the missing pieces featured a drooping, leafless tree and a wilted flower; the other an upright tree teeming with leaves and a flower in full bloom. One of these pieces had to be fitted into a picture showing a miserable-looking man standing in the rain outside a closed shop advertising a sale. Only 7 of the 22 7-year-olds were successful in picking the right one, as opposed to a 100-per-cent success rate at the other two age levels – a dramatic leap. Obviously there is a major shift occurring somewhere in the 8–9-year-old age-group, but we must await more detailed research before we can track down precisely where it comes.

Carothers and Gardner's production tasks followed much the same pattern. The participants now had to finish drawings started by other children, but they were urged to do so 'just like you think the kid who drew it would have finished it' (*ibid.*). One of these tasks concerned sensitivity to the feelings portrayed – a quality that appeared in the work of only 2 of the 22 7-year-olds and just under half the 10-year-olds. In contrast, nearly all the 12-year-olds showed this characteristic in their drawings (at least to some extent).

Two main conclusions stand out from these results and from other data in the study too detailed to include here. The first is that children are sensitive to aesthetic qualities in the artwork of others some time before they are able to represent these qualitities themselves. Second, there is a steady increase in the use of aesthetic symbolism with advancing age.

There is a study by Ives (1984) that also covers part of the same ground. He used a sizeable sample of 128 subjects, 8 male and 8 female, in each of the age-groups 4, 5, 7, 9, 11, 13, 16 and 20. In investigating the ability to express psychological moods, he asked them to draw a happy tree, a sad tree and an angry tree. As expected, competence to express feelings in drawings progressed with age, although not evenly. A surprising 37 per cent of 4-year-olds managed to produce an accurate representation and to convey the emotion asked for, rising to an 87-per-cent success rate at the age of 20, but the most interesting feature of the investigation lies in Ives' analysis of the techniques used to express the various moods.

There were, for example, three main ways of conveying sadness, which are set out in Figure 7.3. A drawing of a child crying with tears rolling down his cheeks is an instance of a literal strategy. There are two forms of

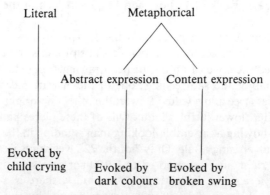

Figure 7.3   Strategies for expressing sadness
(*Source*: Constructed from Ives, 1984.)

metaphorical expression – abstract and content. In abstract expression sadness is commonly conveyed by dark colours or drooping lines. These incidentally, are almost universally interpreted correctly. The term 'abstract' is used here in its artistic sense and is not intended to denote higher-level thinking as it does in psychology. In content expression, sadness is depicted through the content of a drawing, for instance, a barren tree or a broken swing.

Ives' findings are too detailed to report here but results for the 4-year-old and 11-year-old age bands give a good indication of the development trend. Of the 4-year-olds' drawings, 37 per cent were successful in conveying feelings. The strategies used were 13 per cent literal only, 4 per cent literal and abstract, 19 per cent abstract and 0 per cent content expression. In contrast, 69 per cent of the 11-year-olds successfully conveyed the designated feelings. The strategies this group used were 2 per cent literal, 6 per cent literal and abstract, 52 per cent abstract and 9 per cent the content-expression technique.

These two studies and others like it have made useful contributions to our understanding of the development of children's expressiveness in art but, to complement the necessarily contrived experimental investigations now beginning to appear, we also need carefully designed and controlled field studies using artwork children produce under typical classroom conditions. The more we know about how children convey feelings in art spontaneously, the better we shall be able to support their efforts.

Summary Three findings of educational significance emerge from the research as it stands:

1. Children recognize aesthetic qualities in the work of others before expressive features are evident in their own drawings.
2. There is a steady development in efforts to represent feeling as age increases.
3. Children tend to use abstract expression much more readily than they do literal or content expression.

Classroom applications More than anything else, this research underlines the importance of talking to children about the expression of emotions in art and of encouraging them to think carefully about how best to represent feelings in drawing and painting. One way of doing so might be to ask children to try out the experimental tasks described in this section, or something similar to them. This could be justified as an occasional exercise because, as art is used for so many purposes in schools, it is easy to overlook the central role of feelings in some forms of drawing and painting.

A second strategy is to study the work of other artists, both adults and children, and to discuss and evaluate how they expressed emotions.

Children's responses to paintings

I was suprised to discover that interest in children's preferences for paintings goes back at least to the turn of the century when art education consisted of drawing of objects and not much else. Since then, a respectable research literature has been built up, which has been reviewed by N. R. Smith (1982) and Taunton (1982), among others.

There are several ways of studying children's responses to paintings. Machotka (1966) presented fifteen colour reproductions of paintings by post-Renaissance artists from Breughel to Picasso to children of various ages who were invited to indicate which picture they liked best and liked least, and to give reasons for their choices. D'Onofrio and Nodine's (1981) experimental design was similar, but specific questions were asked such as whether it was a good work of art and why the artists chose the methods they used. In studying sensitivity to painting style, Gardner and Gardner (1970) presented children with postcards of four paintings, two of which were executed by one artist and the other two by a second artist. Children then sorted the postcards into two piles, one for each artist.

The development trend in children's preferences for paintings identified by this research takes roughly the following pattern. Younger children like:

1. a subject-matter they can understand and identify with;
2. realistic pictures, simple in composition; and
3. bright and contrasting colours.

This represents the concentrate operational stage in responding to paintings. Later on, less obvious abstract characteristics, for example, style, composition and harmony, emerge as criteria that, according to Machotka (1966), are associated with formal operational thinking.

D'Onofrio and Nodine (1981) see as the high point of aesthetic sensitivity the capacity to infer the artist's point of view from the way he or she has executed his or her painting. The steps along the path to this achievement form the substance of Parson's (1978) theory of aesthetic development, which was used in analysing D'Onofrio and Nodine's data and which gives another slant on the way children extract meanings from paintings. Briefly, the scale consists of the following four levels:

1. *Aesthetic idiosyncracy* Personal and idiosyncratic responses to paintings dominate.
2. *Aesthetic realism* The worth of a painting is now judged by how well

the artist conformed to conventional representations of people and objects. If an artwork does not represent the world literally, then it has failed, even if it was painted by Picasso.

3. *Aesthetic fallacy* Children's judgements become confused and unfocused and there is a reluctance to criticize an artwork. Children often argued that the artist simply wanted to be different and original, a position deriving from a belief that an artist's intention alone is a sufficient criterion for judging a picture. Little heed was given to the intelligibility of a painting to an audience.

4. *Aesthetic perspective* Finally, it was recognized that an artist's formal decisions might have been determined by the desire to make his or her point of view understood. Form, style, subject-matter, skill, colour and emotional factors are all taken into account in offering judgements.

Among the youngest children at level 1, personal associations dominate their response to paintings. At level 2, which seems to cover much of the primary-school age-range, there is a concentration on such characteristics as subject-matter, realism and colour. Older primary-school children, some of whom are at level 3, are beginning to show an increasing interest in the artist's intentions and the emotional content of a work of art.

Scales of aesthetic development are very difficult to construct indeed, because often the same criteria are used at each level but in qualitatively different ways. Take colour as an example. Haysom (1970) studied the likes and dislikes of children aged 5, 8 and 11 and a group of adults for a number of illustrations of the nativity scene widely differing in form and style. Note the progression in the following comments about colour, ranging from the purely subjective to the analytical:

I don't like it very much because it is black and I don't like black [5-year-old]. It [the picture] has nice colours though they are not so striking as in the other picture, they are merging together more [11-year-old]. I don't like the colours, they are unrelated, haphazard, a bit muddly and not particularly well selected. I don't like this red against that one. It is not an intelligent use of colour [Adult].

In Haysom's study, references to realism reached a peak in the 11-year-old group and here, too, there were obvious differences between the age-groups in the nature of their judgements. Actual comments included:

The sun doesn't have a mouth or nose or eyes [5-year-old]. This is best because it is more like real life [7-year-old]. I like a painting that looks like a photograph and shows the real expression, not a sort of made up expression [10-year-old]. This is a little too Ali-Baba, a sort of panto picture, very realistic but in pantomime costume. It doesn't come across as real or evocative at all [Adult].

Incidentally, also in Haysom's (1970) investigation, few children referred to a painting's style and composition unlike the adult group, where these criteria were basic to judging the worth of a work of art.

Summary   The general drift of the research suggests that, in the early years, children expect pictures to have a clear and unambiguous subject-matter. Realism is the principal quality looked for, with colour coming a close second. Nevertheless, there is growing awareness of other factors, such as form and style, particularly in the later years of the primary school.

Classroom applications   This research gives teachers a helpful framework to follow in encouraging close observations of paintings. It singles out the various criteria to focus on, and the basic 'compare-and-contrast' experimental approach could just as easily be used in the classroom. We shall return to this topic in the next section.

Extending Children's Artistic Abilities

I shall begin this section by discussing strategies used to facilitate children's artistic abilities but I must point out that empirical research of consequence in this field is severely limited. I shall then move on to consider how children's sensitivity to paintings might be increased.

Drawing from observation

The research about to be described is not strictly an experimental 'teaching' study but, as it raises issues of unusual significance to art education, it is included here.

Until recently there was an assumption most often appearing in the American literature that memories and impressions ought to form the basis of child art, and not drawing from observation. If you are interested in pursuing the 'to-copy-or-not-to-copy' controversy, I would advise reading Duncum's (1988) analysis of the issue but, for our immediate purposes, it is enough to note that drawing from observation seems to be on the increase in schools both as an aid to learning and to improving children's powers of artistic expression.

Smith (1983) could find little empirical evidence on copy drawing and so she decided to set up an experiment on her own account designed to answer two questions. First, would children choose to draw from observation if given the chance? Second, if they did, in what way would memory drawings differ from observation drawings? Twelve boys and girls aged 7–9 and drawn from a university community were recruited to pursue these objectives. The group met for twelve one-and-half-hour sessions, during which observation drawing was interspersed with other activities. Apart from encouraging the children to observe the models closely and to recall previous experiences of them, the teacher took no other part in the proceedings.

The first significant finding was that, when given a choice of activities, children overwhelmingly preferred to draw from observation. Even allowing for the novelty of the situation, the preference for drawing from life was unexpectedly strong except when the objects selected for copying had no particular appeal to young children.

The second major finding was that observation drawing differed significantly from memory drawing. To begin with, observation drawing tended to be much more detailed than memory drawing. One example Smith gives is of an 8-year-old's effort to draw an iguana. This small drawing, only a few inches long, included the ear patch, dewlap, spiney back, skin texture and facial features all drawn with convincing effect.

Observation drawings were also more sophisticated in the rendering of contour than memory drawing and, in place of using simple geometric shapes, complex outlines were employed. The children's way of working was also intriguing: they began the task by focusing on one point along the edge of the object and worked out from there, looking and drawing carefully all the time until the whole object was sketched.

Summary   Although Smith has discovered significant variations between observation and memory drawings, we need to know much more about the course of development these two forms take and the precise differences between them. However, as things stand at present, recognizing that children draw from life as well as from memory (and sometimes a combination of both) alerts us to the differing demands of each activity and signals the need to structure teaching methods accordingly.

The teaching of techniques in art

We now turn to more general considerations. Paintings have a subject-matter and a formal stylistic content. The former is concerned with what is represented, the latter with how it is represented, and teachers have a responsibility to develop both these aspects. However, as Anderson (1986) reminds us, there is still a lingering yet mistaken view that discussing the meanings of children's artwork is an intrusion into children's privacy and, worse still, that it could stunt genuine, spontaneous expression. Oddly enough, this idea does not seem to have anything like the same currency in teaching written expression, where it is accepted that children have meanings they want to clarify and communicate and that they need help in doing so. The same argument applies with equal force to art education.

There are disappointingly few classroom-based experimental studies concerned with the second aspect of children's paintings, their formal and stylistic content, but a carefully structured teaching programme constructed by Renfrow (1983) is of interest. Eighteen 40-minute sessions were given over to teaching art to gifted pupils between the ages 8 and 11, during which specific help was given in representing perspective and proportion, in expressing shape through shadow and in copying the works of such artists as Klee and Picasso. In contrast with a control group, children undergoing this programme significantly improved in the ability to draw a human head (chosen as the main indicator of progress). Renfrow noticed how dissatisfied children were with the lack of realism in their paintings and how much they appreciated formal, systematic training in skills enabling them to produce work more to their liking.

Renfrow adopted a direct and structured teaching strategy for experimental purposes but many teachers would prefer to build in educative experiences around the problems children meet in trying to achieve their own objectives. Teacher intervention is probably at its best not in teaching skills in isolation, but as the need arises.

Summary   As Renfrow's (1983) research indicates, teachers can influence children's artwork and it suggests that general learning principles are as relevant to children's learning in art as they are to any other curriculum area.

Developing children's understanding of art

Earlier we saw that developmental trends in responding to paintings can be traced with reasonable confidence. First of all there is a shift from a primarily personal reaction to paintings to a more considered response embracing such dimensions as subject-matter, realism and colour. Eventually, some children, but by no means all, come to appreciate the formal characteristics of form and style painters use to produce the effects they are seeking.

There are at least two good reasons for encouraging children to look at and talk about paintings. The first is that it influences child art: as children become more sensitive to technical problems and recognize the influence of form and style, great paintings can provide ideas for executing their own work. Second, artists convey impressions about life in all its complexity, and an early introduction to the serious study of paintings can bring pleasure and enlightenment to young people no less than to adults.

Anderson (1986), whose paper was based in part on the work of Feldman

(1970), gives helpful suggestions about discussing pictures that can be adapted to individual circumstances. His first step involves identifying the artist, title and date of the work, followed by a description of its constituent parts, such as 'green trees', 'a church' and 'a starry night'. So far no value judgements are invited or pursued; comments are restricted to analysis only. In the second stage, form and style become the focus, taking account of such features as balance, colour, harmonies, disharmonies and perspective. Typical probes might be 'What makes the stars show up?' or 'Why does there seem to be so much movement?' At the third stage, the emphasis is on interpretation – the most difficult aspect of all. The key strategy here, Anderson (1986) advises, is to insist on children backing up their judgements with evidence. Children's perceptions of feelings expressed in the picture are just as important as their general interpretation of it, and are probed in the same way. Finally comes the stage of overall evaluation, where the work is judged essentially in terms of its success in achieving what the artist apparently set out to do.

Anderson (*ibid.*), who obviously knows children well, explains that the object of the four steps is to damp down immediate 'like-and-don't-like' reactions in favour of a systematic analysis of the work before making value judgements. In his experience, he says (*ibid.*) 'if children are given a system and an opportunity, the depth of their critical abilities is often amazing'.

Walshe (1980) carried out a programme of education in visual awareness among a group of 23 11- and 12-year-old middle-school pupils. It consisted of five elements: visits to art galleries (many of which, incidentally, are making serious efforts to accommodate to primary-school children); individual work on reproductions of paintings; group work based on assignments and themes; class discussion of slides, filmstrips and art books; and critical discussions of children's own artwork.

It soon became clear that children did not take readily to what were dubbed 'brown gravy' pictures, defined as 'those works epitomised by Rembrandt containing strong forms yet midst dark backgrounds often following a religious theme' (*ibid.*). Whenever children came across a picture of that style in the National Gallery, and dismissed it as boring, the group stopped, listened to the guide and then discussed the work. This tactic proved to be a useful counter to the instant-rejection tendency Anderson (1986) mentions.

Incorporated into the class-based work was a slide-and-sound production component, where pupils were asked to find a picture they particularly liked, and to select fitting music to go with it. The mixing of two art forms is a risky and delicate matter but in this case it seemed to work well. One girl elected to talk about a painting called 'Christina's World' by Andrew

Wyeth, which depicts a solitary figure in an open landscape gazing towards a single house. She began her description (*ibid.*) with these words:

> I like this picture because it looks as though it is in the middle of nowhere and that the end of the field goes down towards a cliff. I like the way the cottage is painted. It just seems like a very windy day in the middle of the moor, nowhere.

Angela Walshe (*ibid.* p. 87) then takes up the story:

> She then played a very soulful pop record at the sound of which a very special kind of silence descended upon the class. It was the sort of silence rarely, and not easily achieved in the middle of a busy school, as the class gazed upon the solitary figure in the field and the music infused meaning into the picture.

Over the period of the study the most significant shift in responses to painting recorded was a decline in the use of realism and colour as evaluative criteria and a corresponding increase in references to contrast, harmony, style, composition, pattern and movement. The quality of pupils' comments in general also improved. For instance, on seeing a picture filled with birds, one boy (*ibid.*) remarked, 'it's really clever how he's positioned the birds in different ways ... they make a pattern'. And the beginnings of understanding of abstract art is suggested by this (*ibid.*) comment, 'though the shapes and colours look simple, I don't really think it is. The artist took time planning'. Others could identify more general movements in paintings as evidence by the (*ibid.*) comment, 'that picture looks as if it was painted by an impressionist painter'.

Summary   In ending this section it is only necessary to point out that developmental stages in children's interpretation of art are quite well defined and that, with sensitive teaching, pupils' judgements become more refined and sophisticated. The inability to paint does not preclude the appreciation of paintings and this is the one aspect of art education where teachers who are poor artists themselves can really make their mark. Finally, because the interpretation of art is another of those activities that can be easily overlooked in the rush of the school day, there is a strong case for including a section on looking at and appraising art and craft in the craft design and technology (CDT) guidelines to ensure it does not escape attention.

SUMMARY AND CONCLUSIONS

It is more than ordinarily difficult to pin down the nature of art. To Canaday (1980, p. 3), the question 'What is art?' is especially daunting because 'Art has so many aspects, takes so many directions, serves so many purposes in such a variety of ways that the question is about as big as the biggest question of all "What is life?" '

All I have tried to do in this chapter is to pick out in simple and abbreviated form some of the major features of painting. As a generalization, art is to do with the construction and understanding of meanings and with the expression of thoughts and feelings through symbols that enable us, to quote Canaday (*ibid.* p. 5) again, 'to clarify, intensify, or otherwise enlarge our experience of life'. Art can force us to look at things we think we know well and to see them in a new light. Sometimes the process brings added pleasure but it could just as easily provoke and disturb, for art, as life itself, encompasses the ugly as well as the beautiful.

In schools, art serves both intrinsic and extrinsic purposes and in the interests of a balanced art education these purposes need to be made explicit. To that end, the Schools Council Art Committee's (1978) categories - recording, analysis, communication and expression - or something similar could provide a useful model for analysing the content of pupils' artwork and planning subsequent activities.

Psychological research has some contribution to make to art education. The study of children's conceptions of art we examined points to the desirability of discussing the nature of art in schools, not least in promoting the idea that it is not a break from 'real' work but an exercise that demands hard thinking about both the subject-matter of the painting and how its message is to be expressed.

There is enough evidence from experimental studies and other sources to enable the landmarks in the development of children's drawings to be defined with reasonable accuracy. More than that, it has been possible to demonstrate an association between artistic expression and general cognitive abilities that makes diagnosis of developmental stages in drawing a little easier. Evidence of egocentricism in its various manifestations can easily be detected in children's art, as can operational thinking, associated with a heavy emphasis on realism in children's drawings. Distinct differences between children's observation and memory drawing have also been noted; and a start has been made in charting the development of the expression of feelings in art. Lastly, a respectable literature available on children's responses to paintings is now building up, which suggests that, in the early years, children want realism in pictures above all else and that it is not until later childhood and adolescence that such factors as form and style exercise a significant influence.

The few classroom-based studies that do exist in this area give no cause to doubt that children's abilities to express themselves in drawing and painting can benefit from direct teaching, although a strong case can be made for learning and practising expressive skills in the context of children's own ongoing work. Children also have clear ideas about adult art that can be sharpened by discussions based on close observations of paintings.

In the final analysis, techniques have to be learnt and mastered if children's efforts at creating are to be effective and satisfying – and that means serving a long, arduous, but exciting and profitable apprenticeship in the discipline.

FURTHER READING

In addition to the references in the text, useful sources on the nature of art are Aldrich (1963) and Canaday (1980), and there are good discussions of art education in Eisner (1974) and A. Dyson (1983a).

For a description of general trends in drawing, see Schirrmacher (1980), Rogers and Sloboda (1983) and general sources, such as Lowenfeld and Brittain (1987).

Texts on the teaching of art in schools include Gaitskell, Horwitz and Day (1982) and Barnes (1987).

8
MORAL EDUCATION

INTRODUCTION

Moral education has an uneasy place in the primary-school curriculum. More often than not it is subsumed under religious studies or taught incidentally as moral issues arise spontaneously throughout the day rather than occupying a place in its own right.

There seem to be at least three main obstacles to a systematic approach to moral education. First, there is its lack of clear identity. Certainly, moral education is about deciding between right and wrong, but beyond that, unlike all other curriculum areas, it has no immediately recognizable body of knowledge of its own. Second, the status of moral education is controversial and uncertain. At one end of the continuum are those who believe that choosing between right and wrong is largely a subjective matter where one person's opinion is as good as another's; at the opposite extreme, we find those who believe that morality consists of nothing more than conforming to rules laid down by religious or secular bodies. Third, there are few (if any) teachers specializing in this area in the primary sector, which leaves moral education at a serious disadvantage when it comes to curriculum development.

All these forces militate against effective moral education yet, paradoxically, there seems to be a very real anxiety among the public that schools should take moral learning seriously. At the professional level, too, the interest of philosophers in ethical problems is as strong as ever and the output of psychological research into moral attitudes and behaviour remains remarkably high – far exceeding research in almost any other curriculum area. As for moral education itself, there are now far more authoritative sources available than there were previously, some of which will be introduced shortly.

THE NATURE OF MORALITY AND MORAL EDUCATION

The Nature of Morality

In its most general sense, morality is that branch of knowledge concerned with how people ought to behave. That sounds simple enough, but the going becomes much rougher when we try to justify the moral actions of ourselves and others – a central issue in the study of morality. Fortunately, several philosophers of education, notably Hirst (1974), Peters (1981) and Wilson (1981, 1983), have systematically clarified and appraised the many justifications advanced to support moral claims. We shall concentrate on just two of them – the appeal to authority and the appeal to reason – that have most relevance to education.

The appeal to authority

Morality is not simply a matter of obeying rules laid down by parents, teachers, religious groups or any other body. Doing something because it is a rule is not a convincing moral argument. In the sense in which the term is used here, morality involves making independent judgements based on carefully thought-out moral principles.

Of course, codes of conduct are necessary if communities are to function smoothly and without unnecessary conflict; equally, obedience to authority and learning the value of rules are essential preconditions to moral education proper. The critical point is that when maturity is reached, morally educated people will subject the demands and arguments of authority to rational appraisal and, if found acceptable, adopt them as their own and, if not, the search continues for something better.

There is a further strong objection to relying too much on rules. The range of human experience is so vast that however long a list of rules may be, it can never cover all conceivable situations. Inevitably then, there are times when people are compelled to make choices outside the codes of conduct they have been taught and, deprived of the support of ready-made solutions and with no idea how to go about solving moral problems, they are left helpless in the face of conflicting social pressures.

The appeal to reason

Peters (1981) is a strong advocate of the case for what he calls rational morality. The substance of his argument (*ibid*. p. 45) is as follows:

> To hold a rational code a man must subscribe to some higher order principles
> which will enable him to apply rules intelligently. ... The higher order principles
> which, in my view, are capable of some sort of rational justification, are those of
> impartiality, truth telling, liberty and the consideration of the interests [of
> others].

You might be wondering how Peters came to select these particular criteria
as a basis for rational morality. In an odd way, it seems, they chose
themselves. Peters argues that anyone who is seriously intent on developing
rational grounds for action is forced to apply the principles he proposes.
There is simply no choice in the matter because these principles inevitably
emerge in any serious consideration of moral conduct. In Hirst's (1974, p.
46) words, 'they are shown to be, not a personal assertion of what is being
taken to be ultimate, but an account of what all rational men must accept in
our concern for reasoned actions'.

However, one snag, as Straughan (1982) points out, is that there are some
people who never ask the question 'What should I do?' and so, for them,
the process of rational discussion never gets off the ground. Another
problem is the uncertain status of moral knowledge. The application of
moral principles is very different from using a mathematical formula that
produces one, and only one, right answer. With moral dilemmas several
solutions are sometimes possible because, for one thing, as Hirst (1974)
explains, not all the relevant circumstances may be known to all parties to
the discussion and, for another, moral criteria frequently conflict with each
other and this means that awkward and difficult choices must be made
between the lesser of two evils.

Rationally justifying moral decisions is a ragged and imprecise business
but, when it comes down to it, the only real alternative is to assume that
moral values are entirely an individual matter where one person's beliefs,
however sophisticated or crude, are no better or worse than anyone else's.
The logic of this argument leads us into very murky waters indeed for, in the
absence of a rationally based moral framework, anything goes.

Summary   We have examined two positions on morality: one based on an
appeal to authority and the other on an appeal to reason. The appeal to
authority conceives morality as a matter of obeying laws laid down by
others. Although it may make life simpler for the individual, it does nothing
to advance moral autonomy and therein lies its central weakness.

The appeal to reason puts the responsibility for making moral judgements squarely on the individual. Its strengths are formidable, not least
because of its insistence on giving reasons for actions as opposed to doing

what authority dictates or simply responding to hunches. However, justifying moral decisions rationally is a difficult and demanding exercise at the end of which there may still be room for legitimate disagreements.

The Nature of Moral Education

Although moral questions crop up in all curriculum areas, it is only morality as a form of knowledge in its own right that is centrally concerned with matters of right and wrong. That emphasis is its major characteristics, marking out its justification for inclusion in the school curriculum and the distinctive contribution it makes to it.

Hersh, Miller and Fielding (1980, p. 5) reduce the complexities of moral education to just three main elements: judging, caring and action. The judging aspect takes us back directly to the appeal to reason argument where, once again, we meet what Hirst (1974, p. 46) calls the main planks of rational morality – the principles of fairness, truth telling, freedom and consideration for others – all of which can be conveniently grouped under the general notion of respect for persons. A basic aim of moral education must, therefore, be to create conditions conducive to children acquiring and practising these skills. In principle at least, this should not raise too many difficulties. As Wilson (1983) reminds us, education in general is tied to the notion of improving people by increasing their knowledge and understanding; the same considerations apply in the moral domain where the aim is to give pupils a better grasp of what it means to be moral.

Wilson (1973, p. 27) gives the following three simple rules of procedure for making moral judgements:

1. That we should stick to the laws of logic.
2. That we should use language carefully.
3. That we should stick to the facts.

Now, for the first time, we focus directly on that aspect of morality concerned with emotions. If anything, the tendency to look on thinking and feeling as separate entities is even more pronounced in the moral area than elsewhere because it is often thought that strong emotions interfere with clear and objective thinking. It does happen, of course, but emotions can be educated, refined and harnessed in the service of moral education. In any event, according to Hirst (1974, p. 39), cognition must always be the mainspring of emotion, for as he sees it, 'we are not morally disgusted and so judge the action to be wrong; but it is because we judge the action wrong that we are morally disgusted'. Actually it makes sense to talk about reasoned emotions if only because it gives emotions a legitimacy and status they do not always enjoy.

Cognition and affect working together define a moral stance but the action component is the most significant of all. The morally educated person is not content simply to reflect on moral matters but is anxious to translate thoughts and feelings into appropriate behaviour. In the final analysis, the success of moral education must be judged by the extent to which children put moral principles into practice.

Wilson (1973, 1981) has identified 16 defining characteristics of a morally educated person that, he claims, embody the only proper objective of moral education. The list is too long to reproduce here, but its essence is contained in its four main headings that conveniently form the summary to this section.

Summary According to Wilson (1973, p. 28), moral behaviour depends upon the following.

1. Treating others as equals; that is, giving the same weight to the wants and needs of other people as to one's own.
2. An awareness of one's own and other people's emotions.
3. An awareness of the 'hard' facts relevant to moral decisions.
4. Bringing the above to bear on particular situations, so as to decide and act in accordance with them.

PSYCHOLOGY AND MORAL EDUCATION

Teachers' and Children's Conceptions of Moral Education

There is not much hope of successful moral education unless teachers are clear about what they are supposed to be doing. With that in mind, Wilson (1981) decided to study the concepts of moral education held by teachers and educationalists and, to complete the picture, by pupils and parents as well.

Essentially, most of those interviewed were confused about the justifications for morality and for the most part fell back on the appeal-to-authority position that, as we have just seen, is seriously flawed. To make matters worse, it appears that the professionals (the teachers and educationists) were not much more knowledgeable about moral principles than were the parents and children. This may well be because moral education remains a neglected area throughout the education system, including initial and in-service teacher education, where it continues to receive short shrift.

Nevertheless, there was a brighter side to Wilson's study. He later discussed individually issues integral to making moral judgements with the participating teachers and was surprised to discover that even those who had previously favoured a strong anti-rational or partisan approach to moral education were able, with only a little guidance from him, to master the principles governing a moral education based on rational criteria.

Summary If Wilson's findings are representative of the general situation, it seems that teachers tend to subscribe to the appeal-to-authority model of morality. However, once exposed to a view of moral education based on rationality, they quickly grasp its essential principles and see its compatibility with education in general.

The Development of Moral Thinking

Moral education is particularly rich in psychological studies and, so for once, a rigorous selection has to be made. To set the scene, I shall first outline the currently influential moral-development scale developed by Kohlberg (1976) and say a little about his methodology. We shall then concentrate on just two areas: children's concepts of lying, and the development of the interrelated concepts of role-taking, empathy and altruism.

Kohlberg's moral-development scale

Kohlberg (1976) extended and elaborated Piaget's (1932) stages of moral development in his own, six-stage scale of 'Obedience to Rules', which is given in summary form:

1. Rules are obeyed to avoid punishment.
2. Rules are obeyed because it is in everyone's interest to do so.
3. Conformity to rules results in social approval, non-conformity in social disapproval.
4. Obedience to rules and doing one's duty upholds the social system.
5. Impartial laws that take account of the rights and circumstances of others are approved of and obeyed.
6. One's own ethical principles are now followed even if it means breaking the law of the land.

The 'Heinz and the drug' problem is the most well-known and widely used of all the moral dilemmas Kohlberg (*ibid.*) used in his researches. It concerns a woman, dying of cancer, who could only be saved by a new wonder drug. The chemist who developed it charged ten times the actual cost of the drug but Heinz, the woman's husband, could raise only half that sum. Although he promised to pay the balance as soon as he could, the chemist refused to let him have it and so, in desperation, Heinz stole the drug.

After the story has been told, a battery of questions then follows ranging from the obvious 'Should Heinz steal the drug?' to the more subtle 'It is against the law for Heinz to steal. Does that make it morally wrong?' Responses are then categorized according to the six developmental stages set out above.

Summary Kohlberg's scale provides an overview of development in moral thinking and put the research findings to be reviewed in this chapter in a clear developmental perspective. Basically, the progression is in three broad stages:

1. Rules are obeyed to avoid punishment.
2. Rules are obeyed to gain approval and to conform to society's expectations.
3. Rules (or laws) are endorsed only if they are in accordance with one's ethical principles.

Concept of lying

Lying is probably the most pervasive of all children's actual or supposed misdemeanours and, as it is a source of anxiety to many parents and teachers, it may be helpful to put the matter into a psychological perspective.

Piaget (1932, p. 135) saw telling lies 'as a natural tendency and so spontaneous and universal that we can take it as an essential part of egocentric thought'. Therefore, he argued, lying is bound to bring children into conflict with adults and cause a good deal of tension at home and in school. Piaget questioned about a hundred children on their ideas about lies. The following three-stage sequence was revealed:

1. A lie is a naughty word.
2. A lie is something that is not true, including mistakes.
3. A lie is something that is intentionally false.

At the most primitive level, a lie is defined simply as a naughty word and is grouped along with swear words and other banned (usually rude) expressions. Next comes the definition, 'a lie is something that isn't true', which appears to be straightforward enough but, as we have come to expect, all was not so simple as it seemed. After further questioning, it soon became apparent that children did not always distinguish between deliberate falsehoods and giving incorrect information unintentionally. Finally, children are able to appreciate that a lie is only a lie when it conveys something that is intentionally false.

Piaget went on to explore further aspects of truth and falsehood but we shall move on to two other investigations that illustrate the state of the field fifty years on from Piaget's pioneering work.

Peterson, Peterson and Seeto (1983) minutely examined variations in lying and statements that children might construe as lies. In order to gain the children's interest and co-operation, video tape-recordings of puppet plays were shown to children while an adult narrator spelt out the plot to make sure it was understood. To give an example, in one episode Jan climbed a tree because she was frightened by a chicken and when her friend, Sara, asked her what she was doing, Jan replied that she was chased up there by a chicken as big as an elephant. The question, 'Did Jan tell a lie?' was put to 200 children in the 5–11 age-range, as well as to a group of adults who were persuaded to take part in the experiment to give the mature person's view.

In all, ten videos were shown incorporating ten different kinds of statements or lies. In Table 8.1 you will find results from those four statements that produced least agreement among the five age-groups. It shows the percentages of those taking part at each age level who equated swearing, exaggerating and two variations of guessing with lying.

The identification of swearing with lying among 5-year-olds is quite strong but, contrary to Piaget's belief, this confusion continues with a minority of children throughout the primary-school years and with some even into adulthood.

The findings for the exaggeration stories do not follow a consistent pattern, probably because of the different functions exaggeration serves. Some exaggerations are meant deliberately to mislead but others are intended merely to amuse or to give bite to a story (rather as a metaphor

Table 8.1   Percentages of subjects at each age level who defined various statements as lies

Statement	Age level				
	5	8	9	11	Adult
Swearing	38	12	8	15	2
Exaggeration	60	85	88	95	50
Directions guess	90	69	65	48	30
Age guess	55	45	20	8	5

(*Source*: Adapted from Peterson, Peterson and Seeto, 1983.
© 1983 Society for Research in Child Development Inc.)

does), in which case it might be stretching a point to equate exaggerating with an outright lie. However, for whatever reason, a high percentage of the children took a hard line and firmly linked exaggerating with lying; it was only among adults that a less rigid position was observed.

The 'directions-guess' category, although it is conceptually straightforward, needs a little explanation. The judgement children had to make concerned a lost adult who asked a child for directions. The girl said she didn't know for sure but she *thought* the road in question was the second turning on the left. In fact she was wrong. As you can see, 90 per cent of the 5-year-olds construed this innocent misdirection as a lie.

Incidentally, this is in line with another of Piaget's (1932) findings that, for young children, it is the consequences of an action rather than the intentions of the perpetrator that determine culpability. For example, a helpful boy who makes a big blot in filling an inkwell is considered to be much naughtier than a boy who played with his father's pen without permission and made a little blot (see the further-reading list for details).

However, to return to lying, there is a steady rise in the tendency to take intentions into account particularly from the age of 8 onwards, but even so about a third of the adults still made faulty judgements. Finally, turning to the 'age-guess' category, about half of the 5-year-olds judged a wrong estimate of a person's age to be a lie, a response that became much less frequent as children grew older.

In the next part of the investigation, participants were asked how good or how bad they judged the action of the central character to be. For this purpose a rating scale was constructed that, although slightly bizarre, apparently did its job well. 'Very, very good' was represented by three angels, 'medium good' rated two angels and 'a little bit good', one. 'A little bit bad' was represented by one devil, 'medium bad' by two and 'very, very bad' by three devils. All age-groups gave relatively worse ratings to lies that were motivated by a desire to escape just retribution than they did to white lies, altruistic lies and lies involving practical jokes. Generally speaking, adults also tended to be more lenient in their judgements than children.

We have not yet considered children's reasons for telling the truth or their attitudes towards the consequences of lying – the subject of a study by Peisach and Hardeman (1983), who worked with 144 6-year-old New York children. At the first level of response, children worked on the principle that you tell the truth to avoid punishment and, if you are caught out, they said, the likely consequences of lying included: 'You get in jail'; 'You get caught by the police'; 'You go to hell'; 'You get burned up'; 'Bye, bye electric chair'; 'You will get sent to your room'. Whether or not children really meant what they said is anyone's guess. I suspect that, if pressed hard, we would find they did not but, even so, the distasteful responses children spontaneously produced still make disturbing reading.

During the second stage, awareness of give and take in interpersonal relationships begins to appear. Children now say if you lie, other people will lie to you.

At the third stage, conformity to rules dominates social thinking. Lies break the rules and are therefore conceived as naughty. In contrast, truth telling is associated with approval of others ('If you lie mother won't like it'); with fairness to others ('Lying might get someone into trouble'); and with the need to bind groups together ('People won't believe each other').

You will note that, by and large, truth telling serves one's own ends until stage 3, when such reasons as fairness to others are put forward for not lying.

Summary There are two main points to stress. First, children's conceptions of lies encompass an astonishingly wide range of ideas from the crude to the sophisticated and so it is hardly surprising that adults and children are often at odds with each other as to what constitutes truth and falsehood. Second, the evidence indicates that children consider lying in terms of how it affects themselves before going on to consider its social consequences.

Perhaps the most sobering finding of all was that even some adults have not yet mastered all the conceptual problems associated with lying, including some of an undemanding and elementary nature.

Classroom applications These findings indicate that there is plenty of scope for helping pupils sort out the confusions and semantic difficulties associated with lying. In addition to using opportunities that arise naturally, Peterson, Peterson and Seeto's (1983) stories illustrating swearing and exaggeration could easily be adapted for classroom use and extended to other forms of lying, for example, white lies or lies told to keep oneself out of trouble. The probe question as ever is 'Why do you think that?' and, of course, we would want to know whether children consider it is wrong to tell a lie in all circumstances.

The literature also provides useful sources for conducting sessions on the reason for truth telling and appropriate punishments for lying. An understanding of intentions is basic to moral actions, so problem situations in which good and bad intentions and positive and negative effects are varied could do much to bring this home to children. The further-reading list cites appropriate sources.

Role-taking, empathy and altruism

Readiness to take the thoughts and feelings of others into account is a major defining characteristic of a morally educated person. Although it is now a thriving research area in its own right, the study of social role-taking skills began as an offshoot of Piaget's investigations into children's understanding of physical phenomena. You might recall his 'mountains' problem reported in Chapter 1, where children had to say what they thought they would be able to see from various vantage points around the table without moving from the chair on which they were sitting.

In turning from the physical to the social world, the central question for research is 'At what age or stage are children able to identify the thoughts and feelings of others?' Let me say at once that the answer depends largely on the level of difficulty of the particular role-taking task: some are very simple and cause no trouble even to pre-school children, while others make considerable cognitive demands.

A task at the simple end of the spectrum is described in Borke's (1971) study of children's judgements of the likely emotional reactions of their classmates. Some 200 children in the 3–8-year-old age-range were told stories in which they, the participants, were represented as behaving in ways that might make another child feel happy, sad or angry. Typical situations were the sharing of sweets, refusing to let another child play and pushing another child off a table. Following each presentation, the children had to select the best picture for indicating the feelings of the other child in the story, from three pictures portraying happy, sad and angry faces. Borke's findings indicated that children as young as 3 were generally successful in judging different kinds of reaction in others, especially when they were happy ones.

In Borke's experiment, children were able to report accurately what their own feelings would have been in similar circumstances; but it was not clear from her results if children could recognize the feelings of others when different from their own. This was the focus of a widely reported study by Chandler and Greenspan (1972), who devised much more difficult role-taking tests. In one of them, for instance, a story was told of a boy who was upset when he accidentally dropped a coin down a drain. A friend, who passed by a little later on, knew nothing of the loss and could not understand why the central character was so disgruntled and refused to join in a game of football.

The 86 6–13-year-old children involved in this experiment were invited, first, to relate the whole story from their own viewpoint and, second, to reinterpret the same event from the limited perspective of the late arrival on the scene. The researchers wanted to know if children could set aside their own full knowledge of the sequence of events and adopt the limited perspective of someone who has less information than themselves. For the 6-year-olds, the answer was generally no; in fact, only 15 per cent could do so. For the 13-year-olds, the answer was generally yes; but even at this age, 4 per cent found the task too difficult.

There is a technical controversy about the conditions that must be satisfied before children can be classed as sociocentric thinkers. However, it is enough to point out that role-taking skills vary in the intellectual demands they make and represent a continuum from Borke's test at one extreme to Chandler and Greenspan's at the other. An intermediate stage is filled in by Urberg and Docherty (1976), who devised a test where children had to put themselves in the position of a second character, as in the following instance. A picture is shown illustrating two children fighting over the same toy truck, followed by the presentation of a second picture showing a woman giving the truck to one of the two children. The participants were told (*ibid.*) 'This is a story about you. You and your friend both want to play with that truck. Then the teacher comes over and gives the truck to you. How do you feel? How does your friend feel?' Note that the two parts of the story are kept separate, which makes this task relatively easy.

We have established that role-taking skills can cover a spectrum from easy to difficult. The next step is to consider the similarities and differences between the interrelated concepts of role-taking, empathy and altruism. Role-taking has just been discussed at length and so no more will be said about it. Empathy goes beyond the simple recognition of an emotional state to the next stage, marked by an involvement in the feelings of another – a sharing with them of their pleasure or pain. Going one stage further still, we come to altruism, which has been formally defined by Hoffman (1976) 'as behaviour carried out for the benefit of another ... in the absence of anticipated or expected rewards'. The most important defining characteristic of altruism is its behavioural element. It is not enough to understand how some else feels; feelings must be translated into action. The relationships can be most easily expressed in diagrammatic form, as in Figure 8.1.

Barnett and Thompson (1985) included a measure of empathy in their battery of tests that consisted of such statements as 'It makes me sad to see a boy who can't find anyone to play with'. Children who scored high on this scale tended to be rated by teachers as being more socially supportive than their classmates and to be more concerned about others. However, Barnett and Thompson warn that the ability to identify the feelings of others does not automatically evoke sympathetic understanding. Indeed, they found that sensitivity to the emotions of other people could be used to further one's own ends.

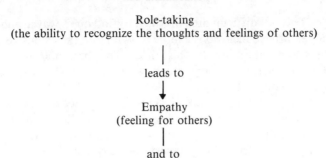

Role-taking
(the ability to recognize the thoughts and feelings of others)

leads to

Empathy
(feeling for others)

and to

Altruism
(selflessly subordinating one's own interests for those of another)

Figure 8.1   Relationships between role-taking, empathy and altruism

Finally we come to altruism that, for the most part, has been investigated in controlled laboratory situations. In a typical experiment, Froming, Allen and Jensen (1985) individually interviewed 222 6–8-year-old children, who were offered a reward of 25 sweets for taking part in the study. Not everyone, they were told, would be asked to help and so some pupils would receive nothing. Next, the lucky ones were given the chance to give some of their sweets to those who had missed out, but it was made clear they were under no obligation to do so. In one condition (that is to say, in one variation of the experiment), the donation was made in the presence of the investigator but, in a second condition, children were really put on the spot by making the donation in private.

The 6-year-olds took no notice whatsoever of the experimenter and ended up giving roughly the same number of sweets in private as they did in public. By the age of 7 and over, however, a sharp increase in public as opposed to private giving occurred, indicating that children now recognized that generous behaviour was approved of by adults. Interestingly, no child in this age-group showed the true spirit of altruism, which entails acting unselfishly in the service of others, whether adults are aware of it or not.

Froming and his collaborators also discovered that children who scored high on a role-taking skills-test gave a great many more sweets than those who found it hard to judge the perspectives of others. That latter group donated the same amount of sweets whether or not they were observed. But (and this is the significant point) those who were good at role-taking tended to be generous only in the presence of an adult. In other words, although the position of the deprived children was recognized, it needed the approval of adults to goad the high role-takers into action.

Summary   This is a difficult area in which to find one's way around, but at least some tentative conclusions can be drawn from the extensive and still-growing research literature in this field. The first and most obvious comment is that there are progressive stages in the ability to identify the thoughts and feelings of others.

Second, high ability in role-taking skills can produce opposite effects. It can evoke sympathy and understanding but it could just as easily result in using knowledge of other people's attitudes to one's own advantage. Role-taking ability, therefore, is a necessary but not a sufficient condition of positive social behaviour.

Third, altruistic behaviour appears to be encouraged in the first instance by adult approval but the eventual hope is that external rewards will become irrelevant in the course of time and that generous acts will occur as an expression of a person's values and for no other motive.

Classroom applications   For teachers, the research just examined gives examples of the various forms and levels role-taking tasks can take that, when suitably modified, can provide a basis for individual, group or class discussion of the issues raised. We will return to this aspect later in the chapter but, before continuing, it is as well to underline that, in the early stages, teacher approval of altruistic behaviour could well play a significant part in its development.

Moral thought and action

The ultimate test of a programme of moral education is its effect on the behaviour of children. We have noted the tenuous relationship between role-taking ability and altruism; we now broaden the discussion to embrace the puzzling discrepancies often found between moral thinking and action. As Rest (1979) reminds us, it is a common-enough phenomenon. He cites (*ibid.*) the Apostle Paul, who wrote (Rom. 7: 19) 'The good that I would I do not; but the evil which I would not, that I do'. However, Rest goes on, there are in contrast great moral leaders, for example, Sir Thomas More and Mahatma Gandhi, whose lives were an outward expression of their beliefs.

But why should there be such uncertainty about the relationships between attitudes and behaviour? The psychological explanations offered are long and complex (Wicker, 1969; Damon, 1977; Rest, 1979) and inevitably hedged around with qualifications. The factors thought to account for the discrepancies can be broadly classed as personal (where individual personalities confuse the issues); situational (where, for one reason or another, the social setting affects people's behaviour); and methodological (where the proper isolation and control of all the factors affecting behaviour creates major problems).

I have chosen Damon's (1977) study of sharing, one of the best of its kind, to represent research in this area. It had its root in a discussion about sharing overheard in a pizza parlour by one of his graduate students. Seven children wearing hockey uniforms ordered a pizza that, for convenience, was cut into eight pieces. Each boy took one piece but the problem then, of course, was what to do with the piece left over. The discussion went this way and that; the claims of the oldest were advanced; a case was made out for favouring a boy who originally had a small piece; and so on. Altogether the episode was a fine example of the dynamics and, indeed, richness of children's relationships. Damon points out that there is no adequate substitute for observing natural occurrences such as these. However, some structured experimentation is necessary. It is wasteful of time and resources to hang around endlessly waiting for something significant to happen; furthermore, it is only in carefully constructed experiments that critical factors can be controlled and analysed.

Damon (*ibid.* p. 99ff.) settled for the next best thing by creating a situation very similar to the pizza episode except that sweets were shared as a reward for services rendered. To begin with, he made a careful distinction in his experimental design between hypothetical moral judgements, real-life moral reasoning and actual conduct, which was put to the test using 18 boys and 18 girls in each of the age-groups 4, 6, 8 and 10.

In variation I (hypothetical judgements) a story was told about four children who were invited to make bracelets. They worked away on the task for about fifteen minutes. At the end of that time not only had Michele made more than anyone else but hers were also the prettiest. John (the biggest boy) and Ellen also made some good bracelets, but George (the youngest child) did not do so well. The children were thanked for their efforts and were given ten candy bars to share among themselves in payment. The participants were then asked how they thought the children in the story should divide the reward, noting particularly whether such factors as age, sex and output influenced decisions.

Variation II (real-life reasoning) closely paralleled the story just outlined. Two months later, three children who took part in the previous experiment – together with a younger child not then a participant – were set to work actually making bracelets. After a suitable interval, they were then asked to decide among themselves how they would share out ten candy bars if they were offered them. The important point to note is that in this variation, no sweets were actually offered.

In variation III (actual conduct), the reward was actually shared out among the children.

It is unnecessary to list here the developmental stages Damon observed in all three conditions. I shall simply highlight the main findings. First of all, a strong but by no means perfect association was discovered between hypothetical judgements (variation I) and real-life reasoning (variation II). This finding was not unexpected, but the results from variation III produced some surprises. All the children, whatever their level of hypothetical reasoning, tended to favour themselves more in practice than they did in theory: a tendency particularly noticeable among younger children. In Damon's view, self-interest frequently seemed to retard moral reasoning so that, in the final analysis, the principle of fairness lost out to selfishness. However, the picture is not all black. Older children favoured themselves much less frequently than did the other age-groups; the self-bias reported was not excessive; and even the most self-centred gave at least something to other members of the group.

Summary   Damon's research illustrates how difficult it is to pin down the relationship between what people say or think they will do and what they actually do in practice. Nevertheless, in spite of the confusion, the essential point for teachers is that reasoning is undoubtedly influential in moral decision-making in real life and, at the very least, it indicates the limits within which the eventual behaviour is likely to occur.

Extending Moral Thinking
Theories of moral learning

This is not the place to review the many, and often competing, theories of moral development. The sources given in the further-reading list fill in the background and so all that is intended here is to sketch in very broad terms the essential differences between the major explanations for moral learning.

The behaviourists attach critical importance to conditioning. Crudely speaking, good conduct is rewarded and bad conduct punished. In the process, children learn to look on adults as models of behaviour, and to identify with their attitudes and values. While behaviourism cannot account for all aspects of moral learning it draws attention to the essential part habit formation plays in the early socialization of children.

Piaget, as we would expect, sees moral development as a particular instance of cognitive development. He sees the peer group as a particularly significant force in accelerating moral thinking. At the concrete operational stage, there is a swing away from a 'What authority says is right' attitude to one where rules emerge in the rough and tumble of everyday life and are the product of group consensus. Piaget's view accords with common sense and, indeed, the power of the peer group in forming values is now generally recognized. However, Piaget, in his turn, has been criticized for playing down the influence of adults in forming moral values.

Kohlberg (1976) is the most well-known follower of the Piagetian tradition. As we shall see shortly, for him, cognitive conflict – often with role-playing as the catalyst – is the primary agent in moral learning. In his turn, Kohlberg has been criticized principally for ignoring the role of habit formation in early socialization and for taking little account of the feeling element in morality.

As you can see, what one theory picks up, another leaves out and, to some extent, therefore, theories of moral learning are complementary.

The cognitive-conflict principle

Kohlberg, whose developmental stages (1976) were briefly referred to in the last section, attaches a great deal of importance to the cognitive-conflict principle. According to this view, an uncomfortable state of dissonance or imbalance arises when it is realized that solutions that worked in the past no longer do so. In the effort to restore equilibrium, so the theory goes, people are forced to think out the situation anew, which, it is hoped, forces their thinking on to a higher plane.

Selman and Lieberman (1975) give a good example of the cognitive-conflict principle in action. A group of 7-year-old children taken from six classes discussed moral problems with their teachers, in the course of which they were exposed to moral reasoning slightly more advanced than their own. The problems, which involved a conflict between two or more principles, were presented in story form using a film-strip backed up by a sound commentary. A similar episode used to test children's moral understanding concerned an 8-year-old girl named Holly who loved to climb trees. One day her father saw her fall off. He asked his daughter to promise not to climb trees again. She made that promise. Later that day, Holly met her friend, Shawn, who was distressed because her kitten was caught in a tree and couldn't get down. Should Holly go back on her promise and rescue the cat?

The classroom discussions were conducted either by 'experts' in moral education, lay informed teachers or by a control group of teachers carrying on as normal (which, in this case, meant the minimum of discussion). The 'experts' and informed lay teachers exposed their classes to a range of levels of reasoning below, at and a little above the level of most of the pupils in the hope that this would improve their moral reasoning. A real attempt was made, therefore, to match the standard of the material offered to the level of children's understanding.

Children's ability to take intentions into account in making moral judgements was measured before and after the experimental teaching. The three stages were as follows:

Stage 0 - where intentions were ignored or confused. Children's responses here were wavering and uncertain.

Stage 1 - where simple intentionality appears. Acts intending good are right and those intending bad are wrong. Thus children at this level will say Holly ought not to be punished because 'she got the kitten down instead of just climbing it for fun'.

Stage 2 - where judgements can take account of the perspectives of both father and daughter and weigh one against the other. Children now recognize that Holly's father will understand why she disobeyed him.

As expected, children in the two experimental groups scored significantly better than the control group in tests of moral reasoning. For example, on the 'ability to recognize intention' dimension, the improvement was estimated at an impressive one-and-a-half developmental stages. Another finding was just as significant: there were no differences of any consequence between the scores of the 'expert' and informed, lay-teacher-led classes. What is particularly encouraging is that the 'informed lay teachers' were expected only to familiarize themselves with the manual of instructions to a moral-reasoning test, nothing more, and yet with that minimum of preparation they were able to bring about a respectable improvement in their pupils' moral thinking.

Note that the informed lay teachers aimed to take the children only as far they could go. This is in complete contrast to a group of teachers studied by Rybash (1980), who seemed to make no allowance at all for the likely developmental stage of their classes. As Rybash explains, some teachers felt duty bound to guide children towards the 'right' course of action and so they deliberately revealed their own 'correct' judgements, justifying what they were doing with such remarks as 'We have to be consistent with our own beliefs'.

Enright's (1982) research, to which we turn next, is in the same mould except in one respect: all the material used to promote moral education came from the observed social behaviour of children because, as Enright argues, disputes that occur naturally in children's peer groups are likely to be more influential than hypothetical problems in sharpening moral thinking.

Only two classes of 6-year-olds and their teachers took part in this project, which was aimed at encouraging teachers to deal with social problems more or less as they arise. Whenever likely problems were identified, teachers would first of all ask the children to give their version of the incident. In the example Enright gives, if Billy has just argued with Tom, the teachers asks Billy what he thinks that might mean to their friendship. If Billy retorts, 'We're not friends because he bothers me', the teacher then tries to raise the discussion to a higher plane by stressing the mutual nature of friendship. He asks, 'Does he have to do something nice for you, then, for you to become friends again, or could you do something nice for him to become friends?' Billy is thus manoeuvred into explaining what that something might be, as well as what he could have done differently to avoid the quarrel. Throughout the exchange, the teacher looks for any discrepancy between thought and action and exploits it to the full.

Wisely, a weekly discussion of hypothetical dilemmas was also included in the research programme for the very good reason that it enabled children 'to think about interpersonal and social problem solving issues while in a more calm state than when being disciplined' (*ibid.*). Various standard measures of moral attitudes and thinking testified to the success of the project but, because both spontaneous and structured sessions were included in the teaching programme, the improved scores cannot be attributed to immediate discussion of social incidents alone.

There is a widespread view among primary-school teachers that incidental rather than planned moral education is more effective. But while it is sensible to exploit to the full the learning possibilities of conflict situations arising spontaneously in schools, there are snags to this approach. In the first place, as Enright recognized, immediate inquests on conflicts and misdemeanours may be counter-productive. Time is needed to allow tempers to cool before sensible discussion can begin and, moreover, teachers often need a breathing space to think out their position rather than give an instant, unconsidered response. Otherwise, moral education could easily become entangled with crisis management. Second, some children may never, or only rarely, be involved in the quarrels and upsets occurring regularly in school and so they may miss out in moral education altogether – all the more so when some discussions are conducted in private out of deference to the feelings of the participants. Third, some major areas may not emerge naturally in particular classes. There is a strong case, therefore, for a more structured scheme to complement the 'on-the-spot' version of moral education.

Hypothetical dilemmas need not necessarily be removed from children's experiences. Incidents that actually happened in the past could be talked over, having the added advantage that no one present would be embarrassed because of personal involvement. Moral issues, too, are inherent in all curriculum areas, notably literature and history, and provide a rich source of material. The planned approach has one clear benefit: it gives teachers a chance to decide in advance which moral issues to introduce and at which level to pitch them.

The discussion of moral problems can be a dangerous business, touching as it does on the deeply held values of teachers, children, parents and the larger society outside the school. There are, too, technical skills in running discussion groups that have to be mastered. Hersh, Miller and Fielding (1980, p. 137) are among those who make a number of common-sense recommendations specific to this area, which include the following:

1. Highlighting the moral conflict and making it real to children.
2. Asking 'why' questions: pressing children to reveal their attitudes and to give reasons for them.
3. Complicating the circumstances. By using probing questions, the complexity of the original problem may be increased.
4. Relating the circumstances of the issue to children's own lives.
5. Using indepth strategies to further the main questions and by posing arguments put in advance of children's thinking.
6. Clarifying and summarizing what the children are saying.

Role-playing

Lastly, we consider role-playing, a technique for sharpening social awareness often used in resolving cognitive conflicts. Hersh, Miller and Fielding (1980) are among many who suggest that acting out and vicariously experiencing what people involved in difficult moral situations have to contend with can lead children to take a more measured and sensitive view of social situations. Certainly a great deal of importance is attached to drama and role-playing in the *Schools Council Moral Education 8–13 Project: Startline* (McPhail, Middleton and Ingram, 1978). Essentially, children are given the information needed to enable them to act out an episode but, at critical points, the teacher interrupts to ask 'As X in this situation, what do you do now?'

The *Startline* material (*ibid*. p. 141) is also designed to give 'children practice in experiencing, understanding, feeling, sympathy, deciding and speaking and acting to convey a message', and it includes an extensive range of material designed to heighten perceptions of other people's needs, abilities and feelings. For example, the photoplay workcards show a variety of facial expressions, body gestures and types of personal relationships that pupils use to identify the kind of person portrayed (angry, bad-tempered or kind and loving) and to make a judgement about how that person's behaviour might affect other people.

Summary   At the beginning of this section it was emphasized that there are radical differences between the various theories of moral development. Nevertheless, they are in some respects complementary and, between them, cover the thinking, feeling and action components of moral learning.

Several matters of practical concern for teachers were also considered. Taking our cue from the psychological literature, we have concentrated on the cognitive conflict principle, a key element in Kohlberg's theory of moral development, which involves deliberately disturbing pupils' existing ideas and forcing a re-examination of them in the light of new information. Experimental studies confirm the effectiveness of this strategy in advancing moral learning in classroom settings.

As it arose directly from the research literature, we touched on the structured versus spontaneous moral-education controversy and concluded that, while it is obviously right to use naturally occurring social problems in educating children morally, pre-planned and structured provision is also necessary. This issue reminds us that moral learning takes place in a social context: in the formal setting of the school, in family and peer groups, and in the wider community.

Finally, the Schools Council *Startline* material was briefly referred to, which emphasizes the role of feeling in moral learning.

SUMMARY AND CONCLUSIONS

Since morality is primarily concerned with how we ought to behave towards each other, a major objective of moral education must be to help children to cope with the difficult and contentious business of arriving at and justifying moral decisions. With that in mind, we examined two different attempts to answer the question, 'How ought I to behave?' – the appeal to authority and the appeal to reason. We concentrated on the appeal to reason, a procedure that attempts to spell out certain higher-order principles, such as fairness and impartiality, which provide a yardstick for judging interpersonal behaviour. This model does not provide easy, straightforward answers to moral questions, but it is probably the best we have and is certainly preferable to the 'one person's view is as good as another's' argument that, if taken seriously, would have worrying and damaging consequences for society. Of course, moral education is not only about judging but it is also about developing a genuine emotional involvement in moral issues and translating one's thoughts and feelings into responsible behaviour. The task of psychology is to assist in accomplishing these ends.

The representative studies we examined revealed the rich and varied nature of children's judgements about lying, sharing and related concepts. As we have seen, the more intensively these areas are explored, the more complex they prove to be. However, such frameworks as Kohlberg's (1976) put these ideas in a theoretical perspective and point to where to begin a learning experience and where to proceed from there. In the section on extending moral thinking, several instances were given of the cognitive-conflict principle in action, and of the role teachers or experimenters can play in making the most of each teaching stimulus.

The relationship between moral thought and action is an under-researched area in schools, partly because of the technical difficulties encountered in disentangling the complex personal and situational relationships involved. Nevertheless, the stark fact remains that the ultimate test of effective moral education is its influence on behaviour in and out of school.

In addition, although it is no business of psychology to dictate what teachers ought to do, research such as Enright's (1982) opens up important issues, for example, whether moral education should be taught incidentally or in a more structured form. However, at the moment moral education often seems to be unplanned and left to chance, which is a pity: the empirical literature includes a wide range of dilemmas of potential value in giving the teaching of morality a progression and continuity it frequently needs. Indeed, if moral education could be structured on philosophical and psychological principles, perhaps it might take its place more confidently alongside other curriculum areas.

FURTHER READING

Hirst's (1974) and Peters' (1981) analysis of the nature of morality and the justifications for moral judgements are essential reading for serious students. See also Wilson, Williams and Sugarman (1967), Hersh, Miller and Fielding (1980) and Straughan (1982). All the above sources also cover the philosophy of moral education.

Reviews of psychological theories of moral learning (including Freud's and the various behaviourist positions I have been unable to refer to in this chapter) are given in Wright (1971) and Graham (1972). All basic textbooks on social psychology also contain an introduction to this field.

Piaget's (1932) pioneering study still repays careful reading. Later assessments of his work are given in Graham (1976) and Duska and Whelan (1977), both of which also refer to Kohlberg's contribution to understanding moral learning. Damon's (1977) *The Social World of the Child* is also strongly recommended.

Additional empirical work on intentionality in moral judgements is given in Costanzo *et al.* (1973) and Leon (1982).

For practical advice on the teaching of moral education, see Wilson (1973), McPhail, Middleton and Ingram (1978) and Hersh, Paolitto and Reimer (1979).

POSTSCRIPT

Our discussion has covered a wide range of concepts in seven curriculum areas and it is now opportune to focus once more on the main themes we have been considering. This book is based on the proposition that a working knowledge of conceptual development, as it relates to the primary curriculum, could significantly help teachers in their day-to-day work in the classroom.

The importance of understanding the nature of the academic disciplines that contribute to the primary curriculum has been emphasized throughout. Despite all the difficulties and uncertainties attendant on trying to pin down the essential characteristics of the different areas of learning, it was an exercise critical to defining educational objectives and to determining what we do in the classroom. Simply knowing, for instance, that language is used both for practical purposes and for reflecting on and ordering human experiences sets a pattern for language teaching and gives it a clearer direction than it might otherwise have had.

The major part of this book describes the development of children's thinking in seven areas representative of the primary-school curriculum. The research effort in this field has been extensive but haphazard. For example, a great deal more is known about young children's moral development than about their overall geographical understanding; similarly, within the separate disciplines, there has been a concentration on some topics to the total neglect of others. Nevertheless, a significant store of information has been built up that, apart from bringing to light the extraordinary variety of children's thinking from the crude to the subtle and from the straightforward to the quirky, also serves well the practical needs of teachers.

Children begin school with their minds well stocked with information and ideas that, although often incomplete or uncertain, provide the foundation on which education in school is built. Teaching is about negotiations of meanings between teachers and pupils and this is why so much stress has been placed here on determining the limits of children's existing knowledge, and on noticing what catches their attention and what does not. Skilled teachers encourage pupils' contributions and look for links between the knowledge children bring to the situation and the new experiences to which they are being introduced. The act of learning then becomes an exchange of viewpoints where the learner works hard on the new material, grafts it on to existing learning and comes out of the experience with fresh insights.

In Chapter 1, the main landmarks in cognitive development were identified that served as a basis for imposing system and order on the many and varied concepts children have acquired. According to Piaget, the thinking of young children is egocentric and tends to be dominated by one feature of the situation to the exclusion of others but, with the onset of the concrete operational stage, egocentricity wanes and thinking becomes more coherent and systematic.

Piaget identified the broad sweep of intellectual development. However, not all research findings fit easily into this pattern. In the fields of written expression and mathematics in particular, some of the developmental scales derived from work with very young children cover a narrow band of ability only and are, necessarily, finely graded. A. H. Dyson's (1983) meticulous analysis of the early stages of learning to write is but one example. There is little point in trying to force such data into a Piagetian mould. It is clear as it is and is much better left alone.

Although a knowledge of conceptual development in itself cannot solve all the problems of teaching, it can help to improve classroom practice. First, this knowledge can be helpful in pitching questions at an appropriate level and in predicting likely answers to them. Second, knowing the developmental sequence can help to ensure a satisfactory match between children's existing levels of ability and the work they are expected to cope with. Third, an awareness of the course of conceptual development can make the use of techniques, such as cognitive conflict, teaching by telling and learning from observation, more precise and efficient.

A promising start has been made in identifying children's concepts in the various curriculum areas but, as research has never been and never will be centrally organized, it is often a matter of chance which concepts attract attention and which do not. Even where the information is available it is unrealistic to expect teachers to keep in their minds the sequence of development for all the hundreds of concepts children have acquired. However, you might recall Selman and Lieberman's (1975) study (referred to in Chapter 8) where teachers were asked to read a manual of instructions to a moral-reasoning test, nothing more, before leading discussions on moral problems. This they did to good effect, which shows that, when research evidence is readily available and in a form easily assimilated by teachers, it can positively influence the quality of teaching.

When information relating to specific concepts is not readily accessible – or, just as likely, when it does not exist – we can still fall back on such theories of cognitive development as Piaget's and Peel's for general guidance. It is not too difficult to spot signs of egocentric thinking, or when only one factor is considered to the exclusion of other relevant data. Even without a basic background in developmental psychology, there is still a great deal to be gained by questioning children about their ideas, assumptions and methods of working.

Nevertheless, there are still many unresolved issues about making the best use of children's concepts in teaching. For instance, we need more precise information about the relative advantages and disadvantages of individual, group and class methods in matching the material to the learner. We also need more practical research to help us determine when it is better to tell rather than to urge children to discover facts or skills for themselves.

But, despite the gaps, existing research throws considerable light on children's thinking as it relates to the primary curriculum: it increases the range of teaching methods open to us; it leads to greater ease of understanding in pupil–teacher communication; and it opens up possibilities for making learning and teaching more stimulating and interesting for both teacher and taught.

REFERENCES AND BIBLIOGRAPHY

Aldrich, V. G. (1963) *Philosophy of Art*, Prentice-Hall, Englewood Cliffs, NJ.
Allen, G. L., Kirasic, K. C., Siegel, A. W. and Herman, J. F. (1979) Developmental issues in cognitive mapping, *Child Development*, Vol. 50, pp. 1062-70.
Anderson, J. (1985) Teaching map skills: an inductive approach, *Journal of Geography*, Vol. 84, no. 1, pp. 25-32.
Anderson, T. (1986) Talking about art with children: from theory to practice, *Art Education*, Vol. 39, no. 1, pp. 5-8.
Anooshian, L. J. and Kromer, M. K. (1986) Children's spatial knowledge of their school campus, *Developmental Psychology*, Vol. 22, no. 6, pp. 854-60.
Anooshian, L. J. and Young, D. (1981) Developmental changes in cognitive maps of a familiar neighbourhood, *Child Development*, Vol. 52, pp. 341-8.
Ashby, R. and Lee, P. (1987) Children's concepts of empathy and understanding in history, in C. Portal (ed.) *The History Curriculum for Teachers*, Falmer Press, Lewes.
Assessment of Performance Unit (1980) *Mathematical Development: Primary Survey Report No. 1*, HMSO, London.
Assessment of Performance Unit (1981a) *Language Performance in Schools: Primary Survey Report No. 1*, HMSO, London.
Assessment of Performance Unit (1981b) *Science in Schools: Age 11 Report No. 1*, HMSO, London.
Association for Science Education (1981) *Policy Statement*, Hatfield, Herts.
Ausubel, D. (1968) *Educational Psychology: A Cognitive View*, Holt, Rinehart & Winston, New York, NY.
Bailey, P. (1986) A geographer's view: contribution of geography to the school curriculum, *Geography*, Vol. 71, no. 3, pp. 193-205.
Bale, J. (1987) *Geography in the Primary School*, Routledge & Kegan Paul, London.
Barnes, R. (1987) *Teaching Art to Young Children 4-9*, Allen & Unwin, London.
Barnett, M. A. and Thompson, S. (1985) The role of perspective taking and empathy in children's Machiavellianism, prosocial behavior, and motive for helping, *Journal of Genetic Psychology*, Vol. 146, no. 3, pp. 295-306.

Baroody, A. J. and Price, J. (1983) The development of the number-word sequence in the counting of three-year olds, *Journal for Research in Mathematics Education*, Vol. 14, no. 5, pp. 361-8.

Barrs, M. (1983) Born again teachers, *The Times Educational Supplement*, 24 June, p. 23.

Bartz, B. S. (1970) Maps in the classroom, *Journal of Geography*, Vol. 69, pp. 18-24.

Beard, R. M. (1963) The order of concept development studies in two fields, *Educational Review*, Vol. 15, no. 3, pp. 228-37.

Bennett, N., Desforges, C., Cockburn, A. and Wilkinson, B. (1984) *The Quality of Pupil Learning Experiences*, Lawrence Erlbaum Associates, London.

Bennetts, T. (1985) Geography from 5 to 16: a view from the Inspectorate, *Geography*, Vol. 70, no. 4, pp. 299-314.

Bergamini, D. (1969) *Mathematics*, Time-Life International (Nederland).

Beveridge, W. I. B. (1980) *Seeds of Discovery*, Heinemann Educational, London.

Bissex, G. L. (1980) *GNYS AT WRK: A Child Learns to Write and Read*, Harvard University Press, Cambridge, Mass.

Blades, M. and Spencer, C. (1987) The use of maps by 4-6 year old children in a large-scale maze, *British Journal of Developmental Psychology*, Vol. 5, pp. 19-24.

Blyth, J. (1988) *History 5 to 9*, Hodder & Stoughton, Sevenoaks.

Boardman, D. (1983) *Graphicacy and Geography Teaching*, Croom Helm, London.

Boardman, D. (1985) Spatial concept development and primary school map work, in D. Boardman (ed.) *New Directions in Geographical Education*, Falmer Press, Lewes.

Bolton, W. F. (ed.) (1975) *History of Literature in the English Language Vol. 10: The English Language*, Sphere Books, London.

Bone, V. (1984) An investigation into children's understanding of historical sequence, unpublished dissertation, diploma in the education of children up to the age of 13 years, University of London.

Booth, M. (1978) Children's inductive historical thought, *Teaching History*, Vol. 21, pp. 3-8.

Borke, H. (1971) Interpersonal perception of young children; egocentrism or empathy?, *Developmental Psychology*, Vol. 5, pp. 263-9.

Bradley, N. (1947) The growth of knowledge of time in children of school age, *British Journal of Psychology*, Vol. 38, pp. 67-78.

Brainerd, C. J. (1979) Concept learning and developmental stage, in H. J. Klausmeier *et al.* (eds.) *Cognitive Learning and Development: Piagetian and Informational-Processing Perspective*, Ballinger, Cambridge, Mass.

Brainerd, C. J. (1983) Modifiability of cognitive development, in S. Meadows (ed.) op. cit.

Brittain, W. L. (1969) Some exploratory studies of the art of pre-school children, *Studies in Art Education*, Vol. 10, no. 3, pp. 14-24.

Britton, J. N. (1984) Viewpoints: the distinction between participant and spectator role language in research and practice, *Research in the Teaching of English*, Vol. 18, no. 3, pp. 320-31.

Britton, J. N., Burgess, T., Martin, N., McLeod, A. and Rosen, H. (1975) *The Development of Writing Abilities*, Macmillan Education, London.

Broster, J. (1979) Children's own perceptions of story-writing, *Language Matters*,

Vol. 1, no. 1, pp. 6–11.
Broudy, H. S. (1966) The case for art education, in E. W. Eisner and D. W. Ecker (eds.) *Readings in Art Education*, Blaisdell, Waltham, Mass.
Brown, A. L. and DeLoache, J. S. (1983) Metacognitive skills, in M. Donaldson (ed.) *Early Childhood Development and Education*, Blackwell, Oxford.
Brown, G. and Desforges, C. (1979) *Piaget's Theory: A Psychological Critique*, Routledge & Kegan Paul, London.
Brown, M. (1979) Cognitive development and the learning of mathematics, in A. Floyd (ed.) *Cognitive Development in the School Years*, Croom Helm, London.
Bruner, J. S. (1983) *Child's Talk; Learning to Use Language*, Oxford University Press.
Bullock Report (1975) *A Language for Life*, HMSO, London.
Buxton, L. (1984) *Mathematics for Everyman*, Dent, London.
Canaday, J. (1980) *What is Art?*, Hutchinson, London.
Carey, S. (1985) *Conceptual Change in Childhood*, MIT Press, Cambridge, Mass.
Carlin, E. (1986) Writing development – theory and practice, in A. Wilkinson (ed.) *The Writing of Writing*, Open University Press, Milton Keynes.
Carothers, T. and Gardner, H. (1979) When children's drawings become art: the emergence of aesthetic production and perception, *Developmental Psychology*, Vol. 15, no. 5, pp. 570–80.
Carr, E. J. (1964) *What is History?*, Penguin Books, Harmondsworth.
Catling, S. J. (1981) Using maps and aerial photographs, in D. Mills (ed.) op. cit.
Century Geographical Readers: Reader VI, The British Colonies and Dependencies (1890) Blackie, London.
Chalmers, A. F. (1976) *What Is This Thing Called Science?*, Open University Press, Milton Keynes.
Chambers, D. W. (1983) Stereotypic images of the scientists: the Draw-a-Scientist Test, *Science Education*, Vol. 67, no. 2, pp. 255–65.
Chandler, M. J. and Greenspan, S. (1972) Ersatz egocentrism: a reply to H. Borke, *Developmental Psychology*, Vol. 7, no. 2, pp. 104–6.
Clay, M. M. (1975) *What Did I Write'*, Heinemann Educational, London.
Clay, M. M. (1981) *The Early Detection of Reading Difficulties*, Heinemann Educational, London.
Clements, M. A. (1980) Analysing children's errors on written mathematical tasks, *Educational Studies in Mathematics*, Vol. 11, pp. 1–21.
Cobb, P. (1985) Two children's anticipations, beliefs and motivations, *Educational Studies in Mathematics*, Vol. 16, pp. 111–26.
Cobb, P. (1987) An investigation of young children's academic arithmetic contexts, *Educational Studies in Mathematics*, Vol. 18, pp. 109–24.
Cockburn, J. (1981) Moral issues in history: the psychology of the matter, *Teaching History*, Vol. 30, pp. 15–17.
Cockcroft Report (1982) *Mathematics Counts*, HMSO, London.
Collis, K. F. (1980) School mathematics and stages of development, in S. Mogdil and C. Mogdil (eds.) *Towards a Theory of Psychological Development*, NFER Publishing, Slough.
Cook, C. J. and Dossey, J. A. (1982) Basic fact thinking strategies for multiplication revisited, *Journal for Research in Mathematics Education*, Vol. 13, no. 3, pp. 163–71.
Copple, C., Sigel, I. E. and Saunders, R. (1979) *Educating the Young Thinker*, Van

Nostrand, New York, NY.
Cordeiro, P. (1988) Children's punctuation: an analysis of errors in period placement, *Research in the Teaching of English*, Vol. 22, no. 1, pp. 62–74.
Costanzo, P. R., Coie, J. D., Grumet, J. F. and Farnill, D. (1973) A reexamination of the effects of intent and consequence on children's moral judgements, *Child Development*, Vol. 44, pp. 154–61.
Cowie, H. (1984) The value of imaginative writing, in H. Cowie (ed.) *The Development of Children's Imaginative Writing*, Croom Helm, London.
Creighton-Buck, R. (1978) New mathematics, in *Colliers Encyclopedia*, Vol. 15, Macmillan Education, New York, NY.
Damon, W. (1977) *The Social World of the Child*, Jossey-Bass, San Francisco, Calif.
Davey, A. (1983) *Learning to be Prejudiced*, Edward Arnold, London.
Dearden, R. (1980) The Primary Survey: an assessment, in C. Richards (ed.) *Primary Education: Issues for the Eighties*, A. & C. Black, London.
Denscombe, M. (1983) Ethnic group and friendship choice in the primary school, *Educational Research*, Vol. 25, no. 3, pp. 184–90.
Dentici, O. A., Grossi, M. G., Borghi, L., De Ambrosis, A. and Massara, C. I. (1984) Understanding floating: a study of children aged between six and eight years, *European Journal of Science Education*, Vol. 6, no. 3, pp. 235–43.
Denvir, B. and Brown, M. (1986a) Understanding of number concepts in low attaining 7–9 year olds: Part I. Development of descriptive framework and diagnostic instrument, *Educational Studies in Mathematics*, Vol. 17, pp. 15–36.
Denvir, B. and Brown, M. (1986b) Understanding of number concepts in low attaining 7–9 year olds: Part II. The teaching studies, *Educational Studies in Mathematics*, Vol. 17, pp. 143–64.
Denvir, B. and Brown, M. (1987) The feasibility of class administered diagnostic assessment in primary mathematics, *Educational Research*, Vol. 29, no. 2, pp. 95–107.
DES (1978a) *Mathematics 5–11: A Handbook of Suggestions*, HMSO, London.
DES (1978b) *Primary Education in England*, HMSO, London.
DES (1982) *Education 5 to 9: An Illustrative Survey of 80 First Schools in England*, HMSO, London.
DES (1984) *English from 5 to 16. Curriculum Matters 1*, HMSO, London.
DES (1985a) *General Certificate of Secondary Education. The National Criteria: Geography*, HMSO, London.
DES (1985b) *History in the Primary and Secondary Years*, HMSO, London.
DES (1986a) *Mathematics from 5 to 16. Curriculum Matters 3*, HMSO, London.
DES (1986b) *Geography from 5 to 16. Curriculum Matters 7*, HMSO, London.
DES (1989) *Science in the National Curriculum*, HMSO, London.
de Villiers, P. A. and de Villiers, J. G. (1979) *Early Language*, Fontana/Open Books, London.
Dickinson, A. K. and Lee, P. J. (1978) Understanding and research in history, in A. K. Dickinson and P. J. Lee (eds.) op. cit.
Dickinson, A. K. and Lee, P. J. (eds.) (1978) *History Teaching and Historical Understanding*, Heinemann, London.
Dickson, L., Brown, B. and Gibson, O. (1984) *Children Learning Mathematics*, Holt, Rinehart & Winston, Eastbourne.
Dieudonné, J. (1978) Mathematics, in *Colliers Encyclopedia*, Vol. 15, Macmillan

Education, New York, NY.

Dixon, J. and Stratta, L. (1986) Argument and the teaching of English: a critical analysis, in A. Wilkinson (ed.) *The Writing of Writing*, Open University Press, Milton Keynes.

Dolgin, K. G. and Behrend, D. A. (1984) Children's knowledge about animates and inanimates, *Child Development*, Vol. 55, pp. 1646-50.

Donaldson, M. (1978) *Children's Minds*, Fontana, London.

D'Onofrio, A. and Nodine, C. F. (1981) Children's responses to paintings, *Studies in Art Education*, Vol. 23, no. 1, pp. 14-23.

Driver, R. (1981) Pupils' alternative frameworks in science, *European Journal of Science Education*, Vol. 3, no. 1, pp. 93-101.

Driver, R. (1983) *The Pupil as Scientist?*, Open University Press, Milton Keynes.

Duncum, P. (1988) To copy or not to copy: a review, *Studies in Art Education*, Vol. 29, no. 4, pp. 203-20.

Dunn, J. R. (1984) A study of developmental stages in children's understanding of maps, unpublished dissertation, diploma in education with special reference to children up to the age of 13 years, University of London.

Duska, R. and Whelan, M. (1977) *Moral Development: A Guide to Piaget and Kohlberg*, Gill & Macmillan, Dublin.

Dyson, A. (ed.) (1983a) *Art Education: Heritage and Prospect*, Bedford Way Papers 14, Institute of Education, University of London (distributed by TINGA TINGA -a branch of Heinemann Educational).

Dyson, A. H. (1983b) The role of oral language in early writing processes, *Research in the Teaching of English*, Vol. 17, no. 1, pp. 1-29.

Eisner, A. (1974) Examining some myths in art education, *Studies in Art Education*, Vol. 15, no. 3, pp. 7-16.

Eng, H. (1931) *The Psychology of Children's Drawings*, Routledge & Kegan Paul, London.

Enright, R. D. (1982) A classroom discipline model for promoting social cognitive development in early childhood, *Journal of Moral Education*, Vol. 11, no. 1, pp. 47-60.

Entwistle, N. (1987) *Understanding Classroom Learning*, Hodder and Stoughton, Sevenoaks.

Feldman, D. H. (1983) Developmental psychology and art education, *Art Education*, Vol. 36, no. 2, pp. 19-21.

Feldman, E. B. (1970) *Becoming Human through Art: Aesthetic Experience in the School*, Prentice-Hall, Englewood Cliffs, NJ.

Ferreiro, E. (1980) The relationship between oral and written language: the children's viewpoints, paper given at the Preconvention Institute, International Reading Association, St Louis, Mo., 6 May, in C. Read (1986) op. cit.

Flavell, J. H. (1979) Metacognition and cognitive mastery, *American Psychologist*, Vol. 34, no. 10, pp. 966-9.

Forrest, M. S. (1983) The teacher as researcher – the use of historical artefacts in the primary school, unpublished MEd dissertation, University of Bath, in J. Blyth (1988) op. cit.

Freudenthal, H. (1972) Recent tendencies in the teaching of mathematics, in W. W. Lamon (ed.) *Learning and the Nature of Mathematics*, Science Research Associates, Chicago, Ill.

Froming, W. J., Allen, L. and Jensen, R. (1985) Altruism, role-taking, and self-awareness: the acquisition of norms governing altruistic behavior, *Child Development*, Vol. 56, pp. 1223-8.

Gaitskell, C. D., Horwitz, A. and Day, M. (1982) *Children and their Art*, Harcourt Brace Jovanovich, New York, NY.

Gallagher, J. J. (1987) Summary of research in science education, 1985, *Science Education*, Vol. 71, no. 3, pp. 271-457.

Galton, M., Simon, B. and Croll, P. (1980) *Inside the Primary School*, Routledge & Kegan Paul, London.

Gardner, H. and Gardner, J. (1970) Developmental trends in sensitivity to painting style and subject matter, *Studies in Art Education*, Vol. 12, no. 1, pp. 11-16.

Garlick, A. H. (1901) *A New Manual of Method*, Longmans, Green & Co., London.

Garofalo, J. and Lester, F. K. (1985) Metacognition, cognitive monitoring and mathematical performance, *Journal for Research in Mathematics Education*, Vol. 16, no. 3, pp. 163-76.

Gelman, R. (1977) Counting in the preschooler: what does and does not develop, in R. S. Siegler (ed.) *Children's Thinking: What Develops?*, Lawrence Erlbaum Associates, Hillsdale, NJ.

Gelman, R. and Gallistel, C. R. (1978) *The Child's Understanding of Number*, Harvard University Press, Cambridge, Mass.

Gentry, J. R. (1982) An analysis of developmental spelling in GYNS AT WRK, *The Reading Teacher*, Vol. 35, pp. 192-200.

Gergen, K. J. and Gergen, M. M. (1981) *Social Psychology*, Harcourt Brace Jovanovich, New York, NY.

Gilbert, J. K. and Watts, D. M. (1983) Concepts, misconceptions and alternative conceptions: changing perspectives in science education, *Studies in Science Education*, Vol. 10, pp. 61-98.

Ginsburg, H. (ed.) (1983) *The Development of Mathematical Thinking*, Academic Press, Orlando, Fla.

Ginsburg, H. P. (1985) Piaget and education, in N. Entwhistle (ed.) *New Directions in Educational Psychology 1: Learning and Teaching*, Falmer Press, Lewes.

Gonner, E. C. K. (1903) Geography, in P. A. Barnett (ed.) *Teaching and Organisation with Special Reference to Secondary Schools*, Longmans, Green and Co., London.

Goodnow, J. (1977) *Children's Drawings*, Fontana/Open Books, London.

Graham, D. (1972) *Moral Learning and Development*, Harper & Row, London.

Graham, D. (1976) Moral development: the cognitive developmental approach, in D. S. Varma (ed.) *Piaget, Psychology and Education*, Hodder & Stoughton, Sevenoaks.

Graves, D. H. (1983) *Writing: Teachers and Children at Work*, Heinemann Educational, London.

Graves, D. H. (1984) Patterns of control of the writing process, in H. Cowie (ed.) *The Development of Children's Imaginative Writing*, Croom Helm, London.

Graves, N. (1980) *Geography in Education*, Heinemann Educational, London.

Greene, J. (1975) *Thinking and Language*, Methuen, London.

Gruber, H. E. and Vonèche, J. J. (eds.) (1977) *The Essential Piaget*, Basic Books, New York, NY.

Gunning, S., Gunning, D. and Wilson, J. (1981) *Topic Teaching in the Primary School*, Croom Helm, London.

Halford, G. S., Brown, C. A. and Thompson, R. McL. (1986) Children's concepts of volume and flotation, *Developmental Psychology*, Vol. 22, no. 2, pp. 218-22.

Hallam, R. N. (1967) Logical thinking in history, *Educational Review*, Vol. 19, no. 2, pp. 183-202.

Hallam, R. N. (1978) An approach to learning history in primary schools, *Teaching History*, Vol. 21, pp. 9-14.

Hallam, R. N. (1979) Attempting to improve logical thinking in school history, *Research in Education*, Vol. 21, pp. 1-23.

Harlen, W. (1982) Matching, in C. Richards (ed.) *New Directions in Primary Education*, Falmer Press, Lewes.

Harlen, W. (ed.) (1985) *Primary Science ... Taking the Plunge*, Heinemann Educational, London.

Harlen, W. and Symington, D. (1985) Helping children to observe, in W. Harlen (ed.) op. cit.

Harpin, W. (1976) *The Second R: Writing Development in the Junior School*, Allen & Unwin, London.

Harré, R. (1983) *Great Scientific Experiments*, Oxford University Press.

Hawney, W. (1763) *The Complete Measurer: or, the Whole Art of Measuring*, Knapton, London.

Haysom, A. E. (1970) A study of children's responses to book illustrations, unpublished dissertation, diploma in primary school education, University of London.

Heege, H. T. (1985) The acquisition of basic multiplication skills, *Educational Studies in Mathematics*, Vol. 16, pp. 375-88.

Herman, J. F., Blomquist, S. L. and Klein, C. A. (1987) Children's and adults' cognitive maps of very large unfamiliar environments, *British Journal of Developmental Psychology*, Vol. 5, pp. 61-72.

Hersh, R. H., Miller, J. P. and Fielding, G. D. (1980) *Models of Moral Education: An Appraisal*, Longman, New York, NY.

Hersh, R. H., Paolitto, D. P. and Reimer, J. (1979) *Promoting Moral Growth*, Longman, New York, NY.

Hiebert, J. and Carpenter, T. P. (1982) Piagetian tests as readiness measures in mathematics instruction: a critical review, *Journal for Research in Mathematics Education*, Vol. 13, no. 3, pp. 329-46.

Hirst, P. H. (1974) *Moral Education in a Secular Society*, University of London Press.

Hodson, D. (1985) Philosophy of science, science and science education, *Studies in Science Education*, Vol. 12, p. 25-57.

Hodson, D. (1986a) Rethinking the role and status of observation in science education, *Journal of Curriculum Studies*, Vol. 18, no. 4, pp. 381-96.

Hodson, D. (1986b) The nature of scientific observation, *School Science Review*, Vol. 68, no. 242, pp. 17-29.

Hoffman, M. L. (1976) Empathy, role-taking and development of altruistic motives, in T. Lickona (ed.) *Moral Development and Behavior*, Holt, Rinehart & Winston, New York, NY.

Howard, M. (1981) Historians may claim to teach lessons – history as such does not, *The Listener*, 12 March, pp. 333-6.

Hughes, E. R. (1979) *Conceptual Powers of Children: An Approach through Mathematics and Science*, Macmillan Education, Basingstoke.

Hughes, M. (1975) Egocentrism in pre-school children, unpublished Phd dissertation, University of Edinburgh, cited in M. Donaldson (1978). op. cit.

Hughes, M. (1981) Can preschool children add and subtract?, *Educational Psychology*, Vol. 3, pp. 207-19.

Hughes, M. (1986) *Children and Number*, Blackwell, Oxford.

ILEA (1979) *Checkpoint Assessment Cards*, ILEA, London.

ILEA (1980) *History in the Primary School*, ILEA, London.

ILEA (1981) *The Study of Places in the Primary School*, ILEA, London.

Ingle, R. and Jennings, A. (1981) *Science in Schools. Which Way Now?*, Heinemann, London.

Inhelder, B. and Piaget, J. (1958) *The Growth of Logical Thinking from Childhood to Adolescence*, Routledge & Kegan Paul, London.

Ives, S. W. (1984) The development of expressivity in drawing, *British Journal of Educational Psychology*, Vol. 54, pp. 152-9.

Jahoda, G. (1963) Children's concepts of time and history, *Educational Review*, Vol. 15, no. 2, pp. 87-104.

Jahoda, G. (1984) The development of thinking about socio-economic systems, in H. Tajfel (ed.) *The Social Dimension*, Vol. 1, Cambridge University Press.

Johnson, N. R. (1982) Children's meanings about art, *Studies in Art Education*, Vol. 23, no. 3, pp. 61-7.

Johnston, R. J. (1985a) Geography in the 1980's, in A. Kent (ed.) *Perspectives on a Changing Geography*, Geographical Association, Sheffield.

Johnston, R. J. (1985b) Introduction: exploring the future of geography, in R. J. Johnston (ed.) *Exploring the Future of Geography*, Methuen, London.

Jurd, M. F. (1978) An empirical study of operational thinking in history-type material, in J. A. Keats *et al.* (eds.) *Cognitive Development*, Wiley, Chichester.

Kellogg, R. (1969) *Analyzing Children's Art*, National Books Press, Palo Alto, Calif.

Kelly, G. A. (1955) *A Theory of Personality: The Psychology of Personal Constructs*, Norton, New York, NY.

Kelvin, P. (1969) *The Bases of Social Behaviour*, Holt, Rinehart & Winston, London.

Kingman, J. F. C. (1986) *Report of the Committee of Inquiry into the Teaching of English*, HMSO, London.

Kohlberg, L. (1976) Moral stages and moralization: the cognitive developmental approach, in T. Lickona (ed.) *Moral Development and Behavior*, Holt, Rinehart & Winston, New York, NY.

Lancaster-Smith, G. E. (1985) A study of the influence of match in mathematics teaching in the middle school, unpublished MA dissertation, University of Surrey.

Landon, J. (1902) *The Principles and Practice of Teaching and Class Management*, Holden, London.

Langer, S. K. (1963) *Philosophy in a New Key*, Harvard University Press, Cambridge, Mass.

Langer, S. K. (1970) Expressiveness, in G. Pappas (ed.) *Conceptions in Art Education*, Macmillan, New York, NY.

Lawson, A. E., Costenson, K. and Cisneros, R. (1986) A summary of research in science education, 1984, *Science Education*, Vol. 70, no. 3, pp. 189-354.

Leon, M. (1982) Rules in children's moral judgments: integration of intent, damage, and rationale information, *Developmental Psychology*, Vol. 18, no. 6, pp.

835-42.

Levstik, L. S. and Pappas, C. C. (1987) Exploring the development of historical understanding, *Journal of Research and Development in Education*, Vol. 21, no. 1, pp. 1-15.

Lewthwaite, G. R. (1986) Geography, in *Encyclopedia Americana*, Vol. 12, pp. 437-43, Grolier, Danbury, Mass.

Light, P. (1983) The use of communication tasks to investigate depiction of spatial relationships in young children's drawings, in D. Rogers and J. A. Sloboda (eds.) op. cit.

Looft, W. R. (1974) Animistic thought in children: understanding of 'living' across its associated attributes, *Journal of Genetic Psychology*, Vol. 124, pp. 235-40.

Lowenfeld, V. and Brittain, W. (1987) *Creative and Mental Growth*, Macmillan, New York, NY.

Luquet, G. H. (1927) *Le Dessin Enfantin*, Alcan, New York, NY.

Machotka, P. (1966) Aesthetic criteria in childhood: justification of preference, *Child Development*, Vol. 37, pp. 877-85.

Mann, B. S. and Lehman, L. B. (1976) Transparencies in children's human figure drawing, a developmental approach, *Studies in Art Education*, Vol. 18, no. 1, pp. 41-7.

Martin, N. (1983) *Mostly About Writing*, Heinemann Educational, London.

Marwick, A. (1970) *The Nature of History*, Macmillan, London.

Matthews, M. H. (1984) Cognitive mapping abilities of young boys and girls, *Geography*, Vol. 69, no. 4, 327-36.

Matthews, M. H. (1985) Environmental capability of the very young: some implications for environmental education in primary schools, *Educational Review*, Vol. 37, no. 3, pp. 227-39.

McClelland, J. A. G. (1982a) Ausubel's theory of learning and its application to introductory science. Part I: Ausubel's theory of learning, *School Science Review*, Vol. 64, no. 226, pp. 157-61.

McClelland, J. A. G. (1982b) Ausubel's theory of learning and its application to introductory science. Part II: Primary science: an Ausubelian view, *School Science Review*, Vol. 64, no. 227, pp. 353-7.

McPhail, P., Middleton, D. and Ingram, D. (1978) *Schools Council Moral Education 8-13 Project: Startline - Moral Education in the Middle Years*, Longman, London.

Meadows, S. (ed.) (1983) *Developing Thinking: Approaches to Children's Cognitive Development*, Methuen, London.

Meadows, S. (1983) An assessment of Piaget's theory of cognitive development in S. Meadows (ed.) op. cit.

Meadows, S. and Cashdan, A. (1988) *Helping Children Learn*, David Fulton, London.

Medawar, P. B. (1967) *The Art of the Soluble*, Methuen, London.

Milburn, D. (1972) Children's vocabulary, in N. Graves (ed.) *New Movements in the Study and Teaching of Geography*, Temple Smith, London.

Mills, D. (ed.) (1981) *Geographical Work in Primary and Middle Schools*, Geographical Association, Sheffield.

Milner, D. (1984) The development of ethnic atttudes, in H. Tajfel (ed.) *The Social Dimension*, Vol. 1, Cambridge University Press.

Mogdil, S. and Mogdil, C. (1976) *Piagetian Research: Compilation and*

Commentary, NFER, Slough.

Morgan, W. and Storm, M. (1989) Uncharted territory, *The Times Educational Supplement*, 24 March, p. 29.

Muir, S. H. (1985) Understanding and improving students' map reading skills, *Elementary School Journal*, Vol. 86, no. 2, pp. 207-16.

Muir, S. P. and Frazee, B. (1986) A developmental perspective, *Social Education*, Vol. 50, no. 3, pp. 199-203.

Newkirk, T. (1987) The non-narrative writing of young children, *Research in the Teaching of English*, Vol. 21, no. 2, pp. 121-44.

Newman, M. A. (1977) An analysis of sixth-grade pupils' errors on written mathematical tasks, cited in M. A. Clements (1980) op. cit.

Nussbaum, J. (1979) Children's conceptions of the earth as a cosmic body: a cross age study, *Science Education*, Vol. 63, no. 1, pp. 83-93.

Nussbaum, J. and Novak, J. D. (1976) An assessment of children's concepts of the earth utilizing structured interviews, *Science Education*, Vol. 60, no. 4, pp. 535-50.

Oakden, E. C. and Sturt, M. (1922) The development of the knowledge of time in children, *British Journal of Psychology*, Vol. 12, pp. 309-36.

Ormell, C. (1980) Mathematics, in R. Straughan and J. Wrigley (eds.) *Values and Evaluation in Education*, Paul Chapman, London.

Osborne, R. (1983) Towards modifying children's ideas about electric current, *Research in Science and Technological Education*, Vol. 1, no. 1, pp. 73-82.

Osborne, R. (1985) Children's own concepts, in W. Harlen (ed.) op. cit.

Osborne, R. J., Bell, B. F. and Gilbert, J. K. (1983) Science teaching and children's views of the world, *European Journal of Science Education*, Vol. 5, no. 1, pp. 1-14.

Osborne, R. and Freyberg, P. (1985) *Learning in Science. The Implications of Children's Science*, Heinemann, Aukland.

Osborne, R. and Wittrock, M. C. (1983) Learning science: a generative process, *Science Education*, Vol. 67, no. 4, pp. 489-508.

Paramour, S. and Wilkinson, A. (1985) The disruption of the probable: narrative writing in children seven to thirteen, *Language Arts*, Vol. 62, no. 4, pp. 391-403.

Parsons, M., Johnston, M. and Durham, R. (1978) Stages in children's aesthetic responses, *Journal of Aesthetic Education*, Vol. 12, no. 1, pp. 83-104.

Partington, G. (1980) Teaching time, *Teaching History*, Vol. 27, pp. 31-4.

Patriarca, L. A. and Alleman, J. (1987) Studying time: a cognitive approach, *Social Education*, Vol. 51, no. 4, pp. 273-7.

Peel, E. A. (1967) Some problems in the psychology of history teaching, in W.H. Burston and D. Thompson (eds.) *Studies in the Nature and Teaching of History*, Routledge & Kegan Paul, London.

Peel, E. A. (1971) *The Nature of Adolescent Judgment*, Staples Press, London.

Peisach, E. and Hardeman, M. (1983) Moral reasoning in early childhood: lying and stealing, *Journal of Genetic Psychology*, Vol. 42, pp. 117-28.

Perera, K. (1984) *Children's Writing and Reading: Analysing Classroom Language*, Blackwell, Oxford.

Peters, R. S. (1981) *Moral Development and Moral Education*, Allen & Unwin, London.

Peterson, C. D., Peterson, J. L. and Seeto, D. (1983) Developmental changes in ideas about lying, *Child Development*, Vol. 54, pp. 1529-35.

Phillips, J. L. (1969) *The Origins of Intellect: Piaget's Theory*, W. H. Freeman, San Francisco, Calif.

Piaget, J. (1929) *The Child's Conception of the World*, Harcourt Brace Jovanovich, New York, NY.

Piaget, J. (1932) *The Moral Judgment of the Child*, Routledge & Kegan Paul, London.

Piaget, J. (1952) *The Child's Conception of Number*, Routledge & Kegan Paul, London.

Piaget, J. (1967) *Six Psychological Studies*, University of London Press.

Piaget, J. (1977) Science of education and the psychology of the child, in H. E. Gruber and J. J. Vonèche (eds.) op. cit.

Piaget, J. and Inhelder, B. (1956) *The Child's Conception of Space*, Routledge & Kegan Paul, London.

Piaget, J. and Inhelder, B. (1969) *The Psychology of the Child*, Routledge & Kegan Paul, London.

Piaget, J. and Inhelder, B. (1970) *The Child's Conception of Movement and Speed*, Routledge & Kegan Paul, London.

Plumb, J. H. (1973) *The Death of the Past*, Penguin Books, Harmondsworth.

Popper, K. R. (1972) *Objective Knowledge. An Evolutionary Approach*, Clarendon Press, Oxford.

Portal, C. (1987) Empathy as an objective for history teaching, in C. Portal (ed.) *The History Curriculum for Teachers*, Falmer Press, Lewes.

Presson, C. C. (1987) The development of landmarks in spatial memory: the role of differential experience, *Journal of Experimental Child Psychology*, Vol. 44, pp. 317-34.

Proctor, N. (1987) History, geography and humanities: a geographer's interpretation, *Teaching History*, Vol. 48, pp. 8-12.

Quam, L. O. and Freeman, T. W. (1980) Geography, in W. D. Halsey (ed.) *Collier's Encyclopedia*, Vol. 10, Macmillan Educational, New York, NY.

Radebaugh, M. R. (1985) Children's perceptions of their spelling strategies, *The Reading Teacher*, Vol. 38, pp. 532-6.

Read, C. (1986) *Children's Creative Spelling*, Routledge & Kegan Paul, London.

Reid, L. A. (1983) Art teaching and conceptual understanding of art, in A. Dyson (ed.) (1983a) op. cit.

Reimer, B. (1970) *A Philosophy of Music Education*, Prentice-Hall, Englewood Cliffs, NJ.

Renfrow, M. J. (1983) Accurate drawing as a function of training of gifted children in copying and perception, *Education Research Quarterly*, Vol. 8, no. 3, pp. 27-31.

Rest, J. R. (1979) *Development in Judging Moral Issues*, University of Minnesota Press, Minneapolis, Minn.

Reynolds, R. E. and Wade, S. W. (1986) Thinking about thinking about thinking, *Harvard Educational Review*, Vol. 56, no. 3, p. 306-17.

Rhys, W. T. (1972) Geography and the adolescent, *Educational Review*, Vol. 24, no. 3, pp. 183-96.

Robinson, E. (1983) Metacognitive development, in S. Meadows (ed.) op. cit.

Rogers, D. and Sloboda, J. A. (eds.) (1983) *The Acquisition of Symbolic Skills*, Plenum Press, New York, NY.

Rybash, J. M. (1980) How teachers help children resolve moral dilemmas, *Journal of Moral Education*, Vol. 10, no. 1, pp. 18-23.

Schirrmacher, R. (1980) Child art, in S. Modgil and C. Modgil (eds.) *Towards a Theory of Psychological Development*, NFER, Slough.

Schools Council Art Committee (1978) *Art 7-11*, Schools Council Occasional Bulletins from the Subject Committees, London.

Schug, M. C. (1987) Children's understanding of economics, *Elementary School Journal*, Vol. 87, no. 5, pp. 507-18.

Scott, L. (1972) Increasing mathematical learning through improving instruction, in W. E. Lamon (ed.) *Learning and the Nature of Mathematics*, Science Research Associates, Chicago, Ill.

Selman, R. L., Krupa, M. P., Stone, C. R. and Jacquette, D. S. (1982) Concrete operational thought and the emergence of the concepts of unseen force in children's theories of electromagnetism and gravity, *Science Education*, Vol. 66, no. 2, pp. 181-94.

Selman, R. L. and Lieberman, M. (1975) Moral education in the primary grades: an evaluation of a developmental curriculum, *Journal of Educational Psychology*, Vol. 67, no. 5, pp. 712-16.

Shemilt, D. J. (1978) Historical understanding at the upper secondary level, *Trends in Education*, spring, pp. 15-20.

Short, E. J. and Ryan, E. B. (1984) Metacognitive differences between skilled and less skilled readers; remediating deficiences through story grammar and attribution training, *Journal of Educational Psychology*, Vol. 76, no. 2, pp. 225-35.

Shymansky, J. A. and Kyle, W. C. (1986) A summary framework in science education, *Science Education*, Vol. 72, no. 3, pp. 249-403.

Slater, F. A. (1973) Content and concepts in geographical education, in D. S. Biddle and C. E. Deer (eds.) *Readings in Geographical Education*, Vol. II, Whitcombe and Tombs, Australia.

Smith, N. R. (1982) The visual arts in early childhood education: development and the creation of meaning, in B. Spodek (ed.) *Handbook of Research in Early Childhood Education*, Free Press, Glencoe, Ill.

Smith, N. R. (1983) Drawing conclusions: do children draw from observation?, *Art Education*, Vol. 36, no. 5, pp. 22-6.

Smith, R. A. (1982) Arts education, aesthetic value, and policy, *Art Education*, Vol. 35, no. 4, pp. 24-6.

Sneider, C. and Pulos, S. (1983) Children's cosmographies: understanding the earth's shape and gravity, *Science Education*, Vol. 67, no. 2, pp. 205-21.

Southgate, V., Arnold, H. and Johnson, S. (1981) *Extending Beginning Reading*, Heinemann Educational, London.

Spencer, F. H. (1938) *An Inspector's Testament*, English Universities Press, London.

Steen, L. A. (ed.) (1978) *Mathematics Today: 12 Informal Essays*, Springer-Verlag, New York, NY.

Steinberg, R. M. (1985) Instruction on derived facts strategies in addition and subtraction, *Journal for Research in Mathematics Education*, Vol. 6, no. 5, pp. 337-55.

Stepans, J. and Kuehn, C. (1985) What research says: children's conceptions of weather, *Science and Children*, Vol. 23, no. 1, pp. 44-7.

Stephan, W. G. and Rosenfield, D. (1978) Effects of desegregation on racial attitudes, *Journal of Personality and Social Psychology*, Vol. 36, no. 8, pp. 795-804.

Sternberg, R. J. (1987) A day at developmental downs, *International Journal of Psychology*, Vol. 22, no. 5-6, pp. 507-30.

Stevens, O. (1982) *Children Talking Politics*, Martin Robertson, Oxford.

Straughan, R. (1982) *Can We Teach Children To Be Good?*, Allen & Unwin, London.

Stubbs, M. (1980) *Language and Literacy: The Sociolinguistics of Reading and Writing*, Routledge & Kegan Paul, London.

Summers, M. K. (1982) Science education and meaningful learning, *School Science Review*, Vol. 64, no. 227, pp. 361-6.

Swift, R. and Jackson, M. (1987) History in the primary school, *Teaching History*, Vol. 49, pp. 29-35.

Tajfel, H. (1981) *Human Groups and Social Categories: Studies in Social Psychology*, Cambridge University Press.

Tamburrini, J., Willig, J. and Butler, C. (1984) Children's conceptions of writing, in H. Cowie (ed.) op. cit.

Taunton, M. (1982) Aesthetic responses of young children to the visual arts: a review of the literature, *Journal of Aesthetic Education*, Vol. 16, no. 3, pp. 93-109.

Temple, C. A., Nathear, R. G., Burrŝs, N. A. and Temple, F. (1988) *The Beginnings of Writing*, Allyn & Bacon, Boston, Mass.

Thompson, A. G. (1984) The relationship of teachers' conceptions of mathematics and mathematics teaching to instructional practice, *Educational Studies in Mathematics*, Vol. 15, pp. 105-25.

Tomlinson, P. (1981) *Understanding Teaching: Interactive Educational Psychology*, McGraw-Hill, Maidenhead.

Travers, R. M. W. (1983) *Essentials of Learning*, Macmillan, New York, NY.

Trowbridge, J. E. and Mintzes, J. J. (1985) Students' alternative conceptions of animals and animal classification, *School Science and Mathematics*, Vol. 85, no. 4, pp. 304-16.

Truscoe, E. S. (1983) Teachers' perceptions of science in the middle school, unpublished MA (education: curriculum studies: primary) dissertation, University of London.

Urberg, K. A. and Docherty, E. M. (1976) Development of role-taking skills in young children, *Developmental Psychology*, Vol. 12, no. 3, pp. 198-203.

Vikainen, I. (1965) The development of time concepts and time schemas, Institute of Education, University of Turka, cited in J. G. Wallace, *Concept Growth and the Education of the Child*, NFER, Slough.

Vygotsky, L. V. (1962) *Thought and Language*, MIT Press, Cambridge, Mass.

Wagman, H. G. (1975) The child's conception of area measure, in M. F. Rosskopf (ed.) *Children's Mathematical Concepts: Six Piagetian Studies in Mathematics Education*, Teachers' College Press, New York, NY.

Walford, R. (1986) Multi-cultural society, in D. Boardman (ed.) *Handbook for Geography Teachers*, Geographical Association, Sheffield.

Walshe, A. J. (1980) Teaching for appreciation in the visual arts: the case for aesthetic education, unpublished dissertation, MA (education: curriculum studies: primary education), University of London.

Welton, J. (1909) *Principles and Methods of Teaching*, University Tutorial Press,

London.

West, J. (1978) Young children's awareness of the past, *Trends in Education*, spring, pp. 8–15.

West, J. (1981) Primary school children's perception of authenticity and time in historical narrative pictures, *Teaching History*, Vol. 29, pp. 8–10.

West, J. (1982) Testing the use of written records in primary school, 1979–80, *Teaching History*, Vol. 32, pp. 32–5.

Wicker, A. W. (1969) Attitudes v. actions: the relationship of verbal and overt responses to attitude objects, *Journal of Social Issues*, Vol. 25, pp. 41–78.

Wickert, P. (1984) I imagine Russia as a fairly dismal place, *The Times Educational Supplement*, 13 March, p. 45.

Wilder, R. L. (1965) *Introduction to the Foundations of Mathematics*, Wiley, New York, NY.

Wilder, R. L. (1972) The nature of modern mathematics, in W. E. Lamon (ed.) *Learning and the Nature of Mathematics*, Science Research Associates, Chicago, Ill.

Wilkinson, A. (1986) *The Quality of Writing*, Open University Press, Milton Keynes.

Wilkinson, A., Barnsley, G., Hanna, P. and Swan, M. (1980) *Assessing Language Development*, Oxford University Press.

Wilson, J. (1973) *A Teacher's Guide to Moral Education*, Geoffrey Chapman, London.

Wilson, J. (1981) *Discipline and Moral Education: A Survey of Public Opinion*, NFER Nelson, London.

Wilson, J. (1983) *Education: An Introduction*, Martin Robertson, Oxford.

Wilson, J., Williams, N. and Sugarman, B. (1967) *Introduction to Moral Education*, Penguin Books, Harmondsworth.

Wolfinger, D. M. (1982) Effect of science teaching on the young child's concept of Piagetian physical causality: animism and dynamism, *Journal of Research in Science Teaching*, Vol. 19, no. 7, pp. 595–602.

Wood, D. M. (1967) Some concepts of social relationships in childhood and adolescence investigated by means of the analysis of the definitions, unpublished MEd thesis, University of Nottingham, in E. A. Peel op. cit.

Wragg, E. C. (1980) Learning to think, in J. Nichol (ed.) *Developments in History Teaching*, Exeter University School of Education, Perspectives 4.

Wragg, E. C. (ed.) (1984) *Classroom Teaching Skills*, Croom Helm, London.

Wright, D. S. (1971) *The Psychology of Moral Behaviour*, Penguin Books, Harmondsworth.

Zutell, J. (n.d.) *Word Sorting Activities*, unpublished course material, University of Ohio, Ohio.

NAME INDEX

Aldrich, V. G.   140, 160
Alleman, J.   102, 110
Allen, G. L.   121, 124
Allen, L.   173
Anderson, T.   155, 156-157
Anderson, J.   135
Anooshian, L. J.   xiii, 123, 125, 137
Arnold, H.   2, 16
Ashby, R.   115
Assessment of Performance Unit   28, 35, 68, 91
Association for Science Education   73
Ausubel, D.   18-9, 90, 94

Bailey, P.   118, 137
Bale, J.   138
Barnes, R.   160
Barnett, M. A.   172
Baroody, A. J.   55-6
Barrs, M.   42
Bartz, B. S.   125-6
Beard, R. M.   79
Behrend, D. A.   76-7
Bell, B. F.   17, 85, 89, 95
Bennett, N.   13-14, 16, 23, 28, 52, 60, 62
Bennetts, T   137
Bergamini, D   47
Beveridge, W. I. B.   72
Bissex, G. L.   37
Blades, M.   126
Blomquist, S. L.   124
Blyth, J.   102, 112, 115
Boardman, D.   135, 137
Bolton, W. F.   45
Bone, V.   102-3
Booth, M.   106
Borke, H.   171-2
Bradley, N.   103-4
Brainerd, C. J.   23
Brittain, W. L.   xiii, 145-6, 160
Britton, J. N.   26-7, 28, 29, 142
Broster, J.   29
Broudy, H. S.   142
Brown, A. L.   23
Brown, C. A.   81
Brown, G.   10, 23
Brown, M.   60, 65-6, 68
Bruner, J. S.   20
Butler, C.   2, 29, 42
Buxton, L.   xiii, 47-8, 67

Canaday, J.   158-9, 160
Carey, S.   77, 95
Carothers, T.   149-50
Carpenter, T. P.   60
Carr, E. J.   98, 115
Cashdan, A.   23
Catling, S. J.   135
Century Geographical Readers: Reader
     VI   116
Chalmers, A. F.   71, 95
Chambers, D. W.   74
Chandler, M. J.   171-2
Cisneros, R.   95
Clay, M. M.   21, 31-2
Clements, M. A.   61, 65
Cobb, P.   51-2
Cockburn, J.   108-9
Collis, K. F.   68
Cook, C. J.   64
Copple, C.   5, 144
Cordeiro, P.   38
Costanzo, P. R.   182
Costenson, K.   95
Cowie, H.   43
Creighton-Buck, R.   68
Croll, P.   23

Damon, W.   174-6, 182
Davey, A.   138
Day, M.   160
Dearden, R.   19
DeLoache, J. S.   23
Denscombe, M.   138
Dentici, D. A.   xiv, 87-9
Denvir, B.   60, 65-6
DES   xi, 13, 19, 26, 50, 69, 73, 97, 99, 107, 115, 119, 131, 135, 139
Desforges, C.   10, 23
de Villiers, P. A.   45
de Villiers, J. G.   45
Dickinson, A. K.   99, 108, 115
Dickson, L.   68
Dieudonné, J.   47-8
Dixon, J.   40
Docherty, E. M., 8, 172
Dolgin, K. G.   xiii, 76-7
Donaldson, M.   9, 23, 57-8
D'Onofrio, A.   152
Dossey, J. A.   64
Driver, R.   92, 95

Duncum, P.   154
Dunn, J. R.   134
Duska, R.   182
Dyson, A.   160
Dyson, A. H.   30-32, 44, 184

Eisner, A.   160
Eng, H.   145
Enright, R. D.   178-9, 182
Entwistle, N.   23

Feldman, D. H.   143
Feldman, E. B.   156
Ferreiro, E.   36
Fielding, G. D.   164, 180, 182
Flavell, J. H.   21
Forrest, M. S.   112
Frazee, B.   125
Freeman, T. W.   118
Freudenthal, H.   68
Freyberg, P.   95
Froming, W. J.   173

Gaitskell, C. D.   160
Gallagher, J. J.   95
Galton, M.   23
Gardner, H.   149-50, 152
Gardner, J.   152
Garlick, A. H.   96
Garofalo, J.   65
Gellistel, C. E.   54-5
Gelman, R.   54-7
Gentry, J. R.   xiii, 36-7
Gergen, K. J.   132, 138
Gergen, M. M.   132, 138
Gibson, O.   68
Gilbert, J. K.   17, 72, 85, 89, 95
Ginsburg, H.   16, 23, 68
Goodnow, J.   142
Gonner, E. C. K.   116
Graham, D.   182
Graves, D. H.   41-3
Graves, N.   137
Greene, J.   45
Greenspan, S.   171-2
Gruber, H. E.   23
Gunning, D.   112-14
Gunning, S.   112-14

Halford, G. S.   81
Hallam, R. N.   106-7, 111
Hardeman, M.   169
Harlen, W.   13, 91-3
Harpin, W.   26, 45
Harré, R.   72
Hawney, W.   46
Haysom, A. E.   153-4
Heege, H. T.   ix-x, 62-3
Herman, J. F.   124
Hersh, R. H.   16, 164, 180, 182
Hiebert, J.   60

Hirst, P. H.   162, 163, 164, 182
Hodson, D.   91, 93, 95
Hoffman, M. L.   172
Horwitz, A.   160
Howard, M.   99
Hughes, E. R.   59
Hughes, M. (mathematics)   23, 57-9, 68
Hughes, M. (psychology)   9

ILEA   99, 115, 135, 138
Ingle, R.   72
Ingram, D.   180, 182
Inhelder, B.   4-5, 8, 53, 79-81, 126-7, 137, 148
Ives, S. W.   xiii, 150-1

Jackson, M.   97
Jahoda, G.   ix, 3, 110, 127-9, 131
Jennings, A.   72
Jensen, R.   173
Johnson, N. R.   143-4
Johnson, S.   2, 16
Johnston, R. J.   137
Jurd, M. F.   106, 115

Kellogg, R.   145
Kelly, G. A.   6
Kelvin, P.   138
Klein, C. A.   124
Kohlberg, L.   166-7, 177, 181, 182
Kromer, M. K.   137
Kuehn, C.   137
Kyle, W. C.   95

Lancaster-Smith, G. E.   14-5, 17
Landon, J.   139
Langer, S. K.   140-1
Lawson, A. E.   95
Lee, P. J.   109, 115
Lehman, L. B.   147
Leon, M.   182
Lester, F. K.   65
Levstik, L. S.   100, 102
Lewthwaite, G. R.   117-8
Lieberman, M.   16-7, 177-85
Light, P.   148
Looft, W. R.   3, 75-6, 78
Lowenfeld, V.   xiii, 145-6, 160
Luquet, G. H.   148

Machotka, P.   152
Mann, B. S.   147
Martin, N.   45
Marwick, A.   96, 115
Matthews, M. H.   xiii, 121-2, 137
McClelland, J. A. G.   18, 90
McPhail, P.   180, 182
Meadows, S.   16, 23
Medawar, P. B.   95
Middleton, D.   180, 182
Milburn, D.   127, 130-1

Miller, J. P. 164, 180, 182
Mills, D. 138
Milner, D. 133, 135
Mintzes, J. J. 95
Mogdil, C. 23
Mogdil, S. 23
Morgan, W. 117
Muir, S. H. 137
Muir, S. P. 125–7

Newkirk, T. 45
Newman, M. A. 61
Nodine, C. F. 152
Novak, J. D. 83,
Nussbaum, J. 83

Oakden, E. C. 102
Ormell, C. 68
Osborne, R. J. 17, 85, 89–90, 95

Paolitto, D. P. 16, 182
Paramour, S. 45
Pappas, C. C. 100, 102
Parsons, M. 152
Partington, G. 102, 110
Patriarca, L. A. 102, 110
Peel, E. A. 6, 11–2, 17, 22–3, 83, 114–15, 128, 185
Peisach, E. 169
Perera, K. 45
Peters, R. S. 162–3, 182
Peterson, C. D. xiii, 168, 170
Peterson, J. L. 168, 170
Phillips, J. L. 23
Piaget, J. xiii, 4–10, 16, 18, 22, 33–4, 53–4, 57, 59–60, 79–81, 83, 95, 109, 111, 124, 126–7, 137, 149, 167–9, 171, 176–7, 182, 184–5
Plumb, J. H. 97, 115
Popper, K. R. 71–2
Portal, C. 99, 107
Presson, C. C. 137
Price, J. 55–6
Proctor, N. 116, 137
Pulos, S. xiv, 83–5

Quam, L. O. 118

Radebaugh, M. R. 38
Read, C. 36, 45
Reid, L. A. 140, 142
Reimer, B. 140–1
Reimer, J. 16, 182
Rest, J. R. 10, 174
Renfrow, M. J. 156
Reynolds, R. E. 21
Rhys, W. T. 127–8, 131
Robinson, E. 23
Rogers, D. 160
Rosenfield, D. 135
Ryan, E. B. 21

Rybash, J. M. 178

Saunders, R. 5, 144
Schirrmacher, R. 145–6, 160
Schug, M. C. 137
Scott, L. 68
Seeto, D. 168, 170
Selman, R. L. xiv, 16–7, 81–2, 85, 177, 185
Shemilt, D. J. 106, 115
Short, E. J. 21
Shymansky, J. A. 95
Sigel, I. E. 5, 144
Simon, B. 23
Slater, F. A. 137
Sloboda, J. A. 160
Smith, N. R. 152, 154–5
Smith, R. A. 140, 141
Sneider, C. xiv, 83–5
Southgate, V. 2
Spencer, C. 126
Spencer, F. H. 24, 116
Steen, L. A. 47
Steinberg, R. M. 64
Stepans, J. 137
Stephan, W. G. 135
Stevens, O, 3, 104
Sternberg, R. J. 10, 23
Storm, M. 117
Stratta, L. 40
Straughan, R. 163, 182
Stubbs, M. 36
Sturt, M. 102
Sugarman, B. 182
Summers, M. K. 90
Symington, D. 91–3
Swift, R. 97

Tajfel, H. 132–3
Tamburrini, J. 2, 29, 42
Taunton, M. 152
Temple, C. A. 45
Thompson, A. G. 51
Thompson, R. McL. 81
Thompson, S. 172
Tomlinson, P. 23
Travers, R. M. W. 23
Trowbridge, J. E. 95
Truscoe, E. S. 73–4

Urberg, K. A. 8, 172

Vikainen, I. 109–10
Vonèche, J. J., 23
Vygotsky, L. V. 20

Wade, S. W. 21
Wagman, H. G. 59
Walford, R. 138
Walshe, A. J. 157–8
Watts, D. M. 72
Welton, J. 47, 96, 139

West, J. 20, 111–13
Whelan, M. 182
Wicker, A. W. 174
Wickert, P. 132
Wilder, R. L. 47
Wilkinson, A. xiii, 25, 27, 32–5, 39, 44–5
Williams, N. 182
Willig, J. 2, 29, 42
Wilson, J. 112–3, 162, 164–6, 182

Wittrock, M. C. 95
Wolfinger, D. M. 86–7
Wood, D. M. 104
Wragg, E. C. 23
Wright, D. S. 182

Young, D., 123, 125

Zutell, J. 40

SUBJECT INDEX

academic disciplines xi–xii, 1–3, 22, 183
  children's conceptions of xi, 1–3, 22
  curriculum and ix–xii
  nature of xi, 183
advance organisers 18–19, 90
  see also meaningful reception learning
altruism 172, 174
  see also egocentricity, role-taking, empathy
art 20, 139–60
  children's conceptions of 143–4
  cognition and 5, 140, 145–9, 159
  egocentricity in 145, 159
  feeling and 140, 149–152
  nature of 139, 140–1, 158, 160
  nature of education in 141–3, 159, 160
  observation drawing 154–5, 159
  responses to 20, 152–4, 156–8, 159
  sequential stages in 145–6, 159, 160
  techniques in 155–6, 159–160
  trends in teaching of 139–40
attitudes 6, 131, 136, 137
  see also concepts, constructs, prejudice, stereotyping

behaviourism 172
Bullock Report 45

child-centred education xii, 25
centration 7, 10, 12, 59, 145
classification 6, 57, 75–6, 92, 112–13
Cockroft Report 50, 68, 188
cognitive conflict 13, 16–18, 23, 89–90, 177–80, 181, 184
concepts ix–x, 3–22, 183, 189
  development of ix–x, 5–12, 183, 184
  discovery of 3–5, 22
  extension of x, 12–22
  nature of 6
  see also attitudes, constructs, prejudice, stereotyping
conservation 8, 10, 59, 79–81, 87

constructs 6
  see also concepts, prejudice, stereotyping
concrete operational thinking 7, 10, 12, 80–1, 87, 106, 129, 145, 152, 176, 184

educational psychology 23
egocentricity 8, 9, 10, 12, 33, 34, 107, 123–4, 145, 184
  see also altruism, empathy, role-taking
embedded thinking 57–9
empathy 107–8, 172, 174, 180
  see also altruism, egocentricity, role-taking

formal operational thinking 83, 106, 127, 145, 152

geography ix, 3, 116–138
  cognitive mapping and 121–5
  counteracting prejudice and 117, 131–3, 135–6, 137, 138
  geographical terms 130
  graphicacy skills 134–5, 137
  logical thinking in 127–8, 137
  map interpretation 125–77
  nature of 117–9, 136, 137
  nature of education in 119–20
  socio-economic concepts ix, 3, 128–30, 137
  trends in teaching of 116–7

history 3, 19, 96–115
  children's conceptions of 100–1, 114
  empathy 107–8
  logical thinking in 106, 111–13, 114, 115
  morality and teaching of 108–9
  nature of 97–9, 114, 115
  nature of education in 99–100, 115
  observation skills in 19, 98, 112, 114
  political terms and 3, 104–5
  time concepts and 101, 102–4, 109–10
  trends in teaching of 96–7

information theory   10

Kingman Report   45

Language (Written Expression)   2, 24–45
  argument in   40
  audience for   27, 34
  children's conceptions of   2, 28, 29, 44
  conference technique and   41–3
  drafting and revising skills and   42
  early stages in development of   30–2
  explanation in   33–35
  grammar and   25, 27, 29
  imagination and   28, 29, 43
  later stages in development of   32–5
  nature of   25–6, 27
  nature of education in   26–7, 44, 45
  punctuation and   29, 38–9
  spelling and   29, 35–9, 40, 45
  style and   34, 35
  teachers' conceptions of   28, 29, 44
  trends in teaching   24

match   13–6, 21, 23, 60, 184
Mathematics   ix–x, 46–68
  children's conceptions of   51–3
  counting skills in   54–9, 64
  learning strategies in   ix–x, 63–7
  metacognition and   65, 67
  multiplication tables and   63–4
  nature of   47–9
  nature of education in   50–1
  'new' mathematics   47, 50, 51, 67
  number concepts and   53–4
  teachers' conceptions of   51–2
  trends in teaching of   46–7
meaningful reception learning   13, 18–9, 22,
    23, 90, 184
  see also advance organisers
metacognition   13, 20–1, 22, 23, 65, 67
moral education   108–9, 135–6, 161–182
  affect and   164–5
  children's conceptions of   165–6
  cognition and   163, 164–5
  cognitive conflict and   177, 181, 182
  history and   108–9
  intentionally in   169, 182
  Kohlberg's moral development scale
    and   166–7, 177, 181, 182
  lying, concepts of and   6–7, 167–170, 182

moral thought and action and   174–5, 182
  nature of morality and   161, 162–4, 181,
    182
  nature of   161, 164–5, 181, 182
  prejudice and   135–5
  role-taking, empathy and altruism
    and   171–4, 180–1
  theories of   176–7, 181, 182
  teachers' conceptions of   165–6

observing,   13, 19–20, 90–4, 98, 112–3, 114,
    184

Piagetian theory   4, 7–10, 22, 23, 184, 185
  methodology   4, 9, 10
  moral thinking and   176
  number concepts and   53–4
  proportionality and   126–7
  stage theory and   7, 10, 184
Peel's model of conceptual
    development   11–2, 22, 128, 185
prejudice   132, 135–6
  see also concepts, constructs, stereotyping
pre-operational thinking   7, 10, 12, 80–1, 87

questioning   3, 5, 17, 22, 23

reversibility   8, 12, 22
role-taking   136, 171–2, 174, 180
  see also altruism, egocentricity, empathy

scaffolding   20
schema   6
scheme   6, 11, 12
Schools Council Art Committee   142, 159
science   3, 69–95
  children's conceptions of   74, 86
  cognitive conflict and   89–90
  flotation concepts in   79–81, 86–7
  gravity and earth concepts in   81–5
  life concepts in   3, 75–8, 85, 95
  meaningful reception learning in   90, 94
  nature of   70–2, 85, 95
  nature of education in   72–3, 95
  observation and   70–1, 72, 94
  teachers' conceptions of   73–4
  trends in teaching   69–70, 94
seriation   53
stereotyping   117, 132, 135
  see also concepts, constructs, prejudice